My Samsung
Galaxy Tab® A

Eric

D1390477

My Samsung Galaxy Tab® A

Copyright © 2016 by Pearson Education, Inc.

ISBN-13: 978-0-7897-5571-1

ISBN-10: 0-7897-5571-8

Library of Congress Control Number: 2015948631

Printed in the United States of America

First Printing: November 2015

Trademarks

All terms mentioned in this book that are known to be trademarks or service marks have been appropriately capitalized. Que Publishing cannot attest to the accuracy of this information. Use of a term in this book should not be regarded as affecting the validity of any trademark or service mark.

Galaxy Tab A images are provided by Samsung Electronics America.

Warning and Disclaimer

Every effort has been made to make this book as complete and as accurate as possible, but no warranty or fitness is implied. The information provided is on an "as is" basis. The author and the publisher shall have neither liability nor responsibility to any person or entity with respect to any loss or damages arising from the information contained in this book or from the use of programs accompanying it.

Special Sales

For information about buying this title in bulk quantities, or for special sales opportunities (which may include electronic versions; custom cover designs; and content particular to your business, training goals, marketing focus, or branding interests), please contact our corporate sales department at corpsales@pearsoned.com or (800) 382-3419.

For government sales inquiries, please contact governmentsales@pearsoned.com.

For questions about sales outside the U.S., please contact international@pearsoned.com.

Editor-in-Chief
Greg Wiegand

Acquisitions Editor
Michelle Newcomb

Development Editor
Charlotte Kughen

Managing Editor
Kristy Hart

Senior Project Editor
Betsy Gratner

Copy Editor
Karen Annett

Indexer
Lisa Stumpf

Proofreader
Debbie Williams

Technical Editor
Christian Kenyeres

Publishing Coordinator
Cindy Teeters

Cover Designer
Mark Shirar

Senior Compositor
Gloria Schurick

Contents at a Glance

Online Bonus Material

Bonus tasks and a complete chapter ("The Galaxy Tab Universe") are available from this book's website, www.informit.com/title/9780789755711. Click the Downloads tab to access them.

Table of Contents

Online Bonus Material

Bonus tasks and a complete chapter ("The Galaxy Tab Universe") are available from this book's website, www.informit.com/title/9780789755711. Click the Downloads tab to access them.

About the Author

Eric Butow began writing books in 2000 when he wrote *Master Visually Windows 2000 Server*. Since then, Eric has authored or coauthored 26 other books. Those books include Addison-Wesley's *User Interface Design for Mere Mortals*, Amacom's *How to Succeed in Business Using LinkedIn*, Wiley Publishing's *Droid Companion*, Wiley Publishing's *Google Glass For Dummies*, Que Publishing's *My Samsung Galaxy Tab S*, and Que Publishing's *Blogging to Drive Business*, Second Edition.

Eric lives in Jackson, California. He has a master's degree in communication from California State University, Fresno, and is the owner of Butow Communications Group (BCG), an online marketing ROI improvement firm.

Website: http://butow.net

LinkedIn: http://linkedin.com/in/ebutow

Dedication

To all the daycare children I've had the pleasure of playing with.
—Eric Butow

Acknowledgments

My thanks as always to my family and friends. I want to thank my awesome literary agent, Carole Jelen, as well as Cindy Teeters, Christian Kenyeres, Joyce Nielsen, Charlotte Kughen, Greg Wiegand, and especially Michelle Newcomb. I'd also like to thank everyone who gave me permission to use their information, particularly the parents of my mother's daycare children for letting me take their pictures for the book.

We Want to Hear from You!

As the reader of this book, *you* are our most important critic and commentator. We value your opinion and want to know what we're doing right, what we could do better, what areas you'd like to see us publish in, and any other words of wisdom you're willing to pass our way.

We welcome your comments. You can email or write us directly to let us know what you did or didn't like about this book—as well as what we can do to make our books better.

Please note that we cannot help you with technical problems related to the topic of this book.

When you write, please be sure to include this book's title and author as well as your name, email address, and phone number. We will carefully review your comments and share them with the author and editors who worked on the book.

Email: feedback@quepublishing.com

Mail: Que Publishing
       ATTN: Reader Feedback
       800 East 96th Street
       Indianapolis, IN 46240 USA

Reader Services

Visit our website and register this book at quepublishing.com/register for convenient access to any updates, downloads, or errata that might be available for this book.

See the differences between the
Galaxy Tab A 8.0 and the Galaxy Tab A 9.7

Understand how to manipulate the screen

Learn how to interact with Android

In this chapter, you discover the different hardware and the common screens on the Galaxy Tab A. This chapter covers the following topics:

→ Investigating the Galaxy Tab A
→ The Galaxy Tab A buttons and switches
→ Galaxy Tab A screens
→ Manipulating the screen
→ Interacting with Android
→ Using the keyboard

Meeting the Samsung Galaxy Tab A

This book covers the two models of the Galaxy Tab A: the 8.0" Tab and the larger 9.7" version.

Galaxy Tab A 8.0

The 8.0" unit, called the Galaxy Tab A 8.0, runs version 5.0 of Google's Android operating system, which is also called Lollipop.

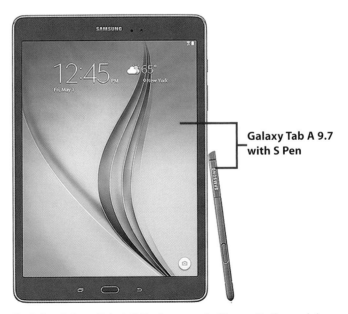

Galaxy Tab A 9.7 with S Pen

The 9.7" unit, called the Galaxy Tab A 9.7, also runs Lollipop. Both models connect to the Internet and/or a network using a Wi-Fi connection.

The Tab A 9.7 model comes in two versions. One version includes the S Pen stylus, which was previously only available on the Samsung Note series of tablets. The other version doesn't include an S Pen. If you have the Tab A 9.7 with S Pen, you can learn how to set up and use the S Pen on the device in Chapter 2, "Setting Up the Galaxy Tab A."

Many tasks throughout the book include information for one model or the other; if there are any differences between the models, there are separate tasks for each. In this case, the headers for each section (or subsection) indicate the model name, such as Galaxy Tab A 9.7". If you don't see the model specified in the section (or subsection) name, the information applies to both models.

Investigating the Galaxy Tab A

Before you work with your Galaxy Tab A, it's important to take it out of the box and examine it so you can learn where all the controls and features are on the unit. If you've used (or tried) another tablet computer in the past, you might already be familiar with some of the features. If this is your first time using a tablet computer or the Galaxy Tab A, though, take the time to read this chapter and enjoy learning about it.

It's Not All Good

Why Do the Galaxy Tab Units Look Different Between Photos?

Both Galaxy Tab A models come in three colors: White, Smoky Blue, and Smoky Titanium. (The Tab A 9.7 with S Pen only comes in Smoky Titanium.) The three different colors of both models appear in photos throughout this book. Some screens may also look different because of app updates or the screen orientation.

Physical Features of the Galaxy Tab A 8.0"

The front of the Galaxy Tab A 8.0" includes the touchscreen for viewing information, a proximity and gesture sensor that can see when someone is near the unit, as well as a camera so you can take photos and/or record video of yourself.

You learn more about using the cameras to take photos in Chapter 10, "Capturing and Managing Photos," and how to record video in Chapter 11, "Playing Music and Video."

Camera viewfinder

Proximity and gesture sensor

Touchscreen

Camera

Cover buttons

The back of the unit has two features:

- A second camera so you can take photos and record video using your Galaxy Tab A.

- Two buttons on the right side that push in so you can attach a cover for your Tab A. You can shop for covers on the Samsung website at www. samsung.com.

There are three buttons below the touchscreen on both the Galaxy Tab A 8.0" and the Galaxy Tab A 9.7". These buttons are covered later in the chapter, in the section titled "The Galaxy Tab A Buttons and Switches." Aside from those three buttons, the Galaxy Tab A 8.0" contains a number of features on the right and bottom sides of the unit:

- A microphone on the right side of the unit so you can record audio on the Tab A without having to use a separate microphone.

- The Power button on the right side of the unit.

- The volume control slider on the right side of the unit.

- A microSD memory card slot also on the right side of the unit.

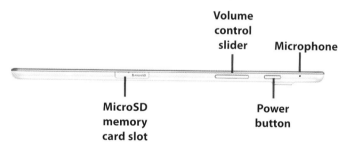

- A dock/charge and sync cable connector that is on the bottom side of the unit. You learn more about docking, charging, and syncing your Galaxy Tab A in Chapter 2.

- A headphone and microphone jack to the left of the dock/charge and sync cable connector. This jack enables you to either listen to audio privately using headphones or record audio into a microphone.

- The audio speaker on the bottom side of the unit.

Speaker

Headphone/
microphone
jack

Dock/charge
and sync cable
connector

Physical Features of the Galaxy Tab A 9.7"

The front of the Galaxy Tab A 9.7" includes the AMOLED touchscreen for
viewing information, a proximity and gesture sensor that can see when
someone is near the unit, and a camera so you can take photos or record
video of yourself.

What Is AMOLED?

AMOLED stands for Active Matrix Organic Light-Emitting Diode, and it's a hybrid
video technology that combines the active matrix features of the older thin-film
transistor liquid-crystal display (TFT LCD) and the newer organic light-emitting
diode (OLED) technology. As a result, you get a screen that's as good as TFT LCD
and also makes moving images more fluid, can be viewed clearly from more
angles, and is more energy efficient.

You learn more about using the cameras to take photos in Chapter 10 and to record video in Chapter 11.

Camera viewfinder

Proximity and gesture sensor

Touchscreen

The back of the unit has two features:

- A second camera so you can take photos and record video using your Galaxy Tab A.

- Two buttons, one each on the top-right and bottom-right sides, that push in so you can attach a cover for your Tab A. You can shop for covers on the Samsung website at www.samsung.com.

Camera

Cover buttons

There are three buttons below the touchscreen on both the Galaxy Tab A 8.0" and the Galaxy Tab A 9.7". Those buttons are covered later in the chapter, in the section titled "The Galaxy Tab A Buttons and Switches." Aside from those three buttons, the Galaxy Tab A 9.7" contains a number of features on the right and bottom sides of the unit:

- If you have the Tab A 9.7 with S Pen, the top end of the S Pen appears on the top-right corner of the unit.

- A microphone is on the right side of the unit so you can record audio on the Tab A without having to use a separate microphone.

- The Power button is on the right side of the unit.

- The volume control slider is on the right side of the unit.

- A microSD memory card slot is also on the right side of the unit.

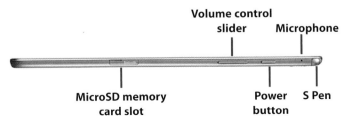

Volume control slider   Microphone

MicroSD memory card slot   Power button   S Pen

- A dock/charge and sync cable connector is on the bottom side of the unit. You learn more about docking, charging, and syncing your Galaxy Tab A in Chapter 2.

- A headphone and microphone jack is to the left of the dock/charge and sync cable connector. This jack enables you to either listen to audio privately using headphones or record audio into a microphone.

- The audio speakers are on the left and right sides of the dock/charge and sync cable connector.

Speaker

Dock/charge and sync cable connector

Headphone/ microphone jack

Speaker

The Galaxy Tab A Buttons and Switches

Both models of the Galaxy Tab A feature two touch buttons on either side of a physical Home button. All three are below the touchscreen. The Power button and volume slider are on the right side of the unit.

Setting Up Your Galaxy Tab A

When you start your Galaxy Tab A for the first time, you go through a series of steps to get your Tab A up and running, including setting up your wireless connection. This book presumes that you have already set up your Tab A using the documentation that came in your Tab A box. If you need help with setting up a Wi-Fi network, you can find that information in Chapter 2.

The Three Galaxy Tab A Buttons

Below the touchscreen are three buttons that you use frequently to manage the device and the applications on it. They are (from left to right) Recent, Home, and Back.

Recent   Home   Back

- **Recent**—The Recent touch button opens the Recent Apps screen and displays a list of apps that are open currently within a stack of tiles. The most recent app you opened appears in the tile at the bottom of the screen. Show an open app on the entire screen by tapping the app tile. Close the Recent Apps screen and return to the app screen within the bottom tile by tapping the Recent touch button again.

- **Home**—The fact that the Home button is a physical button signifies its place of importance with regard to how the Tab A functions. It's probably the button you will use most often because it's the one you press to get out of a specific application, such as the Galaxy Tab A web browser, and move back to the Home screen so you can open another application.

**The Recent Apps screen
with the Calculator app tile
at the bottom of the list**

If you want to hide an application and go back to the Home screen, pressing the Home button is the way to go. Pressing the Home button hides the application you currently have open.

- **Back**—The Back touch button moves you back to the previous screen. For example, if you're on the Home screen and touch the Recent touch button to bring up the Recent Apps screen, you might decide that you don't want to open an app. You can close the Recent Apps screen by tapping the Back touch button.

The Power Button

The Power button performs a number of important functions on your Galaxy Tab A:

- It turns on the unit when you press the button. The Power button is on the right side of both the Galaxy Tab A 8.0" and Galaxy Tab A 9.7" units. The Galaxy Tab A boots up and is ready for you to use in about 5 seconds.

- If you press and hold the button for about 1 second, you see the Device Options window on the screen; you use this window to power off the device, put the device into Airplane mode so Wi-Fi connectivity is turned off temporarily, or restart the device.

- If you press the button and immediately release your finger, the screen turns off and the Galaxy Tab A enters Sleep mode.

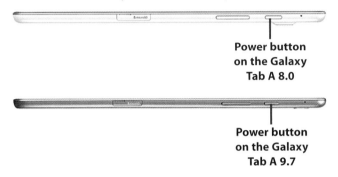

**Power button
on the Galaxy
Tab A 8.0**

**Power button
on the Galaxy
Tab A 9.7**

What Happens If I Don't Turn Off the Galaxy Tab A?

If the Galaxy Tab A is idle for a long period of time, the unit goes into Sleep mode automatically. Sleep mode drains very little battery power, so if the Galaxy Tab A is frequently in Sleep mode, you don't need to recharge your battery as often. Refer to Chapter 17, "Troubleshooting Your Galaxy Tab A," for information about expected battery life and strategies for extending that life span.

Volume Control Buttons

There are two volume control buttons on the left side of the device—one that turns up the volume and one that turns down the volume. What device the buttons control depends on what you have connected to the Galaxy Tab A.

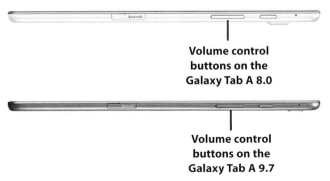

**Volume control
buttons on the
Galaxy Tab A 8.0**

**Volume control
buttons on the
Galaxy Tab A 9.7**

If you're listening to audio through the Galaxy Tab A speakers, the unit remembers the volume settings for the external speakers and sets the volume accordingly. If you decide to connect headphones to the unit, the Galaxy Tab A adjusts to the headphone volume the unit has in memory. When you remove the headphones, the unit readjusts the volume to the speaker volume.

You might want to check your volume settings for your headphones and external speakers so you don't get any nasty surprises. You learn more about setting the volume in Chapter 2.

Galaxy Tab A Screens

Three important screens are the mainstays of your Galaxy Tab A experience no matter which Galaxy Tab A model you use.

The Lock Screen (Galaxy Tab A 8.0")

The Lock screen is the default state of the Galaxy Tab A when it first boots.

The Lock screen shows the current date and time, the current weather for your location, as well as the Wi-Fi connectivity status and battery charge status in the upper-right corner. It might also include the Smart Stay feature icon (it looks like an eye), which indicates that this feature is on. You'll learn more about Smart Stay later in this chapter.

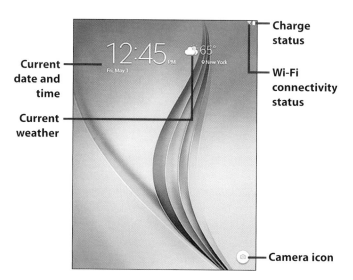

The Camera icon is at the bottom of the screen; tap and hold on the icon and then swipe upward to open the Camera app and take photos using your Tab A. You read more about taking photos in Chapter 10.

All you have to do to unlock your Tab A is hold your finger anywhere on the screen and then swipe in any direction, or you can press and hold on the Home button so the Tab A can read your fingerprint using the Finger Scanner. If your Tab A is password-protected, you need to type your password in the password box. You learn more about password-protecting your Galaxy Tab A in Chapter 3, "Customizing Android to Your Liking."

The Lock Screen (Galaxy Tab A 9.7")

The Lock screen is the default state of the Galaxy Tab A when it first boots.

The Lock screen shows the current date and time, the current status of your Bluetooth and Wi-Fi connections, and the amount of charge you have in your battery. It might also include the Smart Stay feature icon (it looks like an eye), which indicates that this feature is on. You'll learn more about Smart Stay later in this chapter.

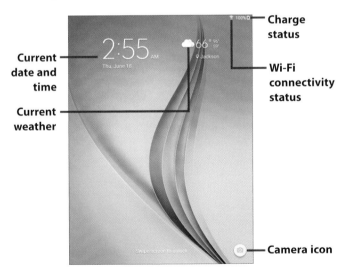

All you have to do to unlock your Tab A is to hold your finger anywhere on the screen and then swipe in any direction. If your Galaxy Tab A is password-protected, the password box appears on the screen. You must type your password and then tap the OK button to open the Home screen or the application you were working on before the unit went to sleep. You learn more about password-protecting your Galaxy Tab A in Chapter 3.

What Is Smart Stay?

Smart Stay detects whether you're looking at the screen. When the Tab A detects that you are looking at it, the device won't go to sleep. If you stop looking at the screen and look back at it after a short period of time, you might see an alert in the status bar that says, "Smart Stay cannot detect your eyes" before the screen turns off.

Why Don't I See the Weather for My Location?

If you don't see the weather for your location on the Lock screen, it means you haven't set up the Weather widget on the Home screen to display the current temperature, forecast high and low temperatures for the current day, and sky conditions outside. You find out how to set up the Weather widget in Chapter 5, "Finding Widgets and Using Flipboard Briefing."

The Apps Screen

The Apps screen is the command center where you can access all the applications available on your Galaxy Tab A. Tap the Apps icon in the lower-right corner of the Home screen to view the Apps screen.

The Apps icon on
the Home screen

If you have more than one page of application icons, buttons appear at the bottom of the screen. You can scroll between pages by tapping one of the buttons or dragging or flicking left and right. You learn more about dragging and flicking later in this chapter.

**Two buttons on the bottom
of the Apps screen**

After you tap an application icon on the Apps screen, the application launches and takes up the entire screen. For example, if you open the My Files application, a list of files and folders on your Tab A appears on the screen.

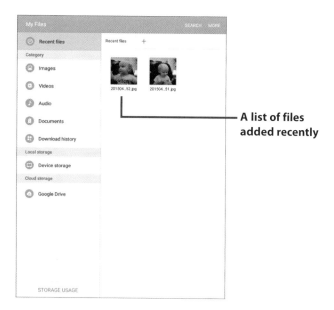

A list of files
added recently

Manipulating the Screen

Like many tablets these days, most of the Galaxy Tab A models don't come with a stylus (essentially a stick) for manipulating elements on the screen. Instead, you use your fingers and change the orientation of the Galaxy Tab A itself to make it do what you want. Although the examples in this section are for the Galaxy Tab A 8.0", you manipulate elements on the Galaxy Tab A 9.7" screen in the same way.

Tapping an Element

Unlike a desktop or laptop computer, your Galaxy Tab A models don't have a mouse installed, so there is no cursor you can see. However, when you quickly tap an element with your finger, the Galaxy Tab A performs an action. For example, when you tap an application icon, the Galaxy Tab A launches the application.

You can also double-tap, which is two quick taps in the same location, to perform a specific function. For example, you can double-tap an image to zoom in and double-tap again to zoom out.

Pinching

Apple set the standard for multitouch screen gesture requirements with its iPad, and the Galaxy Tab A follows the same standard. A multitouch screen can recognize different gestures that use multiple finger touches. One such gesture is the pinching gesture.

You pinch when you touch the screen with both your thumb and forefinger and bring them together in a pinching motion. This is also called "pinching in," and it has the same effect as zooming out. For example, you can view more information in a web page within the browser by pinching. You can also pinch outward, which has the same effect as zooming in, by touching the screen with your thumb and forefinger together and moving them apart.

Dragging and Flicking

You can drag up and down the screen (or even left to right if an app allows it) by touching the top of the screen and moving your finger to drag content the length of the screen. If you want to move more content down the screen, remove your finger, touch the top of the screen, and drag your finger down the length of the screen again. You can drag a page of content up by touch-ing the bottom of the screen and dragging your finger upward.

Dragging can become cumbersome, though, if you have to drag through a long document such as a web page or spreadsheet. The Galaxy Tab A makes it easy for you to drag through large chunks of content by flicking. That is, after you touch the top (or bottom) of the screen, move your finger quickly down (or up) and then lift your finger at the last moment so the content scrolls after you lift your finger. You can wait for the content to stop scrolling when you reach the beginning or end of the content, or you can touch any-where on the screen to stop scrolling.

Screen Rotation and Orientation

Your Galaxy Tab A has two screen orientation modes—vertical and horizontal—and it knows which way it's oriented. By default, the Galaxy Tab A screen orientation changes when you rotate the unit 90 degrees so the screen is horizontal, or you can rotate it another 90 degrees so the screen is vertical again. Nearly all default apps, such as the Chrome app, use both orientations. However, there might be times when you don't want the Galaxy Tab A to automatically change its screen orientation when you move the unit. For example, you might want to view a web page only in vertical orientation.

You can set the screen rotation on or off as you see fit. Here are the steps to follow:

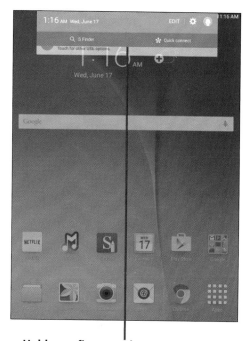

Hold your finger at the top edge of the screen and swipe downward

1. Open the Quick Settings and Notifications screen by holding your finger at the top edge of the screen and then swiping downward.

2. By default, the Screen Rotation button is green to signify that orientation lock is on. Tap the Screen Rotation button. The button turns gray to signify that orientation lock is off.

The green Screen Rotation button indicates orientation lock is on

3. Tap the Screen Rotation button again to turn off orientation lock; the button turns green. The next time you rotate the unit 90 degrees, the screen rotates automatically.

Interacting with Android

Android is a fun operating system to use; it offers a number of common elements, including sliders and buttons, as well as a keyboard you can use to enter and edit text in your Galaxy Tab A.

Sliders

A *slider* is a button that requires a bit of effort for you to activate. Android uses sliders to prevent you from doing something that can lead to unintended consequences. For example, if you open the Quick Settings and Notifications screen, you see the brightness slider for adjusting the brightness of the screen.

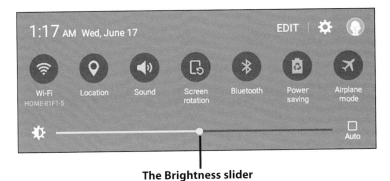

The Brightness slider

Button Bar

You might see a button bar in different locations on the screen, depending on the app you're using. For example, if you read a message in the Gmail app, you see some buttons in the bar at the bottom of the screen that enable you to perform certain tasks, such as putting the message in the trash.

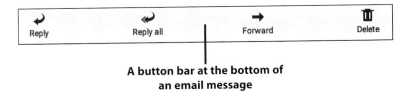

**A button bar at the bottom of
an email message**

Tab Area

Some apps have a tab area that contains a set of buttons that control the app. The area location and buttons vary depending on the app; if the app doesn't have a tab area, you won't see one. For example, when you open the Clock app, you see a tab area at the top of the screen that enables you to view different settings in each tab area category.

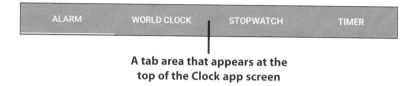

**A tab area that appears at the
top of the Clock app screen**

Using the Keyboard

The Galaxy Tab A doesn't come with a physical keyboard like you find on many smartphones. Instead, you type in the text with something that looks similar to a computer keyboard. The keyboard appears at the bottom of the screen automatically when you want to enter text.

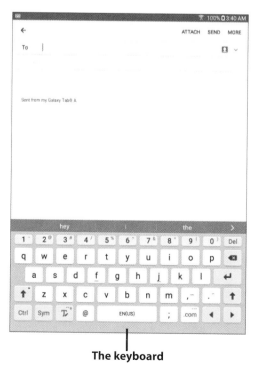

The keyboard

You can type a letter by tapping the letter's key. For example, if you tap the letter *a* on the keyboard, the lowercase letter *a* appears on the screen.

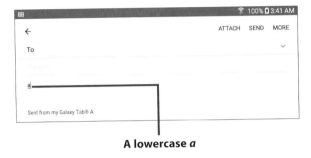

A lowercase *a*

>>>Go Further

HOW DO I CAPITALIZE A LETTER?

There are two ways you can capitalize a letter:

- Tap one of the two Shift keys and then tap the letter you want to capital-ize. Notice that after you tap the Shift key, the Shift key turns blue and all the keys on the keyboard become capitalized.

The Shift keys

- You can capitalize more than one letter by tapping the Shift key twice. The arrow on the Shift key turns blue, and on the left Shift key (the one to the left of the letter Z), the dot in the upper-right corner of the key turns blue as well. This denotes that the Shift key is locked.

You can unlock the Shift key by tapping the key again. You know the Shift key is unlocked not only because the blue arrow on the Shift key is off, but also because all the letter keys on the keyboard are back to lowercase.

Using Special Keyboards and Characters

It's not easy typing on a screen that's only 8.0" diagonally (or even 9.7"), especially with an onscreen keyboard, but Android has a trick to make it a bit easier to add information.

You can't access special characters from the standard Tab A keyboard, but you can access those special character keys by tapping the Sym key to see a variety of symbols.

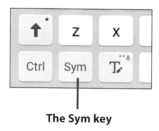

The Sym key

If the symbol you need isn't on the keyboard that displays, you can access an extended symbols keyboard by tapping the 1/2 key on the numbers and symbols keyboard. After you tap this key, the key label changes to 2/2, which signifies that you are on the second of two extended keyboards. When you're on the second extended keyboard, you can return to the numbers and symbols keyboard by tapping the 2/2 key.

After you tap the Sym key to access special character keys, the Sym key is replaced with the ABC key. Tap the ABC key to return to the standard Tab A keyboard.

The 1/2 key ———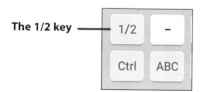

My Keyboard Doesn't Look the Same!

Your keyboard options might change somewhat depending on the app you're in. For example, if you're typing an email message in the Gmail app, you see the @ key to the left of the spacebar because that's a key that you use often when typing an email address.

If you hold down a key on the keyboard, the letter appears, and if there are any related characters, such as a letter with an umlaut (such as ü), you see a character window above the letter key. Hold and drag your finger to the character you want to insert and then release your finger.

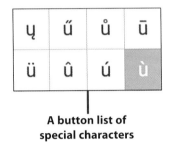

A button list of special characters

What Does the Settings Key Do?

To the left of the spacebar, you see a key that has a T with a pencil next to it. When you tap this key, the Samsung Keyboard Settings screen appears so you can change a variety of keyboard settings, such as selecting a new input language and entering text by sliding your finger across the keyboard instead of tapping each key. When you're finished changing and/or reviewing settings, tap the Back touch button to return to the app that uses the keyboard.

Copy and Paste Text

Android makes it pretty easy to copy and paste text from one app to another. In this example, you learn to copy a term from the Chrome app and paste it into the Search app so you can search for the term not only on the Web but also throughout the Galaxy Tab A.

1. Tap Chrome on the Home screen.

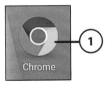

2. This example starts on the Google website. Type a search term into the Google search box.

3. When you're finished typing, tap the Search button.

4. Hold down your finger on the search box for a couple of seconds and then release your finger. The search term is highlighted and bracket buttons appear below and on each side of the term.

5. Tap Copy in the menu bar that appears above the Search box.

6. Tap the Google logo to return to the Google home page.

7. Hold down your finger on the Google box until the Edit Text pop-up menu appears above the Search box and then release your finger.

8. Tap Paste in the Edit Text pop-up menu to insert the copied text.

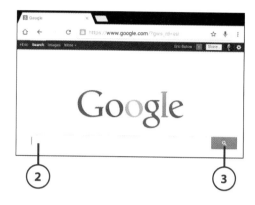

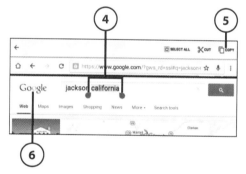

Learn how to get
details about the
Galaxy Tab A

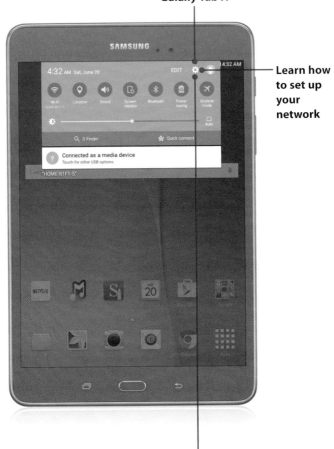

Learn how
to set up
your
network

Learn about
synchronizing the
Galaxy Tab A with
your computer

In this chapter, you discover more about your Galaxy Tab A and how to connect it with other computers and networks. This chapter covers the following topics:

→ Getting details about the Galaxy Tab A
→ Setting up your network
→ Syncing the Galaxy Tab A

2

Setting Up the Galaxy Tab A

You can easily find information about the Galaxy Tab A so you can make changes as needed. When you finish making general changes to the Galaxy Tab A, it's time to set up the network so your Galaxy Tab A can connect with the Internet. Finally, you find out how to synchronize your Galaxy Tab A with other devices, such as your desktop or laptop PC.

Getting Details About the Galaxy Tab A

If you want to get information about the features in your Galaxy Tab A from one place, you can use the About Device section within the Settings app.

1. Open the Quick Settings and Notifications screen by tapping and holding your finger on the top edge of the screen and swiping your finger down.

2. Tap the Settings icon.

3. Swipe down in the settings list on the left side of the screen and then tap About Device.

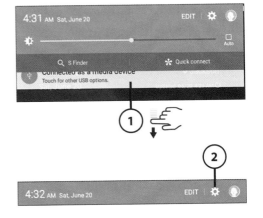

4. See the model number for your Galaxy Tab A.

5. See the Android and Kernel versions.

6. Scroll down (if necessary) to see the build number for your Galaxy Tab A.

7. Scroll back up (if necessary) and tap Status.

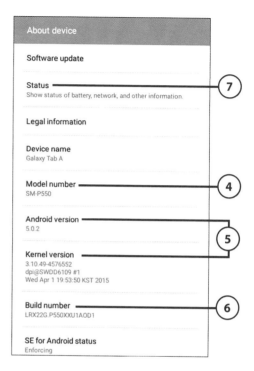

8. View the status of your Galaxy Tab A, including battery status and battery charge level, IP address, your Wi-Fi MAC address, Bluetooth address, and the current up time (that is, how long your Galaxy Tab A has been on continuously).

9. Tap the Back touch button.

10. Tap Legal Information to view a menu that shows Galaxy Tab A legal information, privacy information, and license settings.

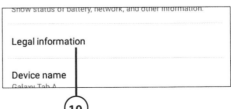

Setting Up Your Network

Now that you're familiar with the details about your Galaxy Tab A and accessing the Settings app, you need to use the Settings app to do one very important setup task: Connect your Galaxy Tab A to the Internet. Depending on the
phone carrier you use, you can link with the Internet through a Wi-Fi connection. You also can link to other devices and networks using a Bluetooth connection or through a virtual private network (VPN).

I Don't Have a Wireless Network…What Do I Do?

If you don't have a Wi-Fi network but you do have a high-speed Internet connection through a telephone (DSL) or cable (broadband) provider, you have
several options. First, call your provider and ask for a new network modem that
enables wireless connections. Second, ask how much the modem costs—some
providers might give you a free upgrade.

Another option is to keep your current box and add a wireless base station of
your own, such as the ones offered by Apple and Microsoft.

Set Up Wi-Fi

The Galaxy Tab A makes it easy for
you to set up a Wi-Fi connection to
access the Internet:

1. On the Home screen, swipe from
    right to left to view the second
    Home screen and then tap Set-
    tings.

2. Tap Wi-Fi if Wi-Fi is not selected already.

3. If Wi-Fi is turned off, you see a slider button within the Wi-Fi entry in the settings list. Turn Wi-Fi on by sliding the button to the right.

4. Tap More in the menu bar.

5. Tap Add Network in the menu.

6. Type the network name.

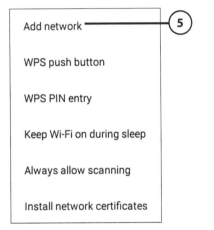

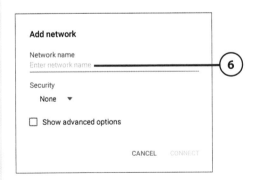

Setting Up Your Network   **35**

7. Tap the Security field to set the security level.

8. Select the security level; the default is None.

9. Tap Connect.

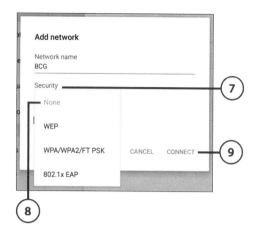

It's Not All Good

Be Secure First!

Your wireless network equipment should have security enabled. You know that security is enabled on the Wi-Fi network when you view the Wi-Fi Settings screen and see a padlock next to the Wi-Fi network in the list. When you select the Wi-Fi network for the first time, you should be asked to supply a password.

If you don't require a password, strongly consider adding one because unsecured networks send unencrypted (plain text) data—such as passwords and credit card numbers—through the air. Anyone else who has a Wi-Fi connection can tap in to your unsecured network and see what you're doing online. If you need more information, consult your network equipment documentation and/or manufacturer's website.

>>>Go Further

DISABLE WIRELESS CONNECTIONS ON A PLANE

When you're flying, the flight attendants always remind you to turn off your wireless devices during takeoffs and landings. You can quickly disable your wireless connections until you get to a safe flying altitude and the pilot gives you permission to turn on wireless devices again. Here's how:

1. On the Home screen, swipe from right to left to view the second Home screen and then tap Settings.

2. Tap Airplane Mode.

3. Using the slider button within the Airplane Mode entry in the settings list, turn Airplane mode on by sliding the button to the right.

The slider button turns green to inform you that wireless connections are disabled. Slide the button to the left to turn off Airplane mode and enable wireless connections.

Set Up Bluetooth

If you connect to another device or a network using a Bluetooth connection, the Galaxy Tab A makes it easy to enable your Bluetooth connection and find Bluetooth-enabled devices.

1. On the Home screen, swipe from right to left to view the second Home screen and then tap Settings.

2.   Tap Bluetooth.

3.   Turn on Bluetooth by sliding the Bluetooth slider button to the right.

4.   If the Galaxy Tab A doesn't find an available device, turn on the Bluetooth device to which you want to connect and then tap Refresh in the Settings menu bar.

5.   Tap a found device to connect with that device. You can rescan for devices by tapping Scan.

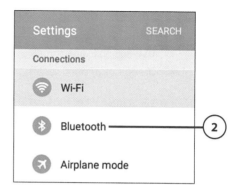

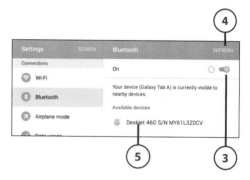

Set Up a VPN

A VPN enables users in a public network (such as the Internet) to transfer private data by making it appear to the users that they're in a private network of their own. For example, you can set up a VPN between yourself and your boss at the office so you can securely send private company data.

1.   On the Home screen, swipe from right to left to view the second Home screen and then tap Settings.

2. Tap More Connection Settings.

3. Tap VPN. If your Tab A is not protected by a password or similar encryption method, you see a dialog box that tells you to set a screen unlock pattern, PIN, or password. Open the Screen Unlock Settings screen and add a password, pattern, or PIN by tapping OK. Refer to Chapter 3, "Customizing Android to Your Liking," for more information about how to add a password, pattern, and PIN.

4. Tap Add VPN in the Settings menu bar.

5. Enter the VPN information, including the VPN name, type, and server address.

6. Tap Save.

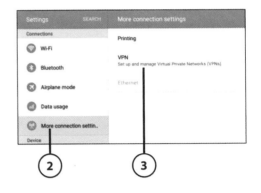

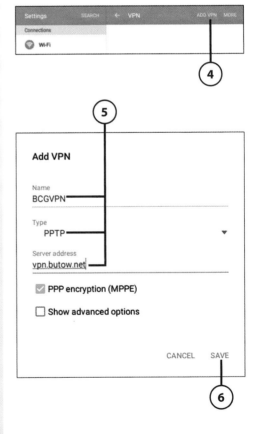

7. Tap the VPN name in the list.

8. Type the VPN username in the Username field and the password in the Password field.

9. Tap Connect.

How to Disconnect from Your VPN

You can begin the VPN disconnection process by opening the Quick Settings and Notifications screen that is covered earlier in this chapter. On the screen, a notification in the list informs you that you're connected to the VPN. Disconnect from the VPN by tapping the notification in the list and then tapping Disconnect.

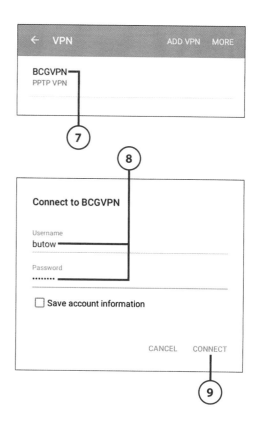

Syncing the Galaxy Tab A

Synchronizing your Galaxy Tab A with your desktop or laptop computer has a number of advantages.

The Galaxy Tab A stores a backup of its contents on your desktop or laptop every time you sync both devices; therefore, if you lose your data on the Galaxy Tab A—or lose the Galaxy Tab A itself—you can restore the data from the backed-up copies on your computer. What's more, if you have music, photos, or video on your computer, you can copy a selection of those files onto your Galaxy Tab A.

Because Windows is the leading operating system for desktop PCs by far, this chapter describes how to sync music with the Galaxy Tab A in Windows. Later chapters cover how to sync other types of data, such as contacts.

Can I Sync Between the Galaxy Tab A and the Mac OS?

Syncing music from iTunes on the Mac OS to the Galaxy Tab A requires that you download additional software for your Mac. JRTStudio (www.jrtstudio. com) produces iSyncr, a utility that syncs what you have in iTunes with Android devices. As of this writing, the main app costs $4.99 in the Google Play Store, and that app enables you to sync your Tab A with iTunes on your Mac by connecting your Tab A to your Mac using the Tab A cable.

Sync Media Files

It's easy to sync music or other media files in Windows Media Player, the default music and multimedia player in Windows, to any model of the Galaxy Tab A.

1. Connect the Galaxy Tab A to your computer with the USB cable that came with your Galaxy Tab A if you haven't done so already. After a short while, your Windows PC informs you that it has installed the drivers to connect with your Galaxy Tab A.

2. Launch Windows Media Player on your Windows PC.

3. Tap the Sync tab; the Galaxy Tab A sync area appears on the right side of the window.

4. Click the folder in the tree that contains the files you want to sync with the Galaxy Tab A.

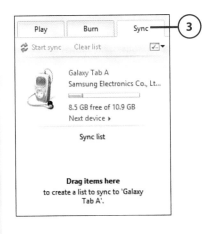

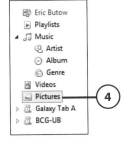

5. Select the files you want to move and then click and drag them to the sync area.

6. Click Start Sync.

7. After Windows Media Player syncs with your Galaxy Tab A, open the app associated with the type of files you synced on the Galaxy Tab A. For example, if you synced image files, open the Gallery app; the Pictures tile shows one of the images you synced. You find out how to use the Gallery app in Chapter 10, "Capturing and Managing Photos."

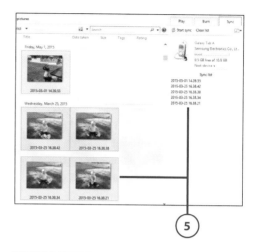

Why Don't I See the Galaxy Tab A Sync Area?

If you have another external device connected to your computer, such as a USB drive, then you might see that external device appear first in the sync area. You can view the next external device Windows Media Player has recognized by clicking Next Device below the device's storage information within the sync area. Continue to click Next Device until you see the Galaxy Tab A in the sync area.

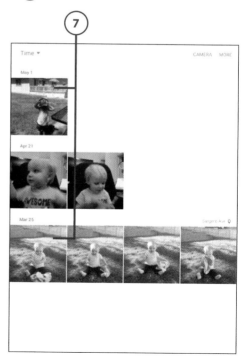

Learn how to set
parental restrictions

Learn how to password-protect your
Galaxy Tab A

Learn about modifying screen wallpaper

Learn about setting alert sounds

Learn how to change keyboard settings

In this chapter, you discover how to change how the Galaxy Tab A behaves, looks, and works. This chapter covers the following topics:

→ Password-protecting the Galaxy Tab A
→ Changing your password
→ Setting parental restrictions
→ Changing the date and time
→ Modifying your wallpaper
→ Setting alert sounds
→ Changing keyboard and voice settings
→ Modifying more settings

Customizing Android to Your Liking

Your Galaxy Tab A isn't just a static system that forces you to work with it. It's malleable, so you can change many attributes of the system to work the way you prefer.

Password-Protecting the Galaxy Tab A

One of the first things you should do when you set up your Galaxy Tab A is to password-protect it so that unauthorized persons can't use it or gain access to the data stored on it:

1. On the Home screen, swipe from right to left to view the second Home screen and then tap Settings.

2. Tap Lock Screen and Security in the settings list.

3. Tap Other Security Settings.

4. Tap Encrypt Device.

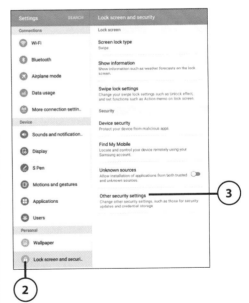

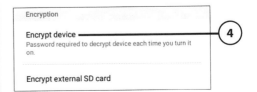

5. The Encrypt Device page on the screen reminds you that the encryption process takes an hour or more, that the device must be plugged in during the entire encryption process, and that interrupting the process risks the loss of some or all of the data stored on the Tab A. When you're finished reading these reminders, tap Set Screen Lock Type.

6. Tap Password.

7. Type your password in the Set Password screen. The password must have at least four characters. One of those characters has to be a letter (either lowercase or uppercase). A couple of seconds after you tap the letter or number, the letter or number turns into a dot to hide what you just entered. Tap Continue.

8. Retype the password in the Confirm Password field and then tap OK.

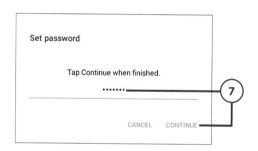

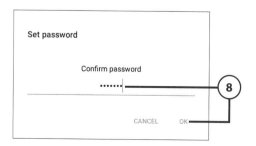

9. By default, the Tab A shows notification content on the Lock screen. If you want to hide the content of these notifications but show the notification title, tap Hide Content.

10. Tap Do Not Show Notifications if you don't want to show notifications.

11. Tap Done after you select the notification option you want.

12. The next time you log in to your Galaxy Tab A, you are prompted to type in your password in the password box.

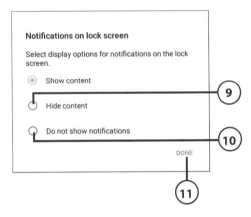

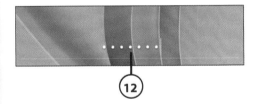

Type your password in the Lock screen

>>>Go Further

WHAT IF I CAN'T REMEMBER MY PASSWORD?

If you can't remember your password, your only recourse is to reset your Galaxy Tab A so that you wipe all the data from it and start from scratch. Unfortunately, this means that all your other data is wiped off the unit as well. Use the following steps to reset your Tab:

1. Turn your Galaxy Tab A off if it isn't already. You might need to remove the battery to turn off the unit.

2. Press and hold the Home and Volume Up buttons.

3. Press and hold the Power button while you're still holding the Home and Volume Up buttons.

4. When you see the Samsung Galaxy Tab A logo, release the Power button but continue to hold the Home and Volume Up buttons.

5. When the recovery screen appears, tap the Volume Down button until Wipe Data/Factory Reset is highlighted.

6. Press the Power button.

7. In the next screen, press the Volume Down button until "Yes—Delete All User Data" is highlighted.

8. Press the Power button.

9. After the Galaxy Tab A wipes the system data, press the Power button to reboot the system.

Changing Your Password

It's a good idea to change your password regularly so you have the peace of mind of knowing that you're keeping one step ahead of potential thieves:

1. On the Home screen, swipe from right to left to view the second Home screen and then tap Settings.

2. Tap Lock Screen and Security in the settings list.

3. Tap Screen Lock Type.

4. Type your password in the Confirm Password screen and then tap Continue.

5. Tap Password.

6. Type your password in the Set Password screen. The password must be at least four characters, including at least one letter (either uppercase or lowercase). A couple of seconds after you tap the letter, the letter turns into a dot to hide what you just entered. Tap Continue.

7. Retype the password in the Confirm Password field and then tap OK. The next time you log in to your Galaxy Tab A, you are prompted to type in your new password.

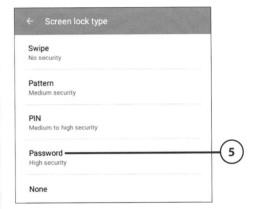

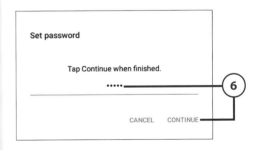

8. By default, the Tab A shows notification content on the Lock screen. If you want to hide the content of these notifications but show the notification title, tap Hide Content.

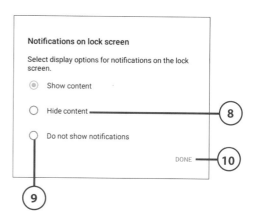

Notifications on lock screen

Select display options for notifications on the lock screen.

◉ Show content

○ Hide content ———————— 8

9. Tap Do Not Show Notifications if you don't want to show notifications.

○ Do not show notifications

DONE — 10

10. Tap Done after you select the notification option you want.

9

>>>Go Further

ENTER A PATTERN OR NUMERIC PIN

The Galaxy Tab A gives you one of three options for password-protecting your unit: a text password, a numeric PIN (such as the one you use for an ATM card), and a pattern that you can draw on the screen. In the Screen Lock Type screen, tap Pattern or PIN to create a new pattern or numeric PIN, respectively. Then follow the step-by-step instructions to set the PIN.

Setting Parental Restrictions

Android 5.0 doesn't include parental restriction settings for specific applications aside from the pattern, PIN, or text password, or the Finger Scanner, used for full access to the Galaxy Tab A.

However, you can find parental control apps in the Google Play Store. Search for "parental control" or "parental controls," read the user reviews for each app, and then decide whether you want to download an app to see if it works for you.

**An example of a parental control app
in the Google Play Store**

Content Filter Settings in the Google Play Store

You can determine what types of apps are shown to anyone who uses your Galaxy Tab A by setting the content filtering settings within the Google Play Store. You can show all apps or you can show apps by maturity level. You find out more about how to do this in Chapter 15, "Finding and Managing Apps."

Changing the Date and Time

You can set the date and time for your Galaxy Tab A, change the time zone, change the date format, and choose whether you want to display the time as standard 12-hour or 24-hour (military) time:

1. On the Home screen, swipe from right to left to view the second Home screen and then tap Settings.

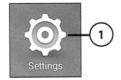

2. Swipe down in the settings list on the left side of the screen and then tap Date and Time.

3. Slide the Automatic Date and Time slider from right to left so the Tab A does not use the network-provided time.

4. The Automatic Date and Time slider and slider button turn gray to let you know the feature is off.

5. Tap Set Date.

6. Set the date by tapping the date within the calendar month on the left side of the Set Date window. Swipe left and right within the calendar to see past, current, and future months. The current date is highlighted with a blue circle.

7. Tap the year to select a new year from the menu.

8. Tap Done.

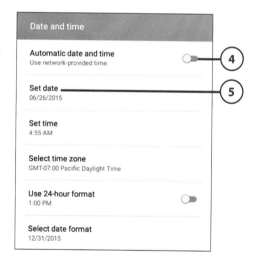

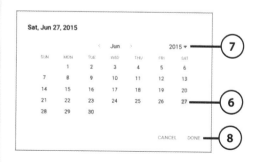

9. Tap Set Time.

10. Tap the hour and/or minute to change the time information. You can also tap the up or down arrow button above and below the hour or minute to move the hour or minute by one hour or one minute, respectively.

11. Tap the AM or PM box to change the time of day between AM and PM.

12. Tap Keypad to open the keypad below the clock, tap the hour or minute, and then type the hour or minute number in the keypad.

13. Tap Done.

14. Tap Select Time Zone to change the current time zone in the Select Time Zone list.

15. Slide the Use 24-Hour Format slider from left to right to change the format to 24-hour time. The slider and slider button turn green to signify the feature is on and the time on the Notification bar reflects the change to 24-hour time. You can return to 12-hour time by sliding the slider from right to left.

16. Tap Select Date Format.

17. Tap one of the four format options to change the date format. If you don't want to change the date format, tap Cancel.

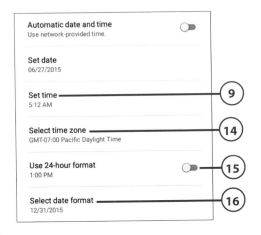

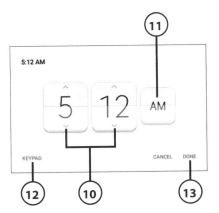

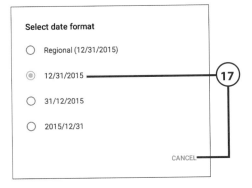

Modifying Your Wallpaper

The standard wallpaper appears behind both the Lock screen and the Home screen. Android makes it easy for you to change the wallpaper to whatever you want:

1. Hold your finger down on the Home screen for a couple of seconds (not shown).

2. Tap Wallpapers.

3. Tap Home Screen, Lock Screen, or Home and Lock Screens depending on where you want to display your wallpaper. This example uses the Home and Lock Screens option.

4. Scroll through the thumbnail images of wallpapers. If you want to preview a wallpaper on the screen, tap the thumbnail image. The current thumbnail image appears above the Set As Wallpaper button and a larger version of the image appears above the thumbnail images.

5. Tap the From Gallery thumbnail image to open the Gallery app and select a photo stored on your Tab A as your wallpaper.

6. When you find wallpaper you want, tap Set As Wallpaper. The new wallpaper appears on your Home and Lock screens.

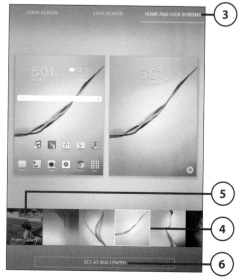

Setting Alert Sounds

If you want the Galaxy Tab A to make noise when you perform different actions, such as when you tap something on the screen, you can change the alert sounds. If you prefer, you can turn them off entirely.

1. On the Home screen, swipe from right to left to view the second Home screen and then tap Settings.

2. Tap Sounds and Notifications in the settings list.

3. You can mute the Tab A by tapping Sound Mode and then tapping Mute in the pop-up menu.

4. Tap Volume.

5. Change the volume for music, video, games, and other media, notifications, and system sounds by dragging the appropriate slider bar to the left (lower volume) or right (higher volume).

6. Tap the Back icon in the menu bar.

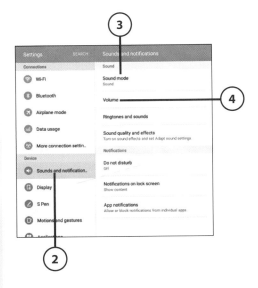

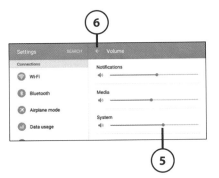

7. Tap Ringtones and Sounds.

8. Tap Default Notification Sound.

9. Set the notification sound from the menu. This sound plays whenever you receive a notification.

10. Tap OK.

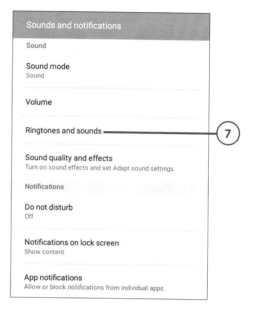

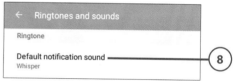

11. Tap Touch Sounds to turn off the feature that plays a sound when you make a screen selection. After you tap Touch Sounds, the slider and slider button turn gray to remind you the feature is off. Turn on this feature again by tapping Touch Sounds.

12. Tap Screen Lock Sounds to stop playing sounds when you lock and unlock the screen. After you tap Screen Lock Sounds, the slider and slider button turn gray to remind you the feature is off. Turn on this feature again by tapping Screen Lock Sounds.

13. Tap Keyboard Sound to stop the Tab A from making a sound when you tap keys on the keyboard and some other user interface features such as the Back touch button.

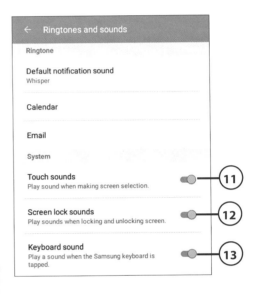

Changing Keyboard and Voice Settings

The Galaxy Tab A gives you two input options: the Samsung keyboard and Google Voice Typing so you can speak commands to the Tab A.

The examples in this book use keyboard settings for the Samsung keyboard, which is the default keyboard the Galaxy Tab A uses when you type text, as well as built-in keyboard settings that apply to all keyboards.

1. On the Home screen, swipe from right to left to view the second Home screen and then tap Settings.

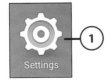

2. Swipe down the settings list on the left side of the screen and then tap Language and Input.

3. Because the default is the Samsung keyboard, open the Samsung Keyboard Settings screen by tapping Samsung Keyboard.

4. Tap Select Input Languages if you want to change the default keyboard input language.

5. Tap Smart Typing.

6. Tap Predictive Text if you don't want the Galaxy Tab A to guess what you're typing and provide suggestions for words. This is similar to the auto-complete feature in word processors.

7. Tap Auto Replace so the Tab A will guess the word you're typing when you tap the spacebar after typing a word.

8. Tap Auto Check Spelling to underline words you type (such as in an email message) with possible spelling errors in red so you can check and fix those errors if necessary.

9. Tap Text Shortcuts to create one or more shortcuts for a phrase that you type often. When you type the shortcut in the app, such as in an email message, the Tab A automatically replaces the shortcut with the phrase you associated with the shortcut.

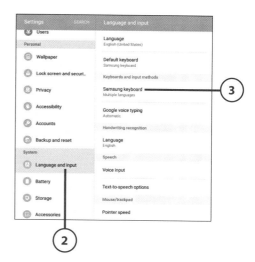

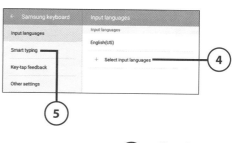

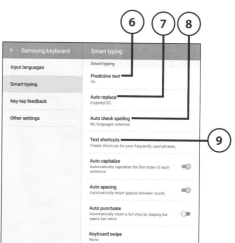

10. Tap Auto Capitalize to turn off auto-capitalization for words; the slider and slider button turn gray to signify the feature is off. By default, the Galaxy Tab A auto-capitalizes the first word in a sentence. If the Galaxy Tab A recognizes a sentence-ending punctuation mark—that is, a period, question mark, or exclamation mark—followed by a space, the next letter is capitalized automatically unless you tap the Shift key to turn it off. (There are exceptions to this rule, such as when you type in the To box when you compose a new email message.) You can turn the feature back on by tapping Auto Capitalization.

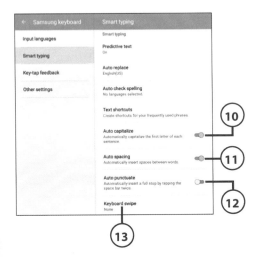

11. Tap Auto Spacing to turn off the automatic insertion of a space between words; the slider and slider button turn gray to signify the feature is off. By default, the Galaxy Tab A monitors your words as you type and automatically inserts a space between words. Turn the feature back on by tapping Auto Spacing.

12. Tap Auto Punctuate to automatically insert a period after a word by double-tapping the spacebar. The slider and slider button turn green to signify the feature is on.

13. Tap Keyboard Swipe to either enter text by sliding your finger across the keyboard or sliding your finger across the keyboard to move the text cursor on the screen.

14. Tap Key-Tap Feedback in the list.

15. Slide the Sound slider from right to left so the Galaxy Tab A makes no sound each time you press a key. The slider and slider button turn gray to signify the feature is off. Turn on the key-tap sound feature by sliding the Sound slider from left to right.

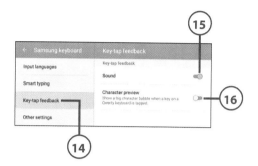

16. Slide the Character Preview from left to right to display the character you're typing on the keyboard in a box above the key for about a second after you tap the key. The slider and slider button turn green to signify the feature is on.

17. Tap Other Settings in the list.

18. If you have the Tab A with S Pen, tap Pen Detection to view the handwriting pad so you can write instead of type, such as when you compose an email message. The slider and slider button turn green to signify the feature is on.

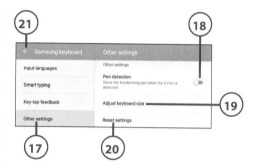

19. Tap Adjust Keyboard Size to adjust the size of the keyboard on the screen so the keyboard is slightly larger or slightly smaller than the default size.

20. Tap Reset Settings if you change your mind after you make settings and decide you want the default settings instead.

21. Tap the Back icon at the left side of the menu bar to return to the Samsung Keyboard Settings screen.

Modifying More Settings

There are too many settings in Android to cover in this book, but here are some of the more important settings that you should know about:

1. On the Home screen, swipe from right to left to view the second Home screen and then tap Settings.

2. Tap Display in the settings list.

3. Set the brightness level by moving the slider in the Brightness area to change the brightness level.

4. Change the brightness to its default level by tapping the Auto check box.

5. Tap Screen Timeout.

6. Select the period of inactivity after which the screen times out and goes dark. The default is 5 minutes. If you don't want to change the time interval, tap Cancel.

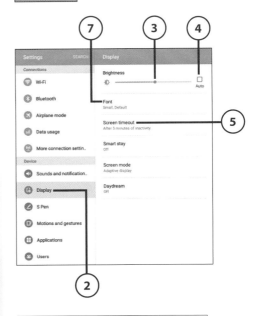

Powering Up Your Screen

After the screen goes dark, you can easily start it again by pressing the Home button or Power button. If your Galaxy Tab A is password-protected (or PIN- or pattern-protected), you must type your password (or PIN or pattern) to start using the Galaxy Tab A again. If the Tab A requires you to scan your finger, you need to place the appropriate finger on the Finger Scanner area so the device can scan it and give you access to the system.

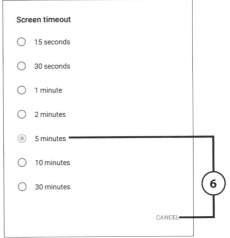

7. Tap Font.

8. Set the font style by tapping the button to the left of the style name. When you select the font style, you can choose from the built-in fonts or you can search for, purchase, and download fonts from the Google Play Store.

9. If you find that the text isn't legible enough, you can enhance clarity of the text by moving the slider from left to right to make the text smaller or larger, respectively.

10. The text above the slider shows you what the text looks like so you can decide if the font size and/or style you selected is right for you.

11. When you select a new font size and/or style, tap OK.

12. After you change the font size and/or style, the new font style and/or size appears within the Settings page after a second or two. If you want to change the font size again, tap Font in the menu and then change the style and/or size in the Font window.

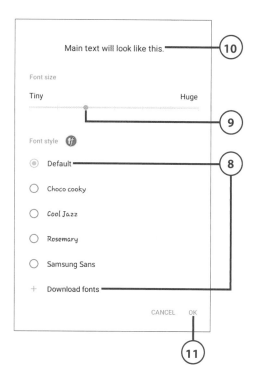

Learn how to browse
widgets and add a widget
to your Home screen

The Galaxy Tab A contains dozens of preinstalled widgets, which act as miniature applications that allow you to perform different
tasks. This chapter covers the following topics:

→ Accessing the Widgets screen
→ Adding a widget to a Home screen
→ Creating a new Home screen
→ Removing a widget

Adding Widgets to Your Home Screen

Widgets are a truly valuable aspect of the Android platform. A *widget* is a small, portable piece of code that you can interact with like
a miniature application. Your Galaxy Tab A has quite a few widgets
from which you can choose that can make your Tab experience
even more convenient.

Accessing the Widgets Screen

You can find widgets on the Widgets screen, where 46 preinstalled
widgets for different tasks are listed. Tapping a widget can provide
you a variety of information, such as stock market news or the
weather. (By default, you have a weather widget on your Home
screen.) A widget can also act as a world clock or initiate
functionality from a parent app, such as Maps, when you tap it.
Although you can apply widgets to a Home screen, some widgets
must be configured.

1. On the Home screen, tap and hold on a blank area within the screen for 2 seconds.

2. Tap Widgets.

3. Swipe left and right through the pages of widgets. The number of pages depends on the Galaxy Tab A model you have and your screen orientation.

Why Do I See More Than 46 Widgets?

If you see more than the 46 widgets described in this chapter, you likely imported widgets from another Android device you own (such as your smartphone) when you set up your Tab A. This chapter discusses only those widgets that come preinstalled on the Tab A.

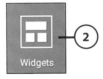

Adding a Widget to a Home Screen

It's easy to add a widget from the Widgets screen to an existing Home screen or a new one that you create. When you add a widget to a Home screen, you can specify where that widget—either an icon or the widget area—will reside on the Home screen. If you decide that you want to move the widget to a different location on the same or a different Home screen, you can drag the widget to that new location on the current Home screen, another existing Home screen, or a new Home screen that you create.

Some widgets also enable you to change their size before you place them on your desired Home screen. If the widget you're trying to add to an existing Home screen won't fit on that Home screen, Lollipop adds a new Home screen automatically and places the widget on that new Home screen.

Place a Widget on a Home Screen

1. On the Home screen, tap and hold on a blank area within the screen for 2 seconds (not shown).

2. Tap Widgets.

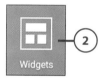

3. Press and hold your finger on the Dual Clock widget.

4. The Edit Home screen appears; the Home screen tile appears in a smaller area of the screen and the widget you're moving appears as an outline on the screen. Underneath the Home screen tile, Lollipop also highlights the corresponding Home screen icon.

5. Move the outline over the Home screen tile to which you want to add the widget.

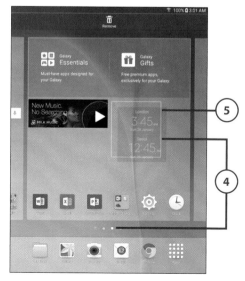

6. Release your finger. The widget appears on the Home screen where you placed it, which in this example is below the Galaxy Apps widget and to the right of the Milk Music widget. If any other widgets appear on the screen, then these other widgets reposition to make room for your widget.

7. The Dual Clock widget lets you configure the information that it displays. Add a new city by tapping the Tap Here to Add a City box.

8. Perhaps a friend has traveled to Paris for the summer and you don't want to call her in the middle of the night. Tap the European continent on the map to see a map of cities.

9. Tap, hold, and drag within the map until you see Paris. Tap Paris to see the current local time.

10. Tap the plus icon to add the city to your clock.

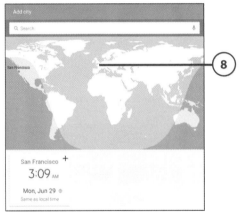

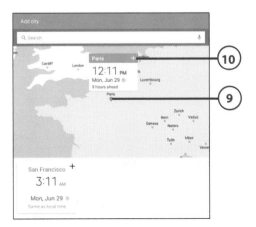

11. Paris is added to the clock, and now you know the current time for the city where your friend is staying.

12. Tap either city to change to a different city.

13. You can search for a city by typing the city name in the Search box.

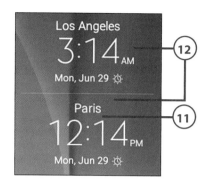

Move a Widget on a Home Screen

You can move a widget to a different location on the same Home screen by tapping and holding the widget within the Home screen. This example shows how to reposition the Dual Clock widget.

1. Tap and hold the widget you want to move. The widget outline appears in the Home screen tile so you can see where you can move the widget.

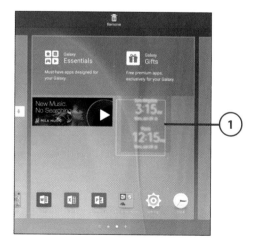

2. Drag the widget to the new location on the Home screen. The Home screen is ordered in a grid format and + signs within the Home screen denote grid corners. As you move the widget to the new location, a lighter copy of the outline appears below and to the right of your widget outline. This lighter outline copy denotes where your widget will reside on the screen. If there's a widget that already resides in the location you want, the widgets reposition themselves on the screen to accommodate your desired location for the widget.

3. Release your finger. The widget appears in your desired location.

Move the Widget to a New Home Screen

You can add the widget to a brand-new Home screen by dragging the widget outline to the right side of the screen until the new Home screen tile appears. Move the widget outline to your desired location within that new Home screen tile. When you're satisfied, release your finger. The new Home screen appears with the widget in your desired location.

Resize a Widget

Some widgets come in a preset size. Others allow you to change the size of the widget when you add it to the Home screen. You can also change the size of an adjustable widget after you add the widget to a Home screen. This example describes how to add the Gmail widget.

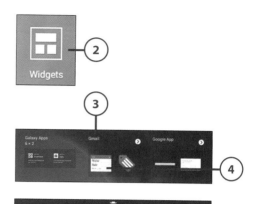

1. On the Home screen, tap and hold on a blank area within the screen for 2 seconds (not shown).

2. Tap Widgets.

3. Navigate to the page that contains the Gmail group widget.

4. Tap the Gmail group widget icon to view all widgets in the group.

5. Press and hold your finger on the Gmail widget. The Home screen tile you chose appears and the widget you're moving appears as an outline within the tile.

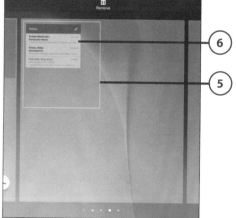

6. Move the outline over the Home screen tile to position the widget within the tile. When you're satisfied with the location of the widget on the Home screen, release your finger.

7. In the Choose Folder window, tap the Gmail folder you want to display in the widget within the list.

8. The widget appears on the Home screen with a blue box around it. Blue circles, or *handles*, appear on all four sides of the box.

9. Resize the widget by tapping and holding on one of the handles and then dragging left and right or up and down, depending on the handle you're moving. For example, if you drag the bottom handle up and down, then you change the height of the widget. If your widget size is too large for the available area on the Home screen, then the box and handles turn red to tell you that the widget is too large for the available space.

Can I Resize More Than One Direction at a Time?

When you resize the widget using one of the handles, you can only drag in the handle's required direction. For example, if you tap and hold the right side handle, you can only drag left and right. After you finish resizing the widget and release your finger, the handles reappear so you can tap and hold on one of the other handles and drag in the required direction.

10. Release your finger. The resized widget appears on the Edit Home screen. If the widget is too large for the area you want, Lollipop automatically resizes the widget to fill the available width or height.

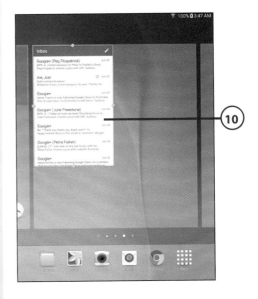

11. Tap the Back touch button. Your widget appears on the Home screen at your desired size.

Resize and/or Move the Widget Again

If you decide that you want to resize the widget, tap and hold on the widget. The Edit Home screen appears so you can resize the widget on the Home screen, move the widget around on the Home screen, or move the widget to a different Home screen.

Creating a New Home Screen

A task earlier in this chapter describes how to create a new Home screen when you add a new widget. There are two other ways to create a new Home screen: from within an existing Home screen and in the Home screen menu.

1. On the Home screen, tap and hold your finger on a blank area within the screen for 2 seconds.

2. Swipe to the right within the page until you see the New Page tile in the menu. (It has a plus sign in the center.)

3. Tap the New Page tile.

4. The new Home page appears in a tile on the screen. The new Home page you're viewing is denoted by a white dot underneath the new Home page tile.

5. Tap the new Home page tile to view the new Home page on the entire screen.

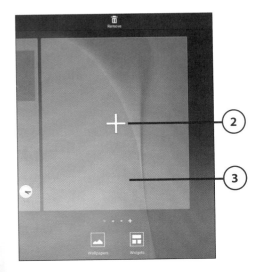

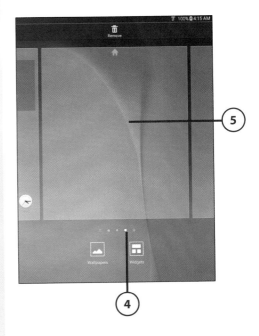

HOW DO I REMOVE A HOME SCREEN?

It's easy to remove a Home screen if you don't want the Home screen and any icons or widgets on that screen. Start by pressing and holding the Recent touch button for a couple of seconds. In the Edit Home screen, tap and hold the Home page tile you want to delete and then drag the button to the Remove icon at the top of the screen. When the button you're dragging turns red, release your finger.

The Home screen disappears from the Edit Home screen. If your Home page has icons or widgets in it when you delete it, Lollipop removes the Home screen and all items within it. Note that if you change your mind, you need to re-create the Home screen and then add the icons and widgets to it.

Removing a Widget

It's easy to remove a widget from a Home screen if you decide that you don't want it any longer.

1. Navigate to the Home screen that contains the widget you want to remove. Tap and hold on the widget.

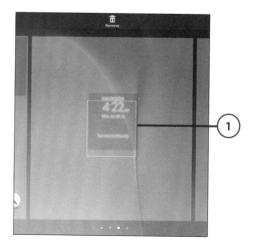

2. Within the Edit Home Page screen, drag the outline of the widget to the Remove icon at the top of the screen. When the Remove icon is highlighted in red, release your finger.

3. The Home screen appears and no longer contains the widget you removed.

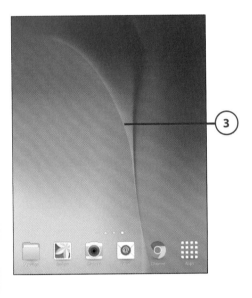

Use widgets designed
for Lollipop and the
Galaxy Tab A

Chapter 4, "Adding Widgets to Your Home Screen," described how to add a widget to a Home screen. Some of these widgets are available on the Home screens by default, and another Home screen houses the Flipboard Briefing news aggregation app. This chapter covers the following topics:

→ Viewing default widgets
→ Using the widgets
→ Using the Flipboard Briefing Home screen

5

Finding Widgets and Using Flipboard Briefing

Your Galaxy Tab A comes with a number of preinstalled widgets you can use. Some of these widgets are new with the latest version of Lollipop and others are unique to the Galaxy Tab A. The widgets include the Weather widget, the Google Chrome Bookmarks widget, and more.

What's more, the Galaxy Tab A comes with the Flipboard Briefing Home screen so you can get the most up-to-date worldwide news from a variety of sources.

Viewing Default Widgets

By default, four widgets appear on the two default Home screens:

- The primary Home screen contains the Weather widget at the top of the screen. This widget displays the current date and time as well as the current weather conditions for your location. Below the Weather widget, the Google Search widget enables you to set up the Google Now app so you can get information you need without having to launch a browser app.

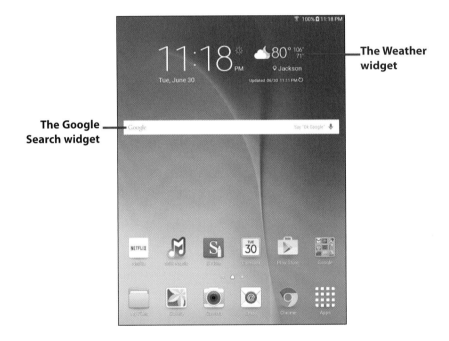

The Weather widget

The Google Search widget

- Swipe from right to left on the primary Home screen to view the Galaxy Apps and Milk Music widgets on the Home screen. The Galaxy Apps widget doesn't display any information because you haven't set up the widget to display suggested apps from the Galaxy Apps Store yet.

The Galaxy — Apps widget

The Milk — Music widget

Find Widgets on the Widgets Pages

The widgets covered in this chapter are also within the Widgets screen pages. Some of them are already on Home screens by default, but it's useful to know where the widgets are within the Widgets screen in case you remove a widget and want to place it on a Home screen again.

1. Tap and hold on a blank area within the Home screen for a couple of seconds (not shown).

2. Tap Widgets.

3. Swipe from right to left to view the Google App widget group on page 2 of the Widgets screen.

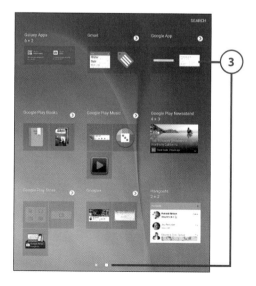

4. Tap the Google App widget group thumbnail image to view the Google App widgets group in the pop-up window. The Google App widget is on the primary Home screen by default.

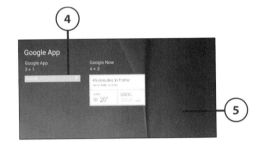

5. Return to page 2 in the Widgets screen by tapping outside the pop-up window.

6. Swipe from right to left to view page 3 in the Widgets screen, which contains the Milk Music widget.

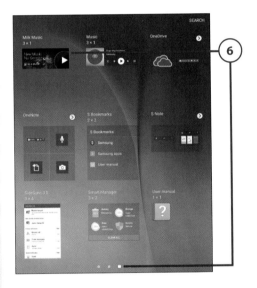

Where Should I Put These Widgets?

You can place these widgets anywhere on Home screens (as described in Chapter 4), and it's presumed that you have added the widgets discussed in this chapter to a Home screen. For the purposes of this chapter, widgets that are not on Home screens by default appear on their own Home screens.

7. Swipe from right to left to view page 4, the last page in the Widgets screen. The Weather widget appears on this page.

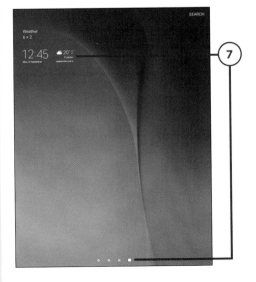

Using the Widgets

All widgets enable you to open the related app on the screen to view more information and make changes to the app. Some widgets have controls within the widget to update and/or change information you view in the widget.

Learn What It's Like Outside with the Weather Widget

Let's begin by viewing the widget that appears on the primary Home screen: the Weather widget.

1. On the Home screen, update the current temperature and sky conditions for your area by tapping the Refresh icon. After a few seconds, the sky conditions image and the current temperature update on the screen. The time and date of your last refresh appear to the left of the Refresh icon.

2. Open the Weather app by tapping anywhere inside the widget.

3. Add a city for which you want to display weather information by tapping Add in the menu bar.

4. If you see the Attention window on the screen that asks you to use the Samsung keyboard personalized data feature, tap OK in the window (not shown).

5. Type the city you're looking for in the Search Cities field. As you type, a list of potential matches appears below the field.

6. Select the city that matches your search term by tapping the city in the list.

7. Swipe up and down the list of cities that match your search term within the list. When you find the city for which you want to display weather information, tap the city in the list.

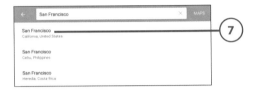

8. Four areas compose the report section at the top of the Weather screen. The top of the screen displays current weather information, including the current sky conditions for your area, the current temperature, the forecast high and low temperatures for the day, the forecast hourly temperatures every four hours during the day, as well as information about precipitation and the ultraviolet (UV) index.

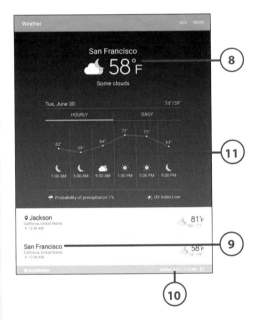

9. Below the report section, you see a list of all cities you're tracking; tap the city name in the list to view the current weather in the report section.

10. Check the bottom of the screen to see the date and time the information was last updated. Tap the Refresh icon to get the most current weather information that appears at the top of the screen.

11. Tap within the report section to view more weather information for your area in either the Internet or Chrome app. This example uses the Internet app.

12. The AccuWeather.com page appears and displays current information for your area. Tap Allow to allow AccuWeather to use your device's location so you can get the most current and accurate weather possible.

13. Swipe up and down the screen to view the temperature, precipitation, and cloud cover forecasts at the beginning of each hour throughout the day. Tap an hourly tile to view more information about the forecast for that hour, including wind speed, humidity level, and the UV index level.

14. Return to the Weather widget screen by tapping the Back touch button (not shown).

15. View more Weather options by tapping More in the menu bar.

16. View a current weather map by tapping Weather Map.

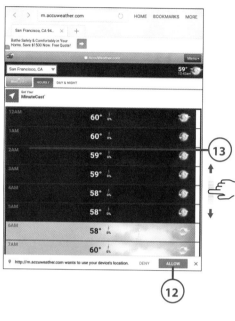

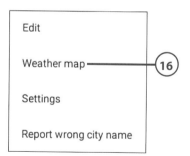

Edit

Weather map

Settings

Report wrong city name

17. A Google map of the larger area around your location appears on the screen. Your current location appears in the center of the map; in this example, it's San Francisco, California.

18. Return to the Weather widget screen by tapping the Back touch button (not shown).

Access Chrome Bookmarks Quickly Using Bookmarks

The Bookmarks widget enables you to store bookmarks within the Chrome browser app. After you set up the Bookmarks widget, you can browse for bookmarks directly within the widget and open the book-marked website in the Internet or Chrome app.

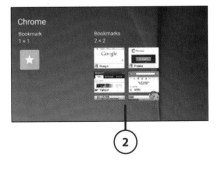

1. Open the Widgets screen, navigate to the first page in the Widgets screen if necessary, and then tap the Chrome tile.

2. Add the Bookmarks (2 × 2) widget to your desired Home screen if you haven't done so already from within the Chrome pop-up window.

3. The Bookmarks widget appears on the Home screen's Setup screen so you can see how the widget will look on the screen. You can move the widget around on the screen and you can resize the widget by tapping, holding, and dragging one of the four resizing handles on the sides of the widget box. For this example, I resized the widget so it appears in the bottom half of the main Home screen.

4. Tap the Back touch button. The widget appears on the screen, but if you haven't set up Chrome yet, there are no bookmarks within the widget.

5. Tap the Chrome icon in the widget.

6. In the Chrome introductory window, tap Accept & Continue.

Do I See the Introductory Window Every Time I Start Chrome?

The introductory windows shown in steps 6 and 7 only appear the first time you start Chrome. The next time, you won't see these windows, and you can proceed to step 8.

Welcome to Chrome

By using this application, you agree to Chrome's Terms of Service and Privacy Notice.

☐ Help make Chrome better by sending usage statistics and crash reports to Google.

ACCEPT & CONTINUE

7. In the second introductory window, tap Done.

8. Return to the Home screen by pressing the Home button (not shown).

9. Tap the folder you want to open within the widget.

10. Swipe your finger up and down within the widget to view all the bookmarks (and any subfolders) contained within the folder. Go back to the previous folder by tapping the folder name at the top left of the folder list.

11. Tap the bookmark that contains the website you want to view.

12. If you see the Open With window, tap the browser app icon to view the website within that browser app. This example uses the Chrome app.

13. Tap Always to open websites from the widget using the selected browser app. If you want the app to ask you to select your browser app each time you open a bookmarked website, tap Just Once.

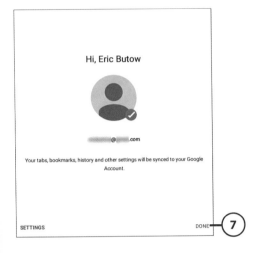

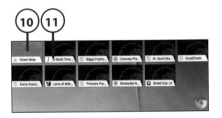

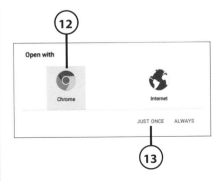

14. The website appears in your desired browser app.

15. Tap the Back touch button to return to the Home screen that contains the Bookmarks app (not shown).

Curious about calculus?
Come take a stroll.
A ∫troll through calculus
by Anthony Barcellos

Author   Reviews   News   Links   Email

A Stroll Through Calculus is an easygoing tour of the main concepts of calculus without fussing over dotting every *i* and crossing every *t*. Despite what many think, the basic content of calculus is understandable at an elementary level. People who aren't afraid of a little high school algebra can discover in these pages why calculus is so important and so powerful—without getting bogged down in

⟨14⟩

Preview New Apps in the Google Play Store Widget

If you want to know what new apps are available and recommended for you without having to go into the Google Play Store app, you can add the Google Play Store widget to the screen and view a slideshow of new apps on your Home screen.

If you find an app you like, tap the widget to open the app information page within the Google Play Store screen. Chapter 15, "Finding and Managing Apps," includes more information about finding apps for your Tab A.

1. Open the Widgets screen, navigate to the third page in the Widgets screen if necessary, and then tap the Google Play Store tile.

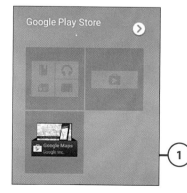

2. Add the Play Store widget to your desired Home screen if you haven't done so already from within the Google Play Store pop-up window.

3. The Google Play Store widget appears on the Home screen's Setup screen so you can see how the widget will look on the screen. Release your finger to place the widget on the page.

4. The widget displays a slideshow of featured apps that include a thumbnail image, the name of the app, and the company that (or individual who) developed the app. The slideshow displays a total of nine apps and displays the next app every 7 seconds in a continuous loop.

5. If you see an app displayed in the slideshow and you want more information about it, tap the widget.

What If I Want to Go Back to Viewing the Featured App in the Google Play Store?

When you tap the Back touch button in the Google Play Store app, you haven't closed it. You can go back to the featured app in the Google Play Store by tapping the Recent Apps touch button and then tapping the Google Play Store tile within the Recent Apps screen.

6. The Google Play Store screen opens and displays information about the app.

7. Swipe up and down the screen to get more information about the app, including user reviews, similar apps, and developer contact information.

8. Tap the Install button to install the free app on your Tab A. If you need to purchase the app before you install it, tap the purchase button, which includes the price of the app within the button.

9. If you prefer to go back to the Home screen and view more featured apps in the widget, tap the Back touch button (not shown).

Using the Flipboard Briefing Home Screen

The Galaxy Tab A contains a specially designed Home screen called Flipboard Briefing, which aggregates news from various sources into one app so you can quickly access news and information that's important to you. The row of Home screen icons at the bottom of the screen also has a unique icon for the Flipboard Briefing Home screen—instead of a button, it's a pair of horizontal bars that look like an equal sign.

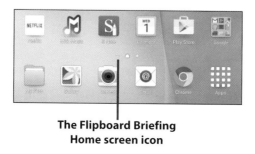

The Flipboard Briefing Home screen icon

Set Up Flipboard Briefing

Before you can use the Flipboard Briefing app, you need to set it up to tell the app what news and information you want delivered.

1. On the main Home screen, swipe from left to right to view the Flipboard Briefing screen.

2. Tap Start Reading.

3. After you see a brief animated introduction, the news feed page appears with the Briefing section at the top of the screen.

4. Swipe up on the screen to view more article headlines, featured stories that include the first few sentences in the article, and other sections such as News and Business. Swipe up to return to the top of the news feed page.

5. Tap the Menu icon.

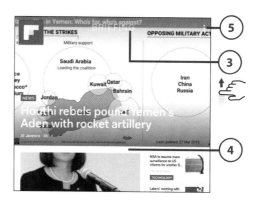

6. You can download the Flipboard app to get all the features of Flipboard by tapping the Get Flipboard Now button. After you tap the button, the Google Play Store screen opens and displays the Flipboard information page.

7. By default, Flipboard Briefing provides notifications of new articles you might want to read. Turn this feature off by sliding the Notifications slider button from right to left; the slider and slider button turn gray to signify that the feature is off.

8. Swipe upward on the screen to view all the news category tiles.

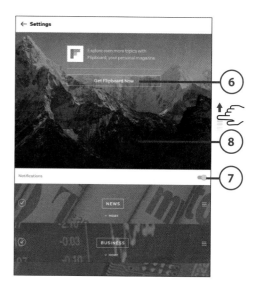

Can I Add More Categories?

If you swipe all the way down to the bottom of the news feed, you see an Explore More Topics section with suggested topics, such as social media, personal finance, and pets. Add a category by tapping the category name button within the section.

9. News categories in the Flipboard Briefing screen appear in the same order as the news category tiles. You can move a category up or down by tapping and holding on the Move button and then moving the category tile up or down. As you move the tile, other tiles move to accommodate the tile you're moving.

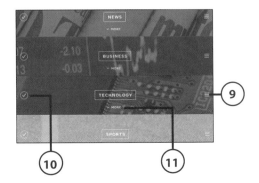

10. If you don't want to view news stories in a category, tap the circle with the check mark. The category tile changes color and the check mark disappears from the circle so you know you won't see articles in that category.

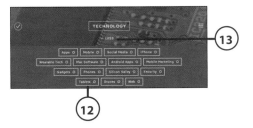

11. Tap More to view subcategories you can add to your news feed.

12. Tap a subcategory button to include more stories about the subcategory topic within the news feed category. After you tap a subcategory button, the button turns white and includes a check mark to the right of the name. Remove the subcategory from the category news feed by tapping the white subcategory button.

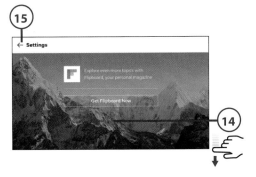

13. Hide the subcategory button list by tapping Less.

14. Swipe down on the screen until you reach the top of the screen.

15. Return to the news feed screen by tapping the Back icon.

Read Stories and Return to the Home Screen

Articles are divided into tiles within the news feed page. Each article tile contains the title of the article and many article tiles contain both photos as well as the first two or three sentences in the article (several sentences in some article tiles) so you can read them and decide if you want to continue reading the article.

1. Swipe up and down the screen until you see article tiles within the category you want to view. If there is room within the article tile, at the bottom of the tile you see the website that produced the article and how long ago the article was published. For example, 2h means the article was published 2 hours ago.

2. When the category name tile reaches the top of the page, the name tile is locked at the top of the page as you swipe. In this example, the Science category name tile appears at the top of the page.

3. Tap the Menu icon to open the Settings screen and change settings as explained earlier in this chapter.

4. Tap the article tile to read the article in its entirety.

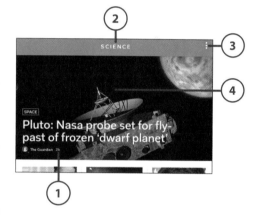

5. Swipe up and down the screen to view the rest of the article on the screen. You can perform tasks available within the web page on the screen, such as sharing the article link on your Facebook profile.

6. Tap Share to share the article with other users or save links to the article in various apps. You can copy the article to the Clipboard, to a Scrapbook app file, as well as to your OneDrive or Google Drive account. You can also send the link to an S Note (or Memo) or OneNote file, to an email message using the Email or Gmail app, to a Google+ post, or in a Google Hangouts or Skype chat. And you can send the link directly to another device using Bluetooth, Wi-Fi Direct, or Samsung Quick Connect.

7. Return to the news feed screen by tapping the Back icon.

8. When you have read one or more articles in a category, the category name tile tells you how many articles you have read. On some article tiles, a check mark appears to the right of the website that produced the article.

9. Swipe downward to view more sections and return to the top of the news feed. When you open a new category as you swipe, that new category name tile appears at the top of the page.

10. Return to the Home screen by swiping from right to left.

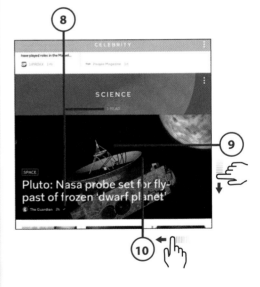

>>>Go Further

IS FLIPBOARD BRIEFING STILL OPEN WHEN I RETURN TO THE HOME SCREEN?

When you return to the Home screen, the Flipboard Briefing app is still open and monitoring your news feeds. When you open Flipboard Briefing again, your news feed will be updated automatically so you can get the latest information in every category. If you want to close the Flipboard Briefing app, tap the Recent touch button and then tap the Close button at the top right of the Flipboard Briefing tile within the Recent screen.

Learn how to browse the Web and view websites using the built-in Internet app

The Galaxy Tab A comes with two built-in browsers: Google Chrome and Samsung's Internet app. This chapter shows you how to browse the Web using the Samsung Internet app, which is designed specifically so you can get the most from the Web on your Tab A. This chapter covers the following topics:

6

→ Browsing to a URL
→ Searching the Web
→ Viewing web pages
→ Bookmarking websites
→ Returning to previously visited pages
→ Deleting bookmarks
→ Filling in web forms
→ Copying text and images from web pages

Browsing the Web

The Galaxy Tab A is a great tool for viewing web pages, whether you're at home or you're on the go. No matter which Galaxy Tab A model you use, the screen is much larger than a mobile phone, so you can see more on the Galaxy Tab A's screen. Because you can touch the screen, you can interact with web content in ways that a computer typically cannot.

Browsing to a URL

It's likely that you already know how to browse to different web pages in your favorite web browser on your computer. The Internet app on the Galaxy Tab A works much the same as the browser on your computer, but there are some differences.

1. On the Home screen, tap Apps.

2. Tap Internet.

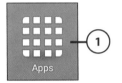

3. Tap the Address field at the top of the screen. The keyboard opens at the bottom of the screen so you can type a uniform resource locator (URL), which can be a website name or a specific page in a website.

4. Start typing a URL, such as samsung.com or play.google.com. You can also select from one of the sites in the list that appears below the Address field.

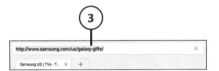

5. Tap Go on the keyboard when you finish typing.

Tips for Typing a URL

The Internet app doesn't require you to type the "http://" or the "www." at the beginning of the URL. For example, if you type samsung.com or www.samsung.com, you still go to the Samsung Home web page. However, there might be some instances when you need to type in "http://" or even "https://" (for a secure web page) at the beginning of the URL. If you do, the Internet app lets you know so that you can type in the "http://" or "https://" in the Address field.

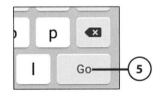

Searching the Web

The Internet app makes it easy for you to search the Web, so you don't need to know every URL of every web page out there (which is good considering there are literally billions of web pages). As you type, the Internet app suggests search terms you've used in the past as well as search terms you might be looking for.

1. On the Home screen, tap Apps.

2. Tap Internet.

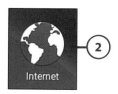

3. Tap the Address field at the top of the screen. The keyboard opens at the bottom of the screen so you can type the URL. Start typing your search term. As you type, a list appears underneath the address bar with suggestions. You can stop typing at any time and scroll down the list to find your search term; tap the search term to select it and start the search.

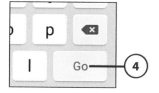

4. If you haven't found what you're looking for, open the Google search page by tapping Go in the keyboard.

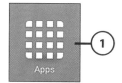

5. The results display in a Google search results page. Tap any link to go to a page; you can also tap one of the links at the bottom of the screen to view more results.

>>>Go Further

TIPS FOR SEARCHING THE WEB

You can search deeper within Google itself. For example, if you put a + in front of a search term, you're telling Google that you require the word in the search results. If you put quotes around a search term ("term"), you're telling Google that you want to search for results that contain that term. Scroll to the bottom of the search page and then tap Help to get more information about how you can get the most from your Google searches.

View popular
articles about
searching with
Google

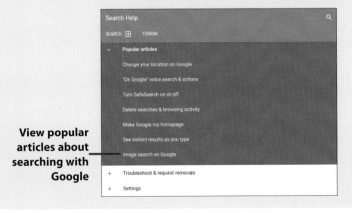

If you look at the top of Google's search results page, you see links so you can search for more than text terms, including Images and Videos. If you click the More link, a pop-up list displays so you can search a variety of other areas within Google.

A list of more areas in which to search within Google

Viewing Web Pages

After you open a website, you can control what you view on the web page in several ways. These techniques enable you to access the entire web page and navigate between web pages in the Internet app.

1. Navigate to a web page using one of the two methods described in the previous tasks in this chapter (not shown).

2. As you view a page, you can drag up and down the page with your finger. You can also flick with your finger to scroll quickly. After you flick, the screen scrolls, decelerates, and then comes to a stop.

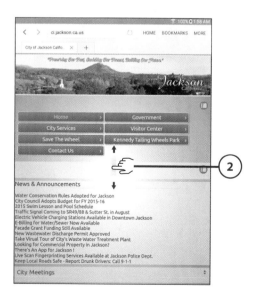

3. Zoom in by double-tapping an area on the screen. Zoom out by double-tapping again.

4. While you're zoomed in, you can touch and drag left and right to view different parts of the web page.

5. Move to another web page from a link in the current web page by tapping a link. Links are usually an underlined or colored piece of text, but they can also be pictures or images that look like buttons.

Hunting for Links

Unfortunately, it isn't always easy to figure out which parts of a web page are links and which ones aren't. Back in the early days of the Web, all links were blue and underlined. As web page elements have become more enhanced over time, it's now more common to find links in any color and any text style. What's more, graphics that are links aren't underlined, either.

On a computer's web browser, it's easy to find out which element is a link when you move the mouse pointer over the link because the pointer changes shape. In Android, there is no cursor, so you can't find out if a web page element is a link unless you tap it and see what happens.

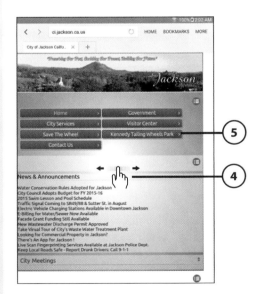

Bookmarking Websites

As you browse websites, you might want to save some of the websites in a list of your favorites so you can go back to them later. In browser parlance, this saving process is called *bookmarking*.

1. Navigate to any page in the Internet app (not shown).

2. Tap Bookmarks at the top of the page. If you see the Sync Bookmarks window, tap Done in the window.

3. The Bookmarks window opens on the right side of the screen. Tap Add.

4. Edit the title of the bookmark. The official title of the web page is filled in and highlighted for you, but you can change the name by typing the new name using the keyboard. To change the folder in which the bookmark is stored, proceed with step 5. Otherwise, skip to step 12.

5. To change the folder in which the bookmark is stored, tap the folder name, which is My Device in this example.

6. Create a new bookmarks subfolder by tapping Create.

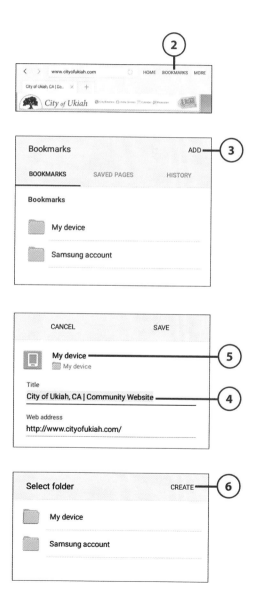

7. Tap the Enter Folder Name field and then type the name of your new subfolder.

8. Tap the parent folder into which your new subfolder will reside. The default is My Device, but you can also save the new subfolder within your Samsung Account folder.

9. Tap Save.

10. Tap the name of the folder into which you want to place the bookmark.

11. Tap Save.

12. Tap the folder name that contains the new subfolder.

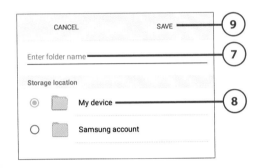

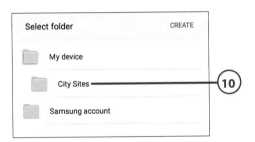

Should I Edit a Bookmark Title?

Because the titles of web pages are usually long and descriptive, it's a good idea to shorten the title to something you can recognize easily in your bookmarks list. Every bookmark also includes a thumbnail picture of what the web page looks like so you can identify the bookmark more easily. If you would rather view your bookmarks by title, tap the Edit button at the bottom of the Bookmarks window. In the Bookmarks screen, tap the Menu icon at the right side of the menu bar and then tap List View in the menu.

13. Tap the subfolder name within the list.

14. The new bookmark appears within the subfolder list.

15. Tap Bookmarks above the subfolder list to return to the main Bookmarks folder.

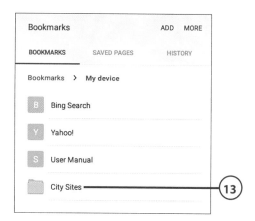

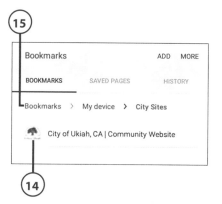

Returning to Previously Visited Pages

It's easy to return to the last page you visited in the Internet app—just press the Back button. As you keep pressing the Back button, you keep going back to pages you visited. In the History page, the Internet app also keeps a list of all web pages you've visited during your browsing session.

Browsing Forward

Like with any web browser, you can browse more recent pages you've viewed in your current browsing session by tapping the Forward button, which is the right-arrow button immediately to the right of the Back button.

1. Visit several web pages in the Internet app if you haven't done so already (not shown).

2. Tap Bookmarks.

3. Tap the History tab in the Bookmarks window.

4. The list of web pages you visited for the current date appears under the Today heading.

Tips for Using History

If you want to hide the history for a specific day so you can see history for another day, tap the header for the specific day. For example, if you want to hide all the web pages for today, click the Today heading above the first web page in the Today list. The Today heading is still visible, but you won't see the web pages. You can view the web pages again by tapping the Today heading.

You can also clear the entire history database by tapping More above the History tab. Within the menu, tap Clear History. After you tap the icon, all websites in the History tab disappear.

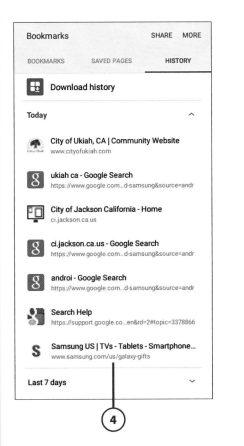

Deleting Bookmarks

If you find there are websites that you don't visit anymore or that go to obsolete or missing web pages, you need to cull your bookmark list. You can delete a bookmark from the Bookmarks list or from the History list.

Delete from the Bookmarks List

The first method uses the Bookmarks list to delete a bookmark.

1. Tap Bookmarks at the top of the Internet app screen as you learned to do earlier in this chapter. The bookmarks you added most recently appear. If you haven't added a bookmark, you see bookmarks and subfolders within the main Bookmarks folder.

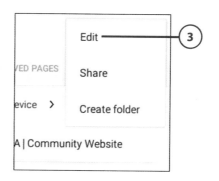

2. Tap More.

3. Tap Edit.

4. Tap the check box to the left of the bookmark name. The check box turns green and a white check mark appears within the check box.

5. Delete the bookmark by tapping Delete. The Internet app deletes the bookmark instantly.

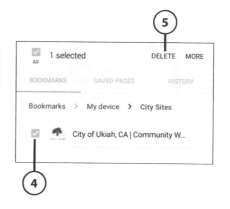

Delete from the History List

The second method uses the History list to delete a bookmark.

1. Tap the Bookmarks button at the top of the Internet screen, as you learned to do earlier in this chapter. The bookmarks you added most recently appear.

2. Tap the History tab. This brings up a list of web pages you've viewed recently.

3. Tap More.

4. Tap Edit.

Sync Your Bookmarks

You can sync the bookmarks in your favorite web browser on your desktop or laptop computer with the Internet app so you have maximum control over your bookmarks. You can read more about syncing your Galaxy Tab A in Chapter 2, "Setting Up the Galaxy Tab A."

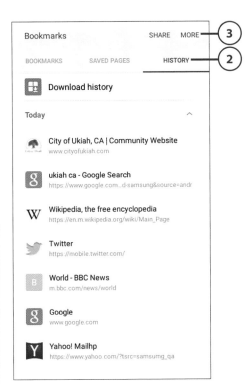

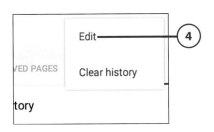

5. Tap the check box to the left of the bookmark name. The check box turns green and a white check mark appears within the check box.

6. Tap Delete. The website no longer appears in the list of web pages.

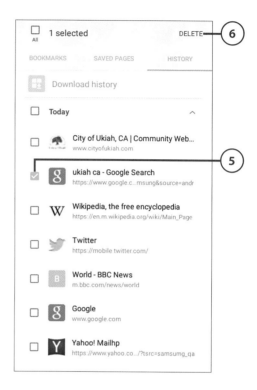

Filling in Web Forms

On many web pages, you are asked to fill in forms, such as for signing up for a company's email newsletter or to get more information about a product. Filling out web forms on your Galaxy Tab A is similar to filling out forms on a computer's web browser, but there are differences.

1. Navigate to a page that you know contains a form. (The sample page is at http://code.google.com/p/android/issues/entry.)

2. Tap in a text box.

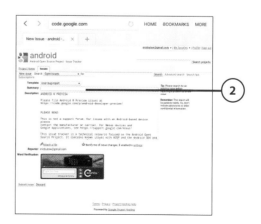

3. The keyboard appears at the bottom of the screen. Use the keyboard to type text into the box; the screen enlarges so you can see the text box more easily. Tap the Go button when you finish typing.

4. Select an item in a pull-down menu by tapping the box.

5. Tap an item in the menu to select it. If the menu list is long, touch and drag up and down to view more selections.

6. The selected item appears in the field.

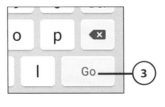

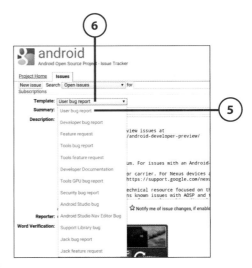

Special Menus

Some websites use special menus that are built from scratch. In these cases, the menu looks exactly like the one you get when you view the web page on a computer. If the web page is well constructed, it should work fine on the Galaxy Tab A. However, it might be a little more difficult to make a selection.

Copying Text and Images from Web Pages

The Internet app treats web pages like other documents. That is, you can copy text and images from a web page you view in a browser to another app.

Copy a Block of Text

You can select text from web pages
to copy and paste into other documents, such as email messages or
your own text documents.

1. Navigate to a web page in the
   Internet app if you haven't done
   so already (not shown).

2. Hold down your finger on the first
   word in the block of text and then
   release your finger. The first word
   is highlighted in green with blue
   "handles" at the beginning and
   end of the word.

3. Hold down your finger on the
   bottom handle (the one on the
   right side of the word) and drag
   over the text you want to copy.
   When you are finished, release
   your finger. The selected text is
   highlighted in green.

4. In the pop-up menu that appears
   above the selected text, tap the
   Copy icon. Android informs you
   that the text has been copied to
   the Clipboard. You can now go to
   another application, such as Email
   (or an email form on another web
   page), and paste the text into
   a text area. For example, in the
   Email app, you tap and hold on
   the cursor in the message for a
   second or two and then tap Paste
   in the pop-up menu that appears
   above the cursor.

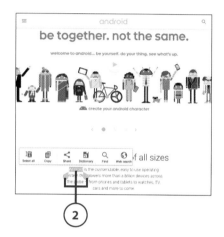

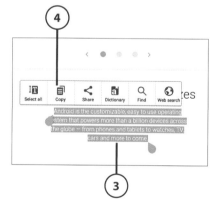

Copy an Image

In addition to being able to copy and paste text from the Internet app, you can also copy images from a web page and save them to an email message or a photo collection.

1. Go to a web page that includes an image on the page (not shown).

2. Tap and hold your finger on that image for a couple of seconds and then release your finger. The image menu window appears on the screen.

3. Tap Save. This saves your image to the Galaxy Tab A so you can view and use it in any app where you select images from your photo albums. Note that the menu options may differ depending on the image you select.

4. As the file downloads, the download icon appears in the status bar. When the file finishes downloading, the status bar disappears.

5. Return to the Home screen by pressing the Home button (not shown).

6. Hold your finger on the status bar and swipe down to open the Quick Settings and Notifications screen.

7. Tap the image filename to open the file in the Gallery or Photos app.

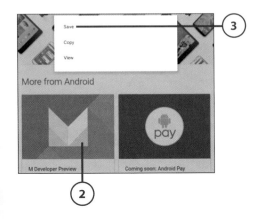

Send and receive email from
your ISP or an email service

Send and receive
instant messages

Your Galaxy Tab A makes it easy for you to read and respond to email and instant messages when you're on the go. This chapter covers the following topics:

→ Configuring email
→ Reading email
→ Composing a new message
→ Creating your own signature
→ Deleting messages
→ Searching through email
→ Configuring email settings
→ Sending and receiving instant messages
→ Configuring Google Hangouts settings
→ Reading email messages in the Email widget

Sending Email and Instant Messages

The built-in Email app on your Galaxy Tab A makes it easy for you to check email messages from various accounts on the device. Before you start, though, you need to configure your email account(s) and then figure out how to use the built-in Email app.

Email isn't the only way to communicate. The Galaxy Tab A also contains the built-in Google Hangouts app so you can chat in real time using text and/or audio and video with other Google+ users.

Configuring Email

Following is a complete list of the information you need to set up your Galaxy Tab to use a traditional email account. If you have an email service such as Exchange, Google Gmail, or Yahoo!, you don't need all this. However, if you don't configure the email settings, you can't use webmail services in other apps (such as Gmail) to email web page links or photos, for example, so you need some of the following information no matter what:

- Email address
- Account type (POP or IMAP)
- Incoming mail server address
- Incoming mail user ID
- Incoming mail password
- Outgoing mail server address
- Outgoing mail user ID
- Outgoing mail password

>>>Go Further

DO I USE POP OR IMAP?

If you're not sure whether to use POP or IMAP as your account type, keep the following in mind:

Post Office Protocol, or *POP*, retrieves and removes email from a server. Therefore, the server acts as a temporary holding place for email. If you receive email using both your Galaxy Tab A and your computer, it's more difficult to share your email messages using POP. You need to either set up your email to go to one device and some to another device, or you need to set up one device so it doesn't remove email from the server so another device can retrieve that email as well.

Internet Message Access Protocol, or *IMAP*, makes the server the place where all messages are stored. Your Galaxy Tab A and computer display all email messages on the server. This is the better situation if you have multiple devices retrieving email from the same account.

When you have the information you need to add your email account, you can open the Email app. The Set Up Account window appears automatically the first time you start the app so you can begin configuring your email account.

1. On the Home screen, tap Apps.

2. In the Apps screen, tap Email.

3. Type the email address in the highlighted Email Address field using the keyboard at the bottom of the screen.

4. Tap Next on the keyboard.

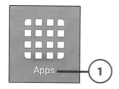

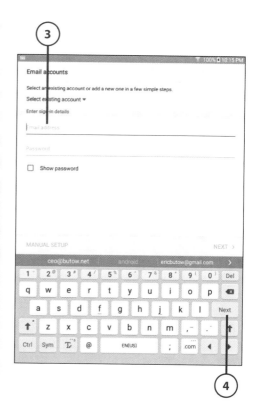

5. Type the password for your email account in the Password field. As you type in the password characters, they become dots so that the password is hidden right away.

6. Tap Done on the keyboard.

7. Tap the button that corresponds to the account type you have.

8. Type the incoming server settings into the appropriate fields.

9. Tap Next.

10. After the Galaxy Tab A checks your incoming server settings, type the outgoing server settings into the appropriate fields.

11. Tap Next.

12. You can uncheck the Notify Me When Email Arrives check box if you don't want to be notified when you have new messages.

13. Tap the Period to Sync Email field to change the amount of time the Email app keeps messages on your Tab A. The default time is 2 weeks, but you can have the Tab keep messages on the Tab A for 1 day, 3 days, 1 week, or 1 month. You can keep all messages on your Tab A by tapping All.

14. Tap the Sync Schedule field to change the checking frequency at which your Tab A checks for new messages. The default frequency is to check your inbox every 15 minutes. You can have the Tab check for new email automatically when new messages are received. If that's too often, you can have the Tab check every 10 minutes, 15 minutes, 30 minutes, every hour, every 2 hours, every 4 hours, or once per day. You can set the time yourself by tapping Manual.

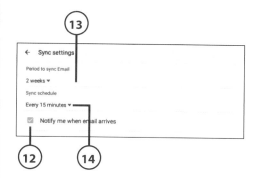

Watch Your Memory Storage

If you have more than one email account and you keep messages from all the accounts for a long period of time (1 to 2 weeks or longer), you will take up more memory on your Tab A. This may affect your ability to store data and run apps on your device.

15. Tap the checking frequency in the list.

16. Tap Next.

What's the Peak Schedule?

The Peak Schedule field reflects how often the Email app checks for new messages. The default frequency is 15 minutes during working hours, which are from 8:00 a.m. to 5:00 p.m. The "Configuring Email Settings" section, later in this chapter, explains how to change the working hour start and stop times.

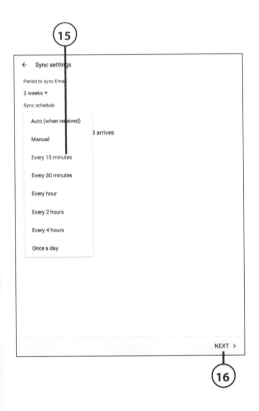

17. Type an optional name into the Account Name (Optional) field.

18. Type your name as you want it to be displayed in outgoing messages.

19. Tap Done. A list of your email messages appears in your Inbox screen.

What Happens If the Settings Won't Verify?

If your settings don't verify, a dialog box displays, asking you to tap the Edit Details button to return to the previous screen and double-check all the information you entered. When something is wrong, it often comes down to misspelled information, such as a misspelled word or a letter that needs to be capitalized, or other incorrect information, such as a different outgoing server port number.

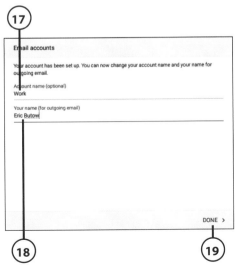

Can I Add a Gmail Account to the Email App?

The Gmail app is preinstalled on your Tab A, but you can still add one or more Gmail accounts in the Email app if you prefer to check all your accounts from one app. Before you add a Gmail account, be sure to set up your Gmail password within your Google account at https://myaccount.google.com/ and then tap the Password in the Account Settings list. Note that you won't see some of the steps listed in this section when you configure a Gmail account, such as incoming and outgoing server settings.

Reading Email

You use the Email app to navigate, read, and type your email messages.

1. Open the Email app, as described earlier in this chapter.

2. The Inbox folder name for the selected email account appears at the top-left corner of the screen. The number of new messages appears below the Inbox folder name.

3. New, unread messages appear in the list with a white background; read messages have a gray background.

4. Close the Tips tile by tapping the Close icon in the upper-right corner of the tile.

5. Tap a message in the list to view the entire message on the screen.

6. The message includes the sender information and message subject at the top of the screen and the body of the message in the center of the screen.

How Do I Get Back to the Message List?

Tap the Back icon at the top-left corner of the screen to return to your list of messages.

7. Tap the sender's name at the top of the page.

8. Tap Create Contact to add the sender to your list of contacts.

9. Tap the account to which you want to add the contact. This example uses Device. Note that if you see an Attention window that says sync is not available, tap OK in the window.

10. Type information into the fields of the Create Contact window if you want. (Chapter 13, "Using Productivity Apps to Simplify Your Life," covers more about adding a contact.) Tap Save to save the new contact and return to the message list.

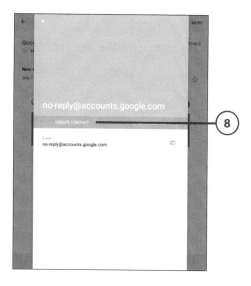

no-reply@accounts.google.com

CREATE CONTACT — **8**

Email
no-reply@accounts.google.com

Save contact to

Device — **9**

Google
@   .com

Samsung account
@   /   .com

ADD NEW ACCOUNT

10

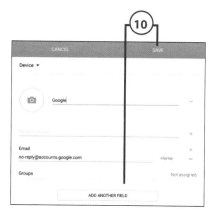

CANCEL   SAVE

Device ▾

Google

Email
no-reply@accounts.google.com   Home

Groups   Not assigned

ADD ANOTHER FIELD

11. Tap the Back icon at the top-left corner of the screen to return to your list of messages and folders.

11

12. View another account (if you have more than one account in the Email app) by tapping the Inbox folder name in the upper-left corner of the screen.

12

13. In the Mailbox window, tap the account name in the list. Open the Mailbox window again by tapping the Inbox folder name again to view the list of mailboxes and folders.

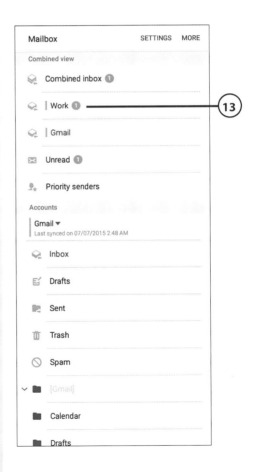

13

14. If there are new messages in a folder, the number of new messages appears in an orange circle to the right of the folder name.

15. Scroll down the folder list to view folders within the Inbox and tap a folder to view messages within that folder.

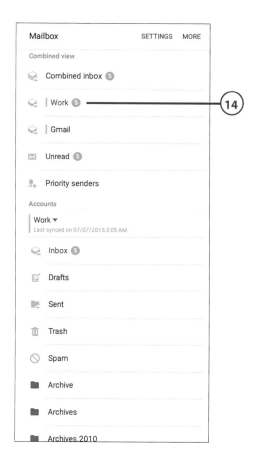

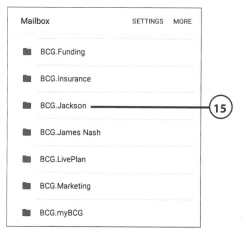

16. The number of unread messages in the folder appears below the folder name.

17. Tap the folder name in the upper-left corner of the screen.

18. Swipe down within the folder list until you see the Inbox folder. Tap it.

19. The Email app automatically searches for any new messages. Any new messages that have come in appear at the top of the list.

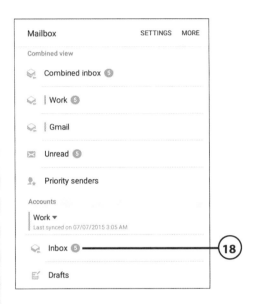

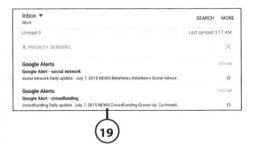

>>>Go Further

HOW DO YOU CREATE FOLDERS?

You can't create folders inside the five default email folders at the top of the folder list—that is, the Inbox, Drafts, Sent, Trash, and Spam folders. If you have an email account that allows you to create folders, you can create subfolders within existing folders within the Mailbox window, like so:

1. Tap More in the upper-right corner of the window.

2. Tap Add Folder in the drop-down list. Note that if your email account doesn't support folder creation, you won't see Add Folder in the drop-down list.

3. Within the Create Folder window, scroll down in the Select Where to Create Folder section and then tap the folder in which you want to add the subfolder.

4. Type the new folder name in the Create Subfolder window.

5. Tap Add.

How Do I Combat Spam?

The Galaxy Tab A has no spam filter built in. However, most email servers filter spam at the server level. If you use a basic POP or IMAP account from an ISP, unfortunately you might not have any server-side spam filtering. If you use an account at a service such as Gmail, you get spam filtering on the server, and spam mail goes to the Spam folder, not your Inbox.

Composing a New Message

The processes for composing a new message and for composing a reply to a message are similar. This section covers composing a message from scratch.

1. Tap the New Mail icon at the lower-right corner of the screen.

2. Type the recipient's address in the To field.

3. Tap the Contacts button to select the recipient(s) from your list of contacts.

4. Tap in the Subject field and then type a subject for the email.

5. Tap below the Subject field in the body of the email and then type your message.

6. Tap Send.

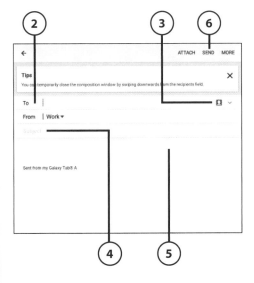

Add Attachments

You can add a file to an email as an attachment, just as you can with any email program on your computer. Just tap Attach in the menu bar at the top of the screen. Then you can pick your text, image(s), contacts, or location from the Attach drop-down list.

HOW DO I REPLY OR FORWARD A MESSAGE?

When you're reading a message, you can choose to reply to the sender or forward the message to another recipient.

In the menu bar at the bottom of the screen, you see a series of four icons. The Reply icon appears as an arrow pointing left. After you tap the icon, you see the reply message screen so that you can type your response to the message. The Subject field contains the "RE:" prefix that denotes you're replying to the original message. View the original message by swiping down the screen. Send the message by tapping Send in the menu bar.

The Forward icon appears as an arrow pointing right. After you tap the icon, you see the forward message screen. You can type the recipient in the To field. Tap the down arrow at the right side of the To field to add any recipients you want to copy or blind copy in the Cc/Bcc field. You can also type a message to the recipient within the body of the email. Any attachments that came with the original message are also attached to the forwarded message. You can view the original message by swiping down the screen. When you finish composing your forwarded message, tap Send in the menu bar.

The Reply icon   **The Forward icon**

Creating Your Own Signature

You can create a signature that automatically appears at the end of your messages. You create your signature in the Email app.

1. Open the Email app, as described earlier in this chapter.

2. Tap More in the menu bar.

3. Tap Settings in the menu.

4. In the Email Settings screen, tap your account name in the list.

5. Tap Signature.

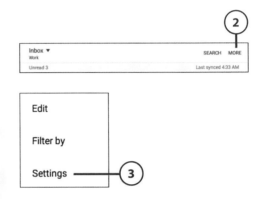

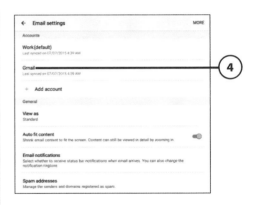

6. You can disable the signature field in your email messages by moving the slider from right to left. The slider and slider button turn gray, which signify the feature is off. You can turn the feature back on by sliding the bar to the right so the slider and slider button turn green.

7. The existing signature appears under the Signature heading. Edit the signature by tapping Signature.

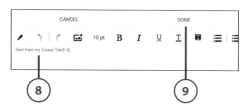

8. Type what you want the signature to say (such as your full name) in the Edit Signature screen. You may want to select the entire existing signature and then type the new signature.

9. Tap Done.

10. The signature as it will appear in your Message Composition field appears under the Signature heading.

11. Tap the Back icon to return to the Account Settings screen.

12. Tap the Back icon in the Account Settings screen to return to the Email Settings screen.

13. Tap the Back icon to return to the message list.

Can I Have Multiple Signatures?

You can have only one signature per email account on your Galaxy Tab A, so technically you can't have multiple signatures. However, the signature is placed in the editable area of the Message Composition field, so you can edit it like the rest of your message and create multiple signatures that way.

Deleting Messages

When you view a message, you can tap the Delete icon and move the message to the trash.

1. In the Email app, open the Mailbox window, as described earlier in this chapter.

2. Go to any mailbox and any subfolder, such as your Trash folder.

3. In the Trash folder message list, tap More.

4. Tap Edit in the menu.

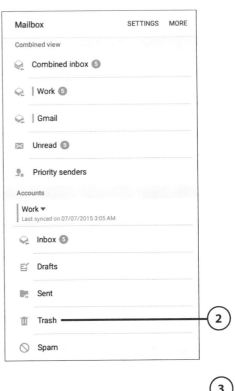

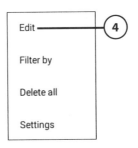

5. Tap a check box at the left side of the message entry that you want to delete. You can select multiple check boxes if you want to delete multiple messages.

6. Delete the messages by tapping Delete.

Searching Through Email

By default, the Galaxy Tab A doesn't let you search through your email messages. You can change this setting quickly and then search text in your email messages.

1. Open the Email app and then open the Mailbox window, as described earlier in this chapter.

2. Open a folder or subfolder and then tap Search.

3. Type the search term(s) into the Search field.

4. As you type, the parts of messages in the list that match your search term appear highlighted in orange. In my example, I opened the BCG.Marketing subfolder and typed **econ** into the field, and portions of messages that contain "econ" appear in red.

5. If you don't find the search results you want after you scroll to the bottom of the message list, tap More.

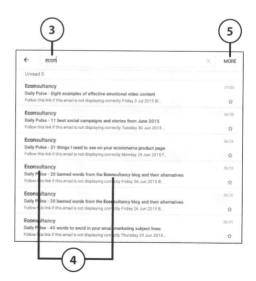

6. Search the mail server for any messages that might not have been downloaded to your Tab A by tapping Search Server.

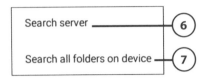

Search server ———————— 6

Search all folders on device —— 7

7. Continue searching for messages that match your search term(s) on all connected devices by tapping Search All Folders on Device.

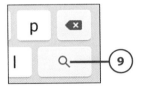

9

8. Close the menu by tapping the Back touch button (not shown).

9. When you finish typing your search term(s), tap the Search button in the keyboard.

11

10. The message list displays all recent email messages in this folder that match your search term. Messages appear in the list so you can read a message by tapping it. Note that it might take a few seconds for all folder messages to appear in the list.

11. Tap the Back icon to return to the folder message list.

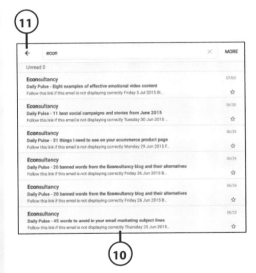

10

Configuring Email Settings

The Galaxy Tab A enables you to update your email account settings as needed.

1. Follow the steps from earlier tasks in this chapter to open the Email app if you aren't there already.

2. Tap More.

3. Tap Settings.

4. Tap Email Notifications to specify whether the Galaxy Tab A should notify you when email arrives for one or more of your email accounts. This feature is activated for all email accounts by default.

5. Tap the email address for which you want to set notifications; you can also change how you want the Email app to notify you when you receive an email message from a sender you've identified as a priority sender.

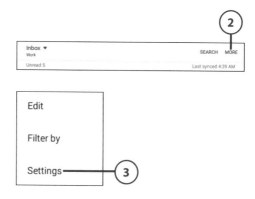

How Do I Add a Priority Sender?

When you read a message on the screen, as described earlier in this chapter, you can tap More in the upper-right corner of the screen. In the menu that appears, tap Add to Priority Senders. Messages from your priority senders appear at the top of the Inbox folder message list.

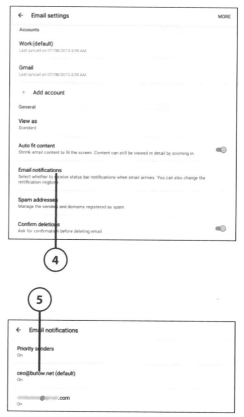

6. You can disable email notifications by moving the slider from right to left. The slider and slider button turn gray, which signify the feature is off. You can turn the feature back on by sliding the bar to the right so the slider and slider button turn green.

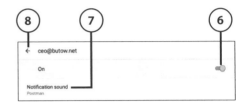

7. Tap Notification Sound to select a ringtone or to designate that there should be no ringtone at all. Select the ringtone from the Notification Sound pop-up window. The default ringtone is Postman.

8. Tap the Back icon.

9. Tap the Back icon in the Email Notifications screen.

10. Tap the email account for which you want to change settings.

11. Tap Sync Schedule.

12. Tap Set Sync Schedule and then select the time interval in the Sync Schedule window as described in the "Configuring Email" section earlier in the chapter.

13. Slide the Peak Schedule slider button from right to left if you don't want to set a separate email syncing schedule. When the slider and slider button turn gray, the app disables all the options in the Peak Schedule Settings section underneath the Peak Schedule setting.

14. Tap Set Peak Schedule to change the peak schedule syncing interval in the Set Peak Schedule window. Tap the appropriate interval for syncing during the peak schedule. (Each interval is the same as in the Sync Schedule field.)

15. By default, the peak days are Monday through Friday, and the peak days are highlighted in green. Tap a day to select or deselect it to add or delete it from the peak schedule, respectively.

16. Change the peak start time by tapping the From button.

17. Change the time by tapping on the up and down arrows above or below (from left to right) the hour, minute, and AM/PM settings.

18. Tap Keypad to use a numerical keypad to enter the hour and minute.

19. When you finish setting the time, tap Set.

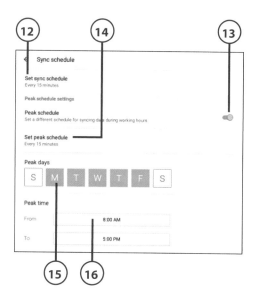

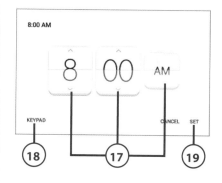

20. Your new peak start time appears. Change the peak end time by tapping the To button.

21. Change the peak end time in the window as you did with the peak start time and then tap Set. The new peak end time appears.

22. Go back to the main Settings screen by tapping the Back icon in the menu bar.

23. Tap Limit Retrieval Size.

24. In the Limit Retrieval Size screen, you can change the default amount of data you can receive in an email message. When you receive messages, the Email app downloads all the data in a message by default. You can choose from 2KB to 300KB, limit the size to headers only, or have no size limits to messages and file attachments. If the message has more than the allotted amount of data, then at the bottom of the message the app asks if you want to download the rest of the message.

25. Return to the account settings screen by tapping the Back icon in the menu bar.

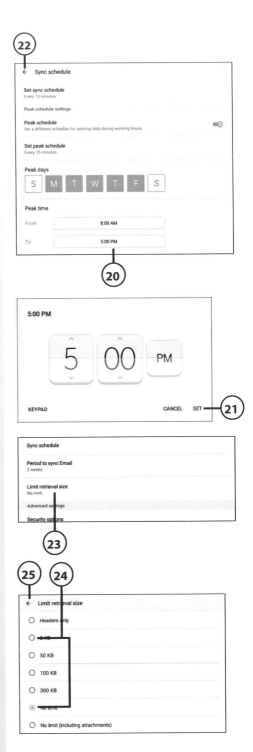

26. Tap Account Name to change your account name.

27. Tap Your Name to add or change your name.

28. Tap Always Cc/Bcc Myself and then select Cc or Bcc in the pop-up window if you always want to add your email address in the Cc or Bcc box.

29. Tap the Signature field to change your signature. Read the "Creating Your Own Signature" task earlier in this chapter for more information about signatures.

30. Tap Show Images to stop showing images automatically in a message when you view it. After you tap Show Images, the slider and slider button are gray to signify the feature is off. Turn the feature on again by tapping Show Images.

31. Tap Auto Download Attachments to download file attachments in a message to the app automatically. After you tap Auto Download Attachments, the slider and slider button are green to signify the feature is on.

32. Swipe up in the screen to view more settings.

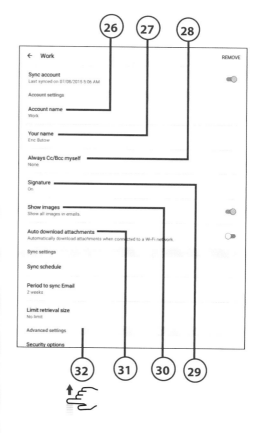

33. Set advanced security options by tapping Security Options. In the Security Options screen that appears, you can encrypt all outgoing email, sign all outgoing email, and create and manage encryption keys for keeping your email messages private.

34. Change your incoming server settings (as you did with a new account earlier in this chapter) by tapping Incoming Server Settings.

35. Change your outgoing server settings (as you did with a new account earlier in this chapter) by tapping Outgoing Server Settings.

36. Go back to the main Settings screen by tapping the Back icon in the menu bar.

37. The word Default appears next to the account that sends your email messages automatically. If you don't want to send email from that account, tap More in the upper-right corner of the screen.

38. Tap Set Default Account.

39. Tap the account you want as the default.

40. Tap Done.

41. The word Default now appears next to the account you selected as your default.

42. Return to the message folder list screen by tapping the Back icon.

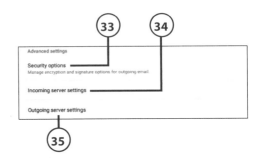

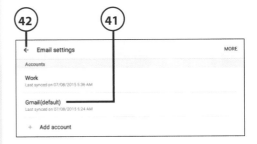

Sending and Receiving Instant Messages

You can send and receive instant messages using the built-in Hangouts app from Google.

You Need a Google+ Account

You need to have an existing Google+ account that is tied to your primary Gmail account. If you don't have a Google+ account, Google Hangouts has you set up your Google+ account before you continue setting up Google Hangouts.

1. On the Home screen, tap the Google icon.

2. Tap Hangouts in the Google pop-up window.

3. If you see a window in the center of the screen inviting you to use Hangouts Dialer to make free phone calls, tap Skip in the window (not shown).

4. If you see a window telling you about what's new in Hangouts, tap "Okay, Got It" in the window (not shown).

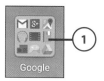

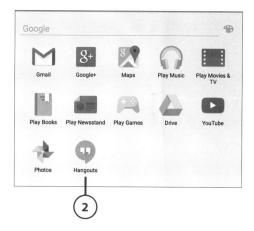

5. Close the menu window on the left side of the screen by tapping outside the window.

6. Tap the plus icon to select the circles or names with which you want to connect in the Contacts window.

7. Tap the recipient field and then type the name of the person with whom you want to chat.

8. As you type, matches appear in the drop-down list above the field. Tap the name of the person with whom you want to chat.

9. Add more people you want to include in the conversation by tapping Anyone Else? Then scroll down the list of users or Google+ groups in the window and add the user or group to the recipient field by tapping the user or group name.

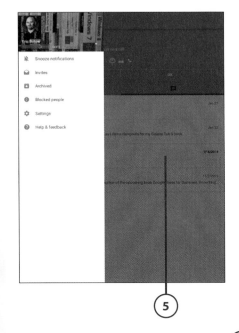

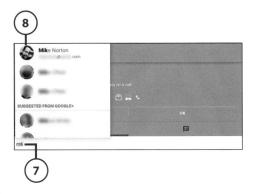

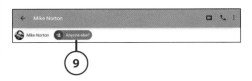

10. Type your message in the Send Hangouts Message field.

11. Add an emoticon to better convey the meaning of your message by tapping the Emoticon icon to the right of the Send Hangouts Message field.

12. Swipe down the section of emoticons and then tap the emoticon you want. The emoticon appears at the end of your message.

13. Return to the keyboard by tapping the ABC key.

14. Tap the Send icon to send your message.

15. Your message appears above the Send Hangouts Message field. If you receive a message from the recipient, your message will be moved up and you will see the recipient's response above the Send Hangouts Message field.

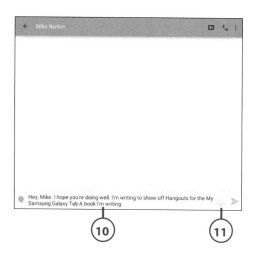

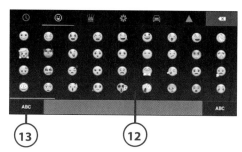

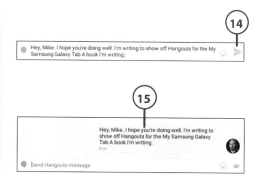

What If I Don't Use Either Google+ or Google Hangouts for Instant Messaging?

If you use a different instant messaging service, then visit the Google Play Store by tapping Play Store on the Home screen. Then search for the instant messaging app you're looking for. If you use Skype, for example, there is a Skype app for Android available that you can download free of charge. You discover more about downloading apps in Chapter 15, "Finding and Managing Apps."

Configuring Google Hangouts Settings

You can change your Google Hangouts settings so you can manage your messages to your liking, determine how you want to be notified of new messages that come into your message Inbox, and change your Google+ profile.

1. On the Home screen, tap the Google icon.

2. Tap Hangouts in the Google pop-up window.

3. Tap the Menu icon in the menu bar.

4. Tap Settings.

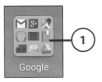

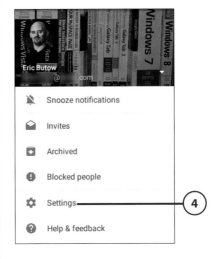

5. Tap your Google account email address in the list, if necessary.

6. Tap Profile Photo to change your Google+ profile photo. You can take a photo using the Camera app or you can choose a photo within the Gallery app.

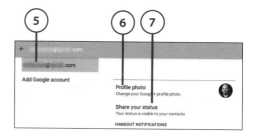

7. Tap Share Your Status if you want to let everyone in your Google+ circles who use Hangouts know what you're doing.

8. Tap the Show My Last Seen check box if you don't want people in your Google+ circles to see when you last used Hangouts.

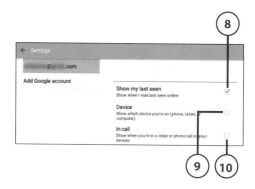

9. Tap the Device check box to have Google Hangouts tell people in your Google+ circles what device you're currently using: a smartphone, tablet, or computer.

10. Tap the In Call check box to have Google Hangouts tell people in your Google+ circles when you're currently busy with a video or phone call on one of your devices.

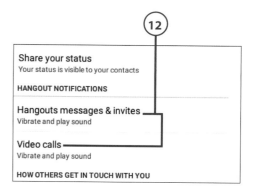

11. Return to the main Settings screen by tapping the Back touch button (not shown).

12. Tap Hangouts Messages & Invites to change what happens when you get messages and invites, and tap Video Calls to change what happens when you get video calls. The options in subsequent steps in this section are the same when you tap Hangouts Messages & Invites or Video Calls.

13. The Notifications and Vibrate check boxes are checked by default so you receive notifications about new Google Hangouts (which are live video chats) started by one of your contacts and when you receive a request to join a Google Hangout. If you don't want to be notified about any Hangouts, tap Notifications to clear the check box.

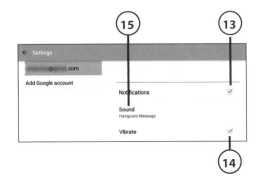

14. Tap Vibrate if you don't want the Tab A to vibrate when you receive a message or invite, or if you receive a video call, depending on the screen you're in. You can turn on vibrations by tapping Vibrate again.

15. Tap Sound to open the Sound window and set a tone that notifies you when someone has joined your Hangout or you have received a request for someone to join your Hangout. By default, you will feel the Tab A vibrate and see a message on the screen.

16. Select from the preselected Hangouts Message ringtone, silent mode, or a number of other ringtones. Scroll up and down the list to view the entire list and tap the button to the right of the tone so you can listen to the sound.

17. Tap OK when you've selected a sound. The name of the selected sound appears within the Sound entry in the Hangout Notifications section.

18. Return to the main Hangout Settings screen by tapping the Back touch button (not shown).

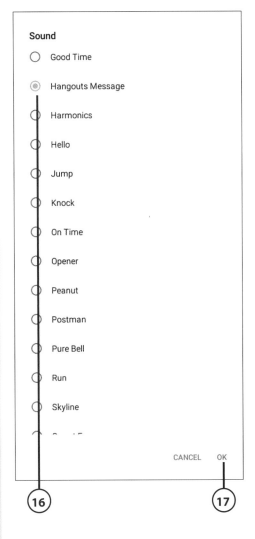

19. Tap Customize Invites to determine who can join your Hangouts.

20. In the Customize Invites screen, you can determine the circles that can join a Hangout with you or request that you accept them as a Hangout participant. Circles include ones that you created in Google+ as well as the default Public circle that includes all Google+ users. Change how users in each circle can request Hangout participation by tapping the circle name in the list.

21. In the circle window, the default request option is selected by default, which in this example is Can Contact You Directly in the Family circle. You can also tap Can Send You an Invite or Can't Contact You. Tap the request option you want for members of this circle.

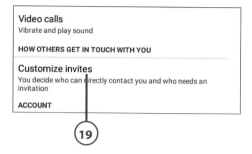

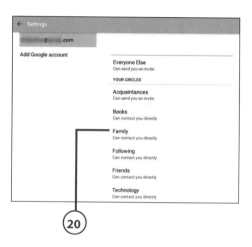

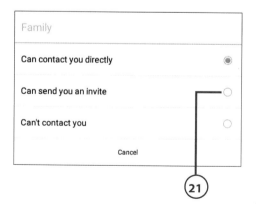

22. After you change the request type, the type appears underneath the circle name.

23. Return to the main Hangout Settings screen by tapping the Back icon.

24. Tap Google+ Profile to change your Google+ profile settings within the Internet browser app.

25. Tap Hidden Contacts to view a list of Google+ contacts you're connected with but who aren't visible on your Google+ profile page.

26. Tap Sign Out to sign out of Google Hangouts and close the Hangouts app.

27. Tap Improve Hangouts to remove the check mark if you don't want to report your usage data to Google to help improve the Hangouts app.

28. Return to the Hangouts screen by tapping the Back icon at the left side of the menu bar.

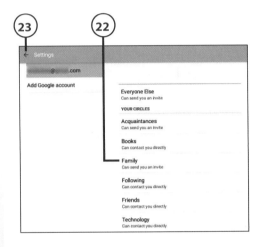

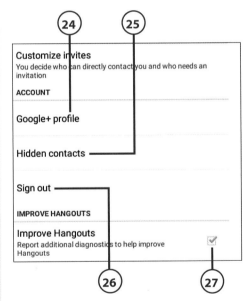

Reading Email Messages in the Email Widget

Chapter 4, "Adding Widgets to Your Home Screen," explains how to add a widget to a Home screen. In this task, you find out how to view your latest email messages in your Inbox folder within the Email widget instead of within the Email app.

1. Tap and hold on a blank area within the Home screen.

2. Tap Widgets.

3. Add the Email widget to a Home screen. If you're not sure how to add a widget, bookmark this page and review Chapter 4.

4. In the Select Account screen, tap the account with the email messages you want to view. If you want to view all messages in all accounts' Inbox folders, tap Combined Inbox.

5. Tap Done in the lower-right corner of the screen.

6. The widget appears on the Home screen with a blue box around it. Blue circles, or *handles*, appear on all four sides of the box.

7. Resize the widget by tapping and holding one of the handles and then dragging left and right or up and down, depending on the handle you're moving. For example, if you drag the bottom handle up and down, then you change the height of the widget. If your widget size is too large for the available area on the Home screen, then the box and handles turn red to tell you that the widget is too large for the available space.

8. After you resize the widget, tap the Back touch button (not shown).

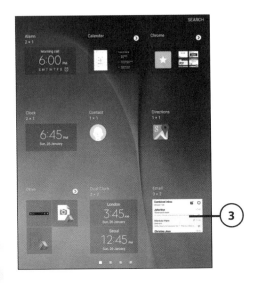

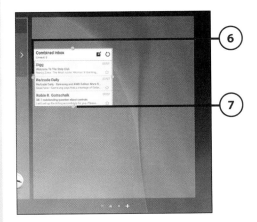

9. Within the Email widget, the Combined Inbox shown in this example displays five messages in the list. Each message tile shows the name of the sender, the message subject, and the first 15 to 25 words of the message.

10. Tap the star outline icon to mark the message as a favorite. After you tap the star icon, the star turns solid gold to signify the message is a favorite. If you don't want the message as a favorite anymore, tap the gold star; the star becomes an outline again.

11. Swipe up and down to view the messages in the list.

12. Open the message and read it in its entirety within the Email app by tapping the message tile.

13. The message screen opens within the Email app so you can swipe up and down and read the message as well as reply, forward, and delete the message.

14. Return to the Combined Inbox message list screen by tapping the Back icon.

15. Return to the Home screen that contains the Email widget by pressing the Home button (not shown).

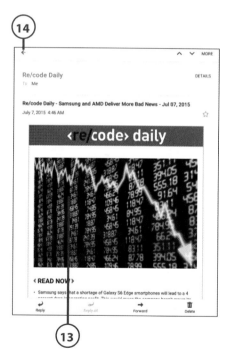

Can I Go Back to the Email App to Read Messages?

When you return to the Home screen that contains the Email widget after viewing a message in the Email app, the Email app remains open. You can return to the Email app to view messages by tapping the Recent touch button and then tapping the Email tile in the Recent Apps screen.

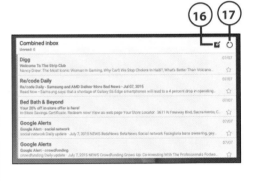

16. Tap the New Mail icon to write a new message in the Email app, as described earlier in this chapter.

17. Tap the Refresh icon to have the widget check for new messages in the Combined Inbox folder.

Connect to other
devices using
Wi-Fi Direct

Connect to the cloud
with the OneDrive app

The Galaxy Tab A is a great tool for sharing with other devices directly using Wi-Fi Direct and also for sharing files and media in the cloud. This chapter covers the following topics:

→ Connecting using Wi-Fi Direct
→ Printing wirelessly
→ Sharing files
→ Sharing music and video

Connecting to the Cloud

The Galaxy Tab A allows you to synchronize data with other devices directly by using Wi-Fi Direct so you don't need to buy a cable or even a wireless router to connect your Galaxy Tab A to another device. You can store and share data with online services on the cloud, which is file storage available on the Internet. What's more, you can share music and video between your Tab A and your computer using a USB cable and the Samsung Smart Switch app.

Connecting Using Wi-Fi Direct

If you need to wirelessly transfer data to or connect with another device such as your smartphone, you can use the Tab A Wi-Fi Direct feature to connect to another device that also has Wi-Fi Direct enabled.

Set Up Wi-Fi Direct

Before you can transfer data between devices, you have to set up Wi-Fi Direct on the Tab A to connect with the other device.

1. On the Home screen, swipe from right to left to view the second Home screen and then tap Settings.

2. Tap the Wi-Fi option in the menu on the left side of the screen if the option isn't selected already.

3. Tap Wi-Fi Direct.

4. The Tab A searches for available devices near you and displays those devices within the Wi-Fi Direct devices list on the right side of the Settings screen.

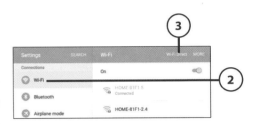

5. Tap the device name to which you want to connect. You may need to confirm connection on the device to which you're connecting.

6. The connected device name text is blue, which means the device is connected.

7. Disconnect from the device by tapping the device name.

How Do I Know I'm Connected to a Device Through Wi-Fi Direct?

If you're not sure you're connected to another device through Wi-Fi Direct, look in the status bar at the top of the screen. The Wi-Fi Direct icon appears to the left of the Wi-Fi icon at the right side of the bar.

The Wi-Fi Direct icon

TROUBLESHOOTING CONNECTION ISSUES

If the Galaxy Tab A can't find your Wi-Fi Direct device, check the other device's Wi-Fi connection and ensure the other device offers Wi-Fi Direct. In the Tab A Settings screen, try connecting to your Wi-Fi Direct device again by tapping Scan at the right side of the menu bar.

You should also check the Wi-Fi Alliance website to learn whether your device is Wi-Fi Direct enabled. The Wi-Fi Alliance is a nonprofit group founded in 1999 that was formed to grow Wi-Fi acceptance in the marketplace, support industry standards, and provide a forum so Wi-Fi companies can collaborate and improve Wi-Fi technologies. You can begin searching for products that include Wi-Fi Direct functionality by opening the Internet app and then accessing the Certified Products page at http://www.wi-fi.org/product-finder.

Printing Wirelessly

It's easy to print a file such as a word processing document or spreadsheet from your Galaxy Tab A. You don't need any cables, and you don't need to transfer your files to another computer, either. There are some limitations to the printing functionality built in to the Tab A, but you can download apps and use web-based services to get around those limits.

Connect a Wi-Fi Printer

Your Tab A automatically scans for wireless printers that are available through a Wi-Fi connection. Note that you might have to enable a Wi-Fi connection on the printer as well. This example uses a Hewlett-Packard (HP) OfficeJet Pro X576dw printer. This OfficeJet Pro requires the user to enable HP Wireless Direct functionality on the printer before any device can see it.

1. On the Home screen, swipe from right to left to view the second Home screen and then tap Settings.

2. Connect to the printer by tapping the printer name in the Wi-Fi networks list.

3. If you need to enter a password, type it in the window and then tap Connect.

4. The Tab A might take a few seconds to find the printer's IP address; after it does, the printer appears at the top of the Wi-Fi networks list and displays the Connected status.

What If the Tab A Can't Find My Wireless Printer?

If the Galaxy Tab A doesn't recognize your wireless printer, you might need to bring your Tab A closer to it. You can scan for the printer again by tapping Scan in the Settings menu bar that appears at the top of the screen. When the wireless printer appears in the Wi-Fi list, connect to the printer by tapping the printer name.

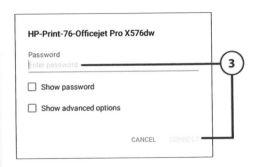

Connect a Bluetooth Printer

If you have a Bluetooth printer, you can also connect that printer to your Galaxy Tab A so you can print wirelessly. The printer in this example is different from the HP OfficeJet Pro used in the previous section.

1. On the Home screen, swipe from right to left to view the second Home screen and then tap Settings.

2. Tap Bluetooth.

3. Swipe the slider button from left to right to turn on Bluetooth connectivity. The Tab A finds your printer.

4. Tap the printer name.

5. Type the printer's PIN in the Bluetooth Pairing Request window using the keypad at the bottom of the screen. If you aren't sure what the PIN is, try 0000 or 1234. If those PINs don't work, you will need to consult your printer documentation and/or the printer manufacturer's website to find the PIN.

6. Tap OK.

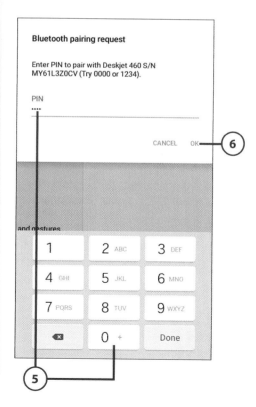

7. The paired Bluetooth printer appears in the Paired Devices section.

8. Tap the Settings icon to the right of the printer name to change the printer name and unpair, or disconnect, the printer from the Tab A.

>>>Go Further

DOWNLOAD A PRINT APP

Samsung boasts that you can print directly from within an app on your Galaxy Tab A to any compatible printer without having to connect to a Wi-Fi or Bluetooth printer. Unfortunately, what Samsung doesn't tell you is that you can only print to Samsung's printers. You find this out when you try to print from an app for the first time and see the message "You can only print to a Samsung printer." Fortunately, apps are available from the Google Play Store that enable you to print to other printers.

For example, if you have a Hewlett-Packard printer, as is used in this chapter, you can download the HP ePrint app. You can search for your printer manufacturer in the Google Play Store to see if a printing app is available. There are also apps available from the Play Store for printing to a variety of devices. One such app is PrinterShare Mobile Print, which is free.

If you find a printing app in the Google Play Store that doesn't work for you (or doesn't work at all), another option is to use Google's Cloud Print service. This service connects your printers to the Web so any web-enabled device, including the Tab A, can access a printer connected to Cloud Print. As of this writing, Google Cloud Print is still in beta test status, so be aware that the service's performance might not match your expectations.

You can access the Google Cloud Print website in the Internet app at www.google.com/cloudprint/learn. After you open the site, you're invited to log in using your Gmail account. After you log in, you can add a printer that's connected to a laptop or PC, or you can add a Cloud Ready printer, which is a printer that connects directly to the Web.

The Google Cloud Print website

Sharing Files

A "cloud storage" service enables you to upload files onto its server computers. Cloud storage services make it easy for you to share large files with others, especially because the maximum file attachment sizes in email messages can vary depending on the email service you use, and downloading email messages with large file attachments can take a long time.

Use the OneDrive App

The Microsoft OneDrive app is preinstalled on your Galaxy Tab A, and you might have set up your OneDrive account when you set up your Tab A. You can give another OneDrive user access to one or more folders in your account so that other users can upload files to and download files from that folder. The OneDrive icon is available on the second Home screen and/or within the Apps screen.

Sign In to OneDrive

When you first start OneDrive, the app takes you step-by-step through setting up your Tab A to work with OneDrive. If you have a Microsoft account, you log in to OneDrive using this account.

1. On the Home screen, swipe from right to left to view the second Home screen and then tap Microsoft Apps.

2. Tap OneDrive in the Microsoft Apps window.

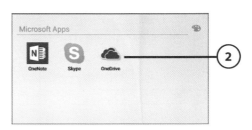

3. Swipe from right to left to view introductory information about OneDrive. Note that if you've already used OneDrive on your Tab A, you can skip ahead to step 5.

4. In the last introductory screen, tap Sign In.

What If I Don't Have a Microsoft Account?

If you need a OneDrive account, tap Sign Up on the last introductory screen and create a free account within the Create Account screen. The app takes you step-by-step through setting up your account. If you have a OneDrive account but haven't signed in, then tap the Sign In link on the last introductory screen.

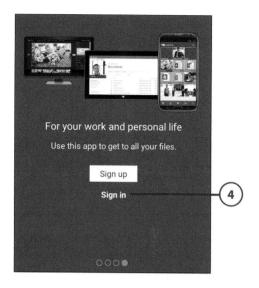

5. Type the email address associated with your Microsoft account.

6. Tap the Done key on the keyboard.

7. Type the Microsoft account password.

8. Tap Sign In.

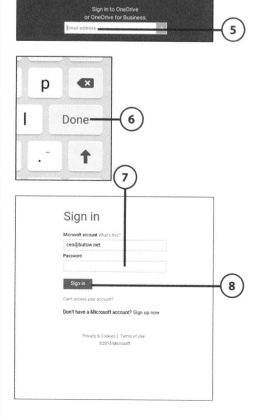

9. You can get 100GB of storage space for two years as a Tab A owner. For now, view the One-Drive screen by tapping Not Now. You can learn about getting more OneDrive space later in this chapter.

10. The OneDrive screen opens and shows all files and subfolders within the Files folder.

Add Galaxy Tab A Images to OneDrive and Create an Album

After you sign in to OneDrive, you can upload images and photos stored on your Galaxy Tab A to OneDrive. Then you can access those photos from any computer or device that has the OneDrive app installed, or from the OneDrive website at onedrive.live.com.

OneDrive uploads photos from the Camera app automatically and you can also upload photos manually. After you upload the images and photos, you can categorize your photos by placing photos into albums with different topics.

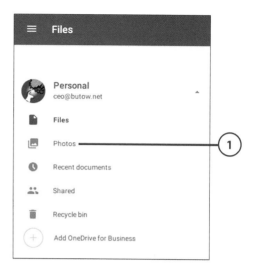

1. Tap Photos in the menu.

2. OneDrive scans the Camera app for all photos you've taken and places them in the All tab within the Photos screen.

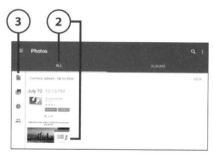

3. Tap the Files icon.

4. Tap the orange Add icon in the lower-right corner of the screen.

5. Tap the Upload icon in the lower-right corner of the screen.

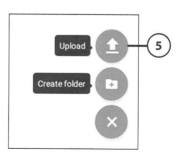

6. Tap Images.

7. Tap the folder that contains the images you want to upload.

8. Tap and hold on a photo in the list for a second or two until you see a check mark in a circle within the photo.

9. After you select the photos you want to upload, tap Open.

10. OneDrive uploads the files. When the process is complete, the files appear in the Files list.

11. Tap the Photos icon in the toolbar.

12. The photos you added appear in the Photos screen.

13. Tap Albums.

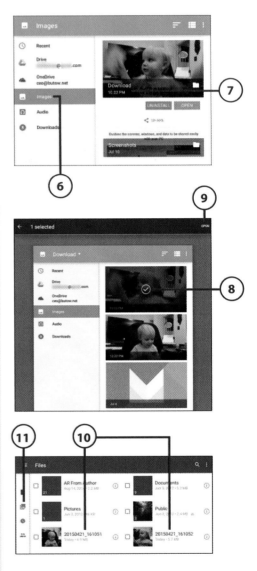

14. Tap the orange Add icon in the lower-right corner of the screen to add photos to an album.

15. Type the name of your album in the Create New Album window.

16. Tap OK.

17. Tap the photo(s) you want to add to the album. The selected photo has a white check mark in the upper-right corner of the photo.

18. After you select the photo(s), tap the check mark icon in the menu bar.

19. The photos appear within the album screen. Tap a photo to view it on the entire screen.

20. View all photos in the All tab by tapping the Photos icon.

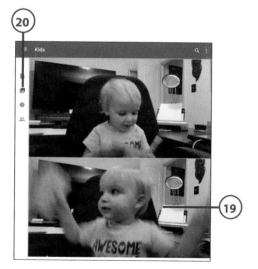

View and Share Files in OneDrive

The OneDrive Files screen contains all files and folders within the OneDrive folder so you can find files easily. You can also share files and all files within a folder with other users.

1. Tap the Menu icon if necessary.

2. Tap Files.

3. Swipe up and down in the screen if necessary to view all the files and folders stored on OneDrive. Each file or folder entry contains a thumbnail image to the left of the file or folder name and an information icon to the right of the name so you can tap the icon to get more information in the Details window. Folders show the number of files contained within the folder in the lower-left corner of the thumbnail image.

4. When you find a file that you want to view, tap the filename to view it. If the file is a photo or image file, as in this example, then the file opens within the built-in OneDrive image viewer.

5. Tap the check box to the left of the thumbnail image for the file or folder you want to share. After you tap the check box, the box turns orange and contains a white check mark.

6. Tap the Share icon.

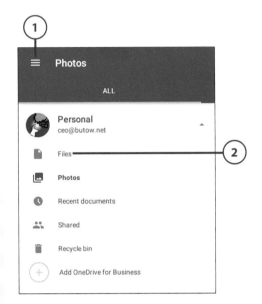

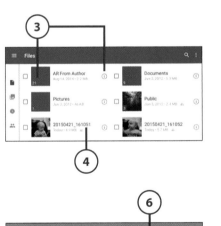

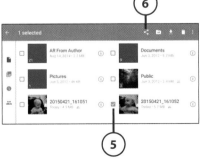

7. Share the link to the file with others by tapping Share a Link.

8. If you want people with whom you share the file to only view it, keep the default View button selected. You can give permission for those people to edit the file by tapping Edit.

9. Tap OK.

10. After OneDrive prepares the link, tap the service or app you want to use to share the link in the Share the Link Via window. You can copy the link to the Clipboard to paste the link elsewhere such as an email message. You can save the link to the Scrapbook app or a note in either the OneNote, S Note (if you have the Tab A 9.7 with S Pen), or Memo app. You can share directly to another device using Bluetooth, Wi-Fi Direct, or Samsung Quick Connect. You can share the link to OneDrive or Google Drive. You can share the link in an Email or Gmail message. You can also share the link in a Google Hangouts or Skype chat or post it to your Google+ account.

11. For now, return to the file and folder screen by tapping the Back touch button (not shown).

12. Tap the Trash icon to send the image to the Recycle Bin folder.

13. Tap the Menu icon to rename the photo file, add the photo to the album, or get details about the file.

14. Deselect all files by tapping the Back icon in the menu bar.

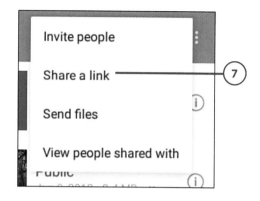

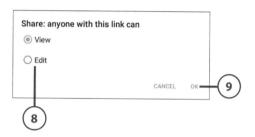

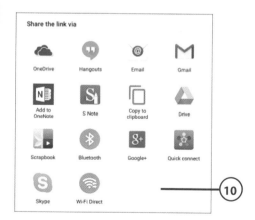

Access Menu Options

You can access a variety of tools and settings for the OneDrive app both by tapping the Menu icon in the OneDrive menu bar and in the menu sidebar on the left side of the screen.

1. Tap the Menu icon to open the menu that appears on the left side of the screen. The Files category is selected by default.

2. Tap the Photos icon to view, add, and delete photos and albums in your OneDrive account.

3. Tap Recent Documents to view all documents you added since the last time you closed the OneDrive app.

4. Tap Shared to view all files and folders you shared with others.

5. Tap Recycle Bin to view files you have marked for deletion; you can restore those files to their original location or delete one or more files from your OneDrive account.

6. Tap Add OneDrive for Business to sign in to your OneDrive business account and manage your files and folders in that account from within the OneDrive app.

7. Tap Settings to open the Settings screen and get information about your account, change your account settings, and learn more about OneDrive.

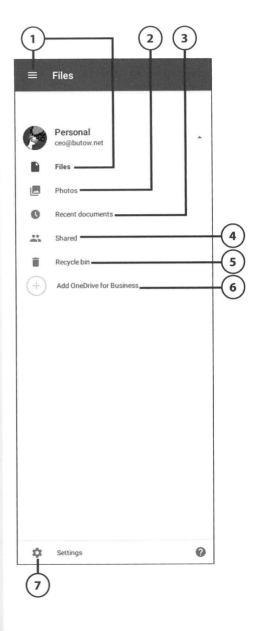

8. Close the menu and view the toolbar by tapping the Menu icon.

9. You can tap one of four icons, from top to bottom: Files, Photos, Recent Documents, and Shared. If you want to view the Recycle Bin or Add OneDrive for Business, you need to open the menu.

10. Open the Settings screen by tapping the Settings icon.

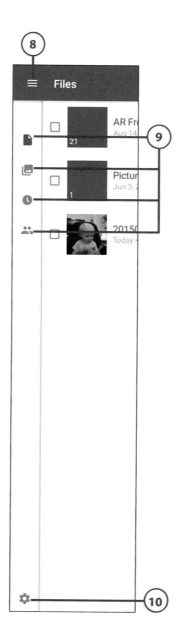

>>>Go Further

GET MORE ONEDRIVE SPACE

As a Tab A owner, you can get 100GB of space (or an additional 100GB of space) in your account for two years at no charge. You can use that extra space on the OneDrive app or website from any computer or device. However, the 100GB of space isn't applied to your account automatically.

Apply the 100GB by tapping Settings in the menu or the Settings icon in the toolbar and then tapping Apply 100GB Samsung Offer within the Settings screen. In the confirmation window that appears, tap OK. After a few seconds, a pop-up box appears on the screen and tells you the total amount of space you have available.

You can view the total amount of space you have at any time by tapping your account name at the top of the Settings list and then viewing the amount within the Account screen.

Find Other Cloud Services

If you prefer to use another cloud storage app other than OneDrive, you can shop the Google Play Store for other cloud storage apps that are optimized for the Android operating system.

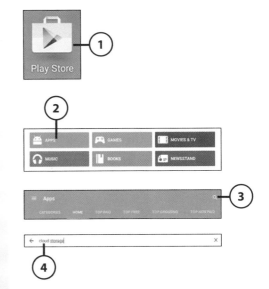

1. Tap Play Store on the Home screen.

2. Tap Apps.

3. Tap the Search icon in the menu bar.

4. Type **cloud storage** in the Search Google Play field.

5. Tap the Search button in the keyboard.

6. Swipe up and down within the list of apps in the search results screen. Tap a tile to view more information about the app. You learn more about shopping for apps in the Play Store in Chapter 15, "Finding and Managing Apps."

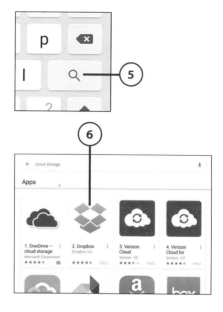

Sharing Music and Video

You have a number of ways to share your music and video between different devices or between your computer and your Galaxy Tab A. If you have a computer that runs Windows, you can connect the Tab A to your computer and copy files with Windows Media Player. You can also connect your Tab A to your Windows computer and tell Windows that your Tab A is a storage device. One other alternative is to connect your PC or Mac to your Tab A with the Tab's USB cable.

Copy Files with Windows Media Player

When you connect your Galaxy Tab A to your PC with the data cable, you can choose how you want to connect and/or synchronize media files with your Tab A. One option is to sync your PC and your Tab A with Windows Media Player. This example connects the Tab A to a PC running Windows 8.1.

1. Connect the data cable from the Tab A to the USB port on your PC (not shown). If an AutoPlay window opens, click the window and then click Sync Digital Media Files to this Device: Windows Media Player in the list. If you don't see this window, open the Windows Media Player app on your PC.

2. Click the Sync tab within the Windows Media Player window.

3. Click and drag the music file(s) you want to copy to the Sync list.

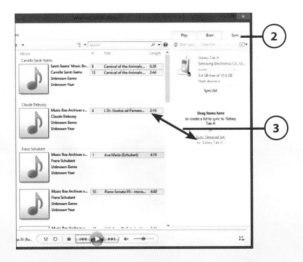

4. The list of music files you select appears in the Sync list. You can deselect any files you do not want to copy by right-clicking the filename and then clicking Remove from List (not shown).

5. Click Start Sync to begin copying the files from your PC to your Galaxy Tab.

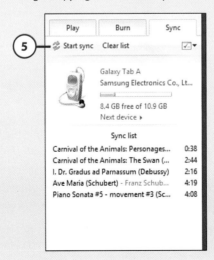

6. After the sync is complete, you can view the music files within the Music app on your Tab A.

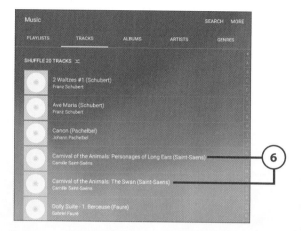

Connect as a Mass Storage Device

You can drag and drop files from a PC to your Galaxy Tab A by connecting as a removable disk. Follow these steps to transfer music files from your PC to your Tab A using the Mass Storage USB mode.

1. Connect the data cable to the Tab A and the USB connector to the USB port on your computer (not shown). If an AutoPlay window opens, click the window and then click Open Device to View Files: File Explorer in the list. If you don't see this window, open the File Explorer app on your computer.

2. Your Tab A appears as a removable disk in the folder tree within the File Explorer window. Double-click the Galaxy Tab A entry in the tree.

3. Open the list of folders on the Tab A by double-clicking the Tablet folder in the tree.

4. Double-click the Music folder in the tree. The list of music files and subfolders appears in the file pane.

5. Locate the files you want to transfer from your computer and then drag them to the Music folder on your Tab A. The files are copied to your device.

6. After you have finished copying files to your Tab from your computer, remove the USB cable from the PC (not shown).

7. When you open the Music app on your Tab, the music you have transferred is available for playback.

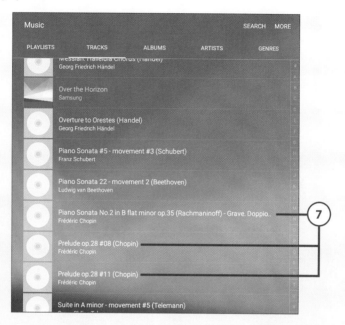

CONNECTING TO A MAC

You need extra software to connect your Tab to a Mac. Android File Transfer
is an application for Macs running OS X 10.5 or later that enables you to view
and transfer files between your Mac and Galaxy Tab A. This application works
with Android devices running Android 3.0 or later. You can download Android
File Transfer from www.android.com/filetransfer/.

Search for locations
and get directions

Locate
businesses
and quickly
receive more
information
about them

Receive turn-by-turn
GPS navigation and
voice-command
directions

In this chapter, you find out how to use the Maps app to find locations, get directions, and connect with friends. This chapter covers the following topics:

→ Enabling GPS
→ Getting around with Maps
→ Getting voice-command directions
→ Finding local information

Using Maps

Your Galaxy Tab A is equipped with the Maps app, which can help you get where you need to go. In Android 5.0 (or Lollipop, if you prefer), Maps is one comprehensive app that combines several apps that were previously separate in earlier versions of Android:

- The app can supply detailed destination directions for a specific address.

- The app can provide voice-guided, turn-by-turn directions to a location.

- You can also use Maps to quickly locate local businesses and access contact information, coupons, and customer reviews.

What's more, the Google+ app enables you to share your location with Google+ friends and view their locations on a map.

Enabling GPS

Before you can begin to use the many features of your Galaxy Tab A that utilize GPS, you must first enable your Tab's GPS capabilities.

1. Open the Quick Settings and Notifications screen by tapping and holding on the status bar at the top of the screen and then swiping down the screen (not shown).

2. Tap Location into the "on" position if it isn't on already. The icon turns green to indicate that GPS is on.

Getting Around with Maps

The Maps app is great when you're planning a trip across town or the nation. You can change your map view by adding layers that include traffic, terrain, satellite imagery, transit lines, and more. You do not even have to have an address for Maps to help you get where you need to go. Just specify the general area on a map and let the Maps app generate directions.

Find a Location with Maps

The Maps app on your Galaxy Tab A gives you the capability to find and pinpoint locations as well as get directions. It also gives you access to features in other apps, such as Navigation, Local, and Location Sharing. The Maps app can help you pinpoint your exact location if you ever find yourself in an unfamiliar place. As soon as you launch Maps, your Tab uses GPS to pinpoint your current location.

1. Tap the Apps icon on the Home screen.

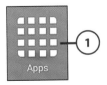

2. Tap Maps in the Apps screen.

3. Tap the Accept & Continue button.

4. Tap the Yes, I'm In button if you want Google to improve your search suggestions.

5. A map displaying your current location opens. The blue dot on the map where your Tab A is located also includes the current address above the dot. After a few seconds, the address disappears and only the blue dot appears on the screen.

6. Tap the Search field at the top of the screen to find a location. If you see a message asking you to store your personal data on the Tab A, tap OK.

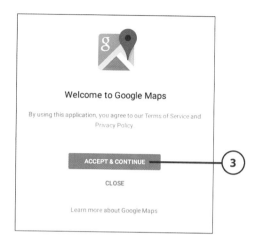

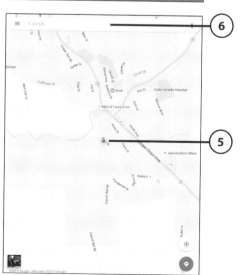

7. Type the address of the location you want to find. As you type, a list of possible locations displays.

8. Tap the correct address in the list. Your Tab A displays the location on the map. If you cannot find the address you need in the list, Maps might not have complete data for that area or the information Google Maps has might be out-dated.

It's Not All Good

Inaccurate or Incomplete Data

The Maps application is not always correct. Some of the directions and navigation data it presents might be inaccurate or incomplete due to changes over time. Complete information might not be available for some locations. Always use your best personal judgment and pay attention to road signs, landmarks, traffic conditions, and closures when following directions generated on your Tab A.

9. View the location on the map by tapping Got It.

Switching Map Views

You can view a location map as a satellite image by tapping Satellite in the menu. You can also overlay a traffic, public transit, or bicycling layer on top of the map or satellite image.

10. View more information about the location by tapping and holding on the white address bar at the bottom of the screen and then swiping up.

11. Tap Save to save this location for future searches. You can access several options from this window, including Share, Directions, Street View, Report a Problem (with the map to Google), and Add a Missing Place (such as adding a business to the map).

12. Tap the Back icon to close the information window.

13. Tap the Menu icon to add additional layers of information to the current map.

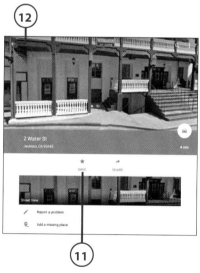

14. Tap the layer of information that you want to add to the map in the menu. The information is added to the map, thus changing the map view.

15. Close the menu by tapping the Back touch button (not shown).

16. Pinch outward to zoom in on the map. You can also double-tap your finger in a specific location on the map to enlarge the area. As you move in closer on the map, you start to notice that new information appears in the map, such as the names of banks and restaurants.

17. Use your finger to physically move the map and pinpoint locations (not shown).

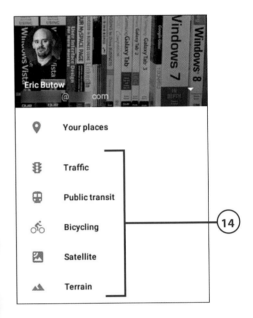

	Your places
	Traffic
	Public transit
	Bicycling	(14)
	Satellite
	Terrain

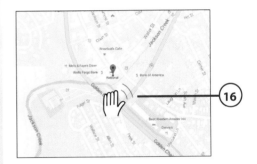

(16)

Get Directions with Maps

Maps can help you get from point
A to point B by providing detailed
directions. You can get step-by-step
driving, public transportation, biking,
and walking directions to a specified
destination by designating addresses
for a starting location and a desired
destination.

1. Tap the Apps icon on the Home
    screen and then tap the Maps icon.
    A street map opens and displays
    your current location as a blue dot.

2. Tap the Directions icon.

3. By default, your Tab A is able to
    pinpoint your current location,
    which appears as Your Location in
    the top field.

4. Tap the address you searched for
    at the top of the Recent History
    list.

5. Your current location appears in
    the From area. The address you
    selected appears in the To area.

6. You can change the address by
    tapping the Close icon and then
    typing a new address in the Search
    field.

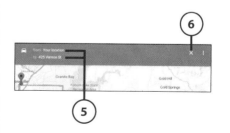

7. By default, the car route is selected
    so you can determine how long
    your trip will take by car (not
    shown).

8. Tap the estimated travel time to
    receive directions. A screen of
    detailed directions appears as
    a list. The estimated travel time
    appears above the list.

9. Swipe up and down the Directions list to move through each step in the directions.

10. Tap any step in the directions to review it on the map.

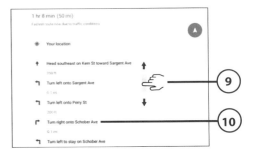

>>>Go Further

UPDATING/MODIFYING DIRECTIONS

After Maps generates the directions, you can instruct Maps to generate new directions that avoid highways and toll roads. View a list of optional routes by tapping in the center of the blue menu bar at the top of the page. Tap a route in the list to view the directions for that route on the page.

Specify Locations with Maps

Maps can help you find locations for which you do not have an address. For example, you might know that a café you would like to visit is located downtown, but you do not know how to get downtown from your hotel. The Maps app enables you to specify a vicinity on a map where you want to go and generates directions from your current location.

1. Tap the Apps icon on the Home screen and then tap the Maps icon.

2. Use your finger to move the map to your desired location and then tap and hold on the location until the pin appears on the location.

3. Tap the location.

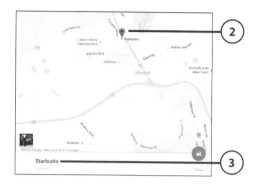

It's Not All Good

Current Location Unavailable

Occasionally, your Tab might not be able to pinpoint your current location because of lack of area coverage or a temporary disruption in the system. If, for some reason, Maps gives you the "Your Current Location Is Temporarily Unavailable" warning, you might have to manually enter your location.

4. The location appears on the map so you can save the location, share it with someone else, or get driving directions. Tap the car icon to get driving directions.

5. Get a map to your destination by tapping the map.

6. Get step-by-step directions by tapping the estimated travel time.

7. Swipe up and down the Directions list to move through each step in the directions.

8. Tap any step in the directions to review it on the map.

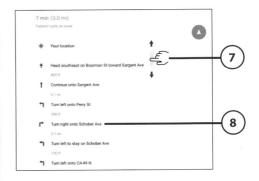

Getting Voice-Command Directions

After you get driving directions, you can turn your Galaxy Tab into a turn-by-turn, voice-command GPS device using the Maps app.

1. Tap the Apps icon on the Home screen.

2. Tap Maps in the Apps screen.

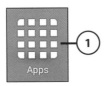

3. Tap the Directions icon.

4. Type the name of the destination for which you need directions in the Choose Destination field or select your destination from the list below the field.

5. If you type the destination in the Choose Destination field, a list of possible destinations appears below the field; tap the correct destination.

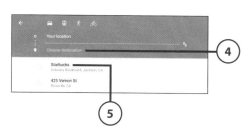

6. A street map appears with a highlighted route; tap the estimated travel time to your destination.

7. If you have a vehicle mount in your car, attach the Tab A to the vehicle mount. Appendix A, "Finding Galaxy Tab A Accessories," has more information about vehicle mounts.

8. Tap the Navigation button. Note that as of this writing, Google Maps Navigation was in beta (that is, testing) mode, so if you see a window that tells you to use caution after you tap the Navigation button, tap Accept in the window.

9. If your destination is a business and you're trying to drive there outside business hours, a pop-up window appears informing you about this. Start driving the route by tapping Start Navigation.

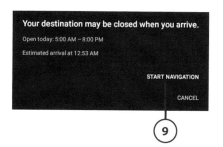

10. Drive the route. Much like a dedicated GPS, your Tab A senses where you are on the route and proceeds to give you instructions verbally and graphically.

11. View step-by-step directions by tapping and holding the black menu bar at the bottom of the screen and then swiping up. Tap the Back touch button to return to the voice directions map.

12. Tap the Menu icon to view more options.

13. Tap Mute to mute voice directions.

14. Tap Traffic to view traffic information on the screen as you drive the route.

15. Tap Satellite to view the map as a satellite image as you drive the route.

16. Return to the voice directions map by tapping the Back touch button (not shown).

17. Return to the highlighted route map by tapping the Close button in the menu bar at the bottom of the screen.

18. Tap the Close button to return to the map without route information.

19. Tap the Menu icon to view the options menu list on the left side of the screen.

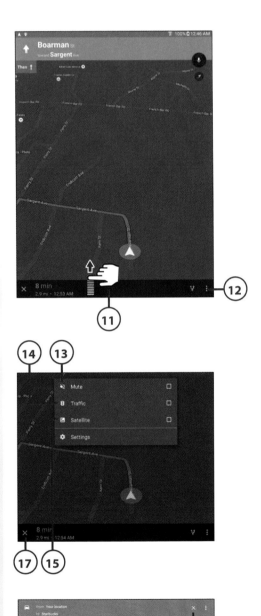

20. Tap to view a list of your places, including your home address, work address, and saved places within the Your Places window.

21. Tap to overlay a traffic status layer on the map.

22. Tap to overlay a public transit route layer on the map.

23. Tap to overlay a bicycling route layer on the map.

24. Tap to view a location map as a satellite image.

25. Tap to overlay a 3D geographic terrain and altitude information layer on the map.

26. Tap to download the Google Earth app and then view your map within the app.

27. Tap to get quick tips and tricks about using the Maps app.

28. Tap to add information about a business to Google Maps so it's easier for Maps users to find that business on the map.

29. Tap to view your account information, edit your home or work address, change location information, view your maps history, change distance units, send feedback, get tutorials and help, and read the terms, privacy policy, and notice information.

30. Tap to launch online tutorials and help for the Maps app.

31. Tap to send feedback about the Maps app to Google.

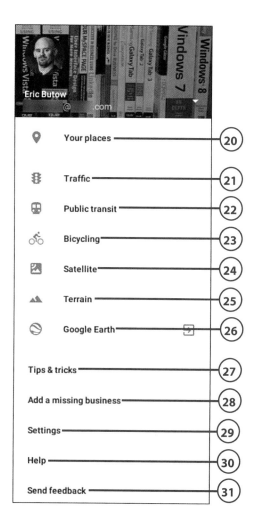

Exploring Route Options

You can access alternate routes by tapping the Map icon immediately to the left of the Menu icon. The map shows your highlighted route as a blue line and alternate routes as gray lines. Tap a gray line on the map to receive voice-command directions for that route. The next time you tap the Map icon, you see the alternate route you selected highlighted as a blue line; resume receiving voice commands for that alternate route by tapping the Back touch button.

>>>Go Further

VIEWING THE MAP

You can find the current step in the voice directions map in the green bar at the top of the screen. Within each direction entry in the list, you can view the direction you are supposed to travel in the current step at the left side of the green bar. Then you see the distance on the black bar at the top of the screen, which gives you the estimated traveling distance for completing the step and the direction to take when you complete the step. Directions take the form of a left turn arrow, straight arrow, right arrow, or a U turn. Tap the left arrow icon to move to the previous step or the right arrow icon to move to the next step. Below the arrow you see the Then arrow, which tells you the direction you'll turn after you complete the current step.

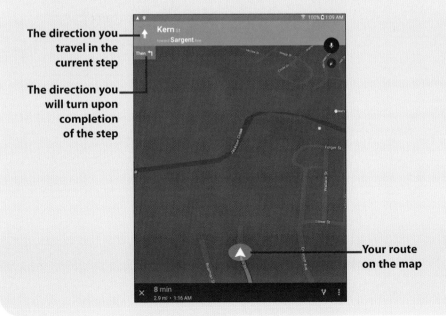

The direction you travel in the current step

The direction you will turn upon completion of the step

Your route on the map

Finding Local Information

The Maps app enables you to locate places of interest and retrieve information such as addresses, hours of operation, and phone numbers for those places. You can use Local to pinpoint the exact locations of restaurants, bars, ATMs, gas stations, and more, or you can create a new location, such as a pharmacy or hospital. The Maps app offers a great way to explore nearby areas with which you might not be familiar.

1. Tap the Apps icon on the Home screen.

2. Tap Maps in the Apps screen.

3. Tap the Directions icon.

4. Type the name of the destination for which you need directions in the Choose Destination field or select your destination from the list below the field.

5. A street map appears with a highlighted route; close the route information by tapping the Close icon.

6. Tap the Search field.

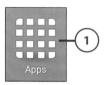

7. The most recent place you searched appears at the top of the list underneath the Search field. You can display a list of related establishments in and around that place by tapping the icon in the Nearby Places icon bar. For this example, I tapped the Restaurants icon to find restaurants.

8. The street map of the area at the top of the Restaurants screen shows various restaurants highlighted on the map. A list of restaurants in the area appears below the map.

9. Swipe up and down the list to view all the results. When you want to find more information about an establishment, tap the appropriate tile.

10. In the restaurant page, the aggregated review ranking based on the number of written reviews appears below the restaurant name. Ratings vary from one star (bad) to five stars (great). To the right of the aggregated ranking, you see how many Google Maps users have reviewed the restaurant.

11. The business type appears under the aggregated review ranking.

12. Tap the car icon to get driving directions to the business location.

13. Tap Save to save this location for future searches.

14. Tap Website to open the business website in the Internet or Chrome browser app.

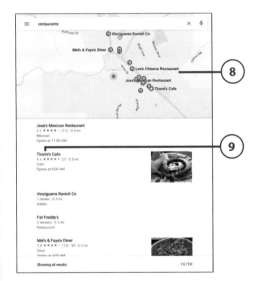

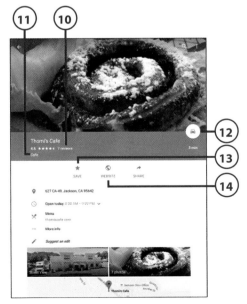

15. Tap Share to share information about this business with other users on Dropbox, ChatON, Email, or Gmail; you can also send it via a Bluetooth or Wi-Fi Direct connection, Flipboard, Google+, Google Hangouts, to your Google Drive account, to your Evernote account, or to the Clipboard.

16. The business address and hours of operation appear below the Save icon.

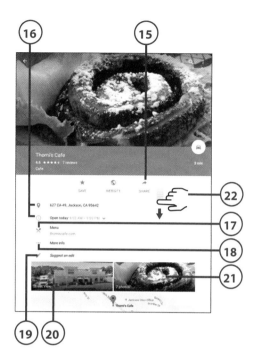

17. If you're viewing a restaurant and a menu is available, tap to view the menu in the Internet or Chrome browser app.

18. Tap to get more information about the business, such as the phone number.

19. Tap to report a problem with the business so Google can update the business entry in Google Maps. For example, if the business listing has the wrong contact details, you can send the correct details to Google. You can also ask Google to notify you when the problem has been resolved so you can check the revised listing for accuracy.

20. Tap to view the street view of the restaurant so you can see what the building looks like.

21. Tap to view photos associated with the restaurant, such as a photo of a featured meal.

22. Swipe down the screen to view more options.

23. Tap to view a map of the location on the entire screen.

24. Tap to take a photo on or add a photo from your Tab A and then add the photo to the restaurant page.

25. Tap to rate and review the business. Your review will be read by other Google Maps users who are interested in visiting the business.

26. Swipe down to read more restaurant reviews from other users.

27. Return to the map by tapping the Back icon.

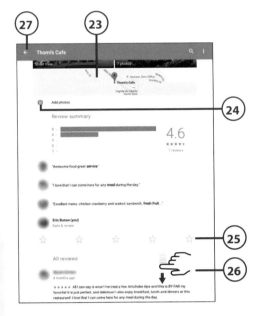

Capture photos

Browse, manage,
and share photos

In this chapter, you find out how to capture photos and screenshots, share photos via email and slideshows, and view and manage photos with Gallery. This chapter covers the following topics:

→ Using the camera
→ Navigating Image Viewer
→ Working with Gallery
→ Creating screen captures

Capturing and Managing Photos

Along with transferring images from other sources, such as your computer or microSD card, to your Galaxy Tab A, you can also take high-quality photos with your Tab A, which can house thousands of photos organized in categories. You also have the capability to take screenshots of the Tab's interface. You can even share pictures via Bluetooth, Gmail, Picasa, and more.

Using the Camera

All Galaxy Tab A models have a 5.0-megapixel rear-facing camera located on the back of the device to take photos, along with a 2.0-megapixel front-facing camera that you can use for self-portraits.

Taking a photo can be as simple as choosing a subject, composing your shot, and pressing a button. The Galaxy Tab A is also equipped with some helpful features commonly found on dedicated photo cameras, including shooting modes, scene modes, manual exposure, white balance, flash, manual exposure, and ISO settings.

1. On the Home screen, tap Camera.

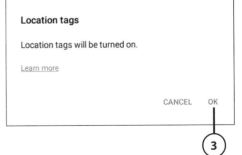

Vertical or Horizontal View?

You can take pictures in the view that's most comfortable for you: vertical or horizontal. The examples in this section starting with step 2 are in vertical view, so when you use the Camera app, keep in mind that the location of features on the screen in horizontal view will be different from what is described here. For example, in vertical view the Settings icon is in the upper-left corner of the screen, but in horizontal view the icon is in the lower-left corner of the screen.

Storage location

An SD card has been inserted. The default storage location will be changed to SD card.

Single shots will be saved to the SD card. Continuous shots will be saved to the device storage.

CANCEL   OK

2. If you insert a microSD card, you can either tap OK to change the storage settings to the SD Card or tap Cancel to use your Tab's storage to store photos and videos.

3. By default, location tags are turned on so each photo you take will have location information embedded in it. That location information is based on your Tab's use of GPS to determine its current location. Tap OK to continue.

Location tags

Location tags will be turned on.

Learn more

CANCEL   OK

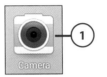

Why Does the Camera App Stop Running on Its Own?

If you don't use the Camera app for two minutes, then the app automatically minimizes and you return to the Home page. This approach helps conserve battery life as the app is resource intensive. You can return to the Camera app by tapping the Recent touch button and then tapping the Camera tile in the Recent Apps screen.

Change Settings

The Camera app contains a variety of settings you can view and/or change. You should check the settings before you start taking photos with the app so you can ensure the camera and the app work the way you want.

Some of the settings allow you to change the video camera, but this section discusses camera settings only. Refer to Chapter 11, "Playing Music and Video," for more information about video settings within the Camera app.

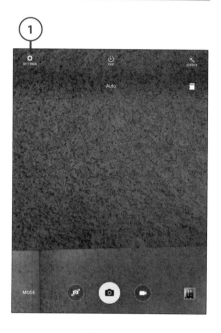

1. In the Viewer, tap the Settings icon to customize camera quick settings.

2. The Camera Settings screen appears with nine settings options.

3. Tap Picture Size (Rear) to change the rear camera size and resolution for your photos. Note that if you switch to the front-facing camera (as explained later in this chapter), this option is Picture Size (Front) so you can change the front camera size and resolution.

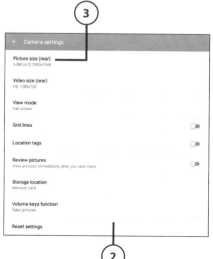

4. In the Picture Size (Rear) window, the default resolution is 5.0 megapixels with 2592×1944 pixel resolution.

5. The aspect ratio, which is the proportional relationship between the photo width and height, appears after the megapixel resolution and the default for 5.0 megapixels is 4:3. You can choose between 4:3, 16:9, and 1:1 ratio.

6. The pixel dimensions that correspond to the megapixel resolution and screen ratio appear to the right of the screen ratio.

7. After you tap one of the six picture sizes you want, you return to the Camera settings screen. If you want to keep the default picture size, return to the Camera Settings screen by tapping the Back icon.

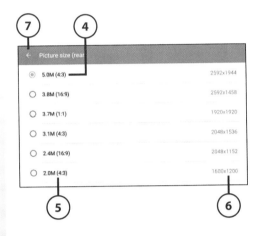

What Happens If I View a 16:9 Aspect Ratio in Full Screen Mode?

If you select a picture size with a 16:9 aspect ratio in Full Screen mode, you will see the scene in the Viewer just as you would in a picture size with a 4:3 ratio. After you take the photo and view it in the Gallery or Photos app, you will see how the scene appears in the 16:9 ratio. The appearance of the scene will be a bit different from how it appeared in the Viewer, so when you view the scene in the Gallery or Photos app, you can decide whether you want to change the View Mode so the photo dimensions in the Viewer match what you see in the scene.

8. Tap View Mode to change the Viewer screen to Standard or use the default Full Screen when taking a picture or recording a video. For example, if you select a picture size with a 16:9 aspect ratio and change View Mode to Standard, you will see the Viewer with black areas on either side of the screen so you'll see how your photo will appear with that aspect ratio.

9. Slide the Grid Lines slider from left (Off) to right (On) to enable an onscreen grid that can help you with composition.

10. Slide the Location Tags slider to the left (Off) or right (On) to disable or enable, respectively, GPS tagging of the photos you capture. Embedded GPS information can come in handy if you use a photo-editing and -managing application such as Photoshop, which enables you to use the location information to manage and showcase photos.

11. Slide the Review Pictures slider to the right (On) or left (Off) to turn the review screen on or off, respectively. If Review Pictures is turned on, you see a preview of the photo you just shot in the Review screen.

12. Tap Storage Location to determine whether the photos you capture are stored on an optional microSD card or on your Tab A.

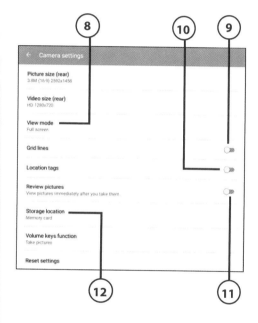

13. Tap Volume Keys Function to determine if the volume key acts as the zoom key, the video recording key, or the camera key. The default is the camera key, shown as "Take pictures" underneath the Volume Keys Function setting name.

14. Tap Reset Settings to reset the Camera settings to their defaults.

15. Return to the Viewer by tapping the Back icon.

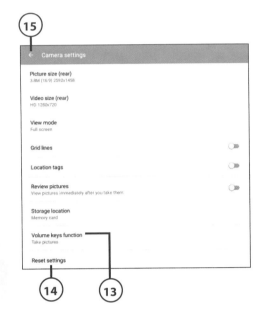

Access Viewfinder Options and Take a Photo

The Viewfinder has several icons that allow you to gain control over how you take photos and how your photos look.

1. Tap the Timer icon to designate how long the Tab A should wait before the camera takes a photo. This is great when you want to set up the shot and then place yourself in the frame.

2. Select the timer option in the Timer pop-up window. The default option is Off, but you can select from 2 seconds, 5 seconds, or 10 seconds.

3. Close the pop-up window without setting the timer by tapping outside the window.

4. Select an effect to apply to your photo after you take the photo by tapping Effect.

5. Tap the selected effect in the pop-up window. You can select from Negative, Sepia, and Grayscale; the default is No Effect.

6. After you tap an effect, a white box appears around the effect tile and a check mark appears in the center of the tile. The Viewfinder also applies the effect on the screen so you can determine if you want to keep the effect or not.

7. Close the pop-up window by tapping outside the window.

8. Change the scene mode by tapping the Mode button.

9. In the Scene Mode screen, tap the scene mode option icon that optimizes the Tab A camera for special shooting situations. For example, Panorama mode enables you to take a picture and then use the onscreen guide to move the Viewfinder and take seven more shots. This is a great mode for capturing wide vistas, such as landscapes and cityscapes. The default mode is Auto.

10. Tap Info to get information about all six screen modes you can choose from.

11. Tap the mode tile you want to use. If you decide you don't want to change the screen mode, tap the Back touch button.

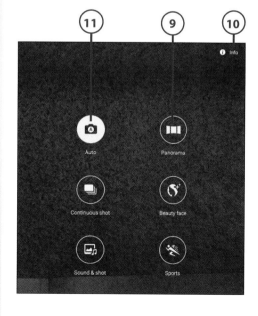

A Second Way to Open and Close the Scene Mode Screen

You can also change the scene mode by tapping and holding on the left edge of the screen and then swiping to the right. Close the Scene Mode screen by swiping from right to left on the screen.

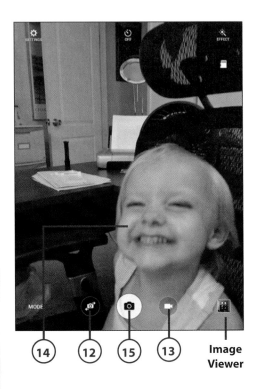

12. Tap to switch between the rear-facing and front-facing cameras. Tap again to return to the previous camera view.

13. Tap to turn on the video camera and record video. Recording video is covered in Chapter 11.

14. Compose the subject in the Viewfinder.

15. Hold your finger on the Camera button, level the shot, and then remove your finger from the button to capture the image. A thumbnail of the image appears in the Image Viewer.

16. Tap the Image Viewer to review the image you just captured. You can also access your photos by tapping the Gallery icon on any Home screen.

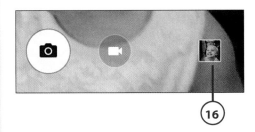

TIPS FOR CAPTURING PHOTOS

Shutter lag is the amount of time that elapses between your press of the shutter release button and the moment the picture is captured. A longer shutter lag is common among most compact cameras and also the Galaxy Tab A. What this means for you is that you have to be particularly mindful of timing your shots when recording moving subjects. Shutter lag can cause you to miss out on a key action if you do not anticipate the shot.

One important thing to know about your Tab is that the shutter does not fire as you place your finger down on the Camera button; the shutter fires when you lift your finger off the button. Use this knowledge to your advantage by pressing your finger on the shutter button and holding while you frame the shot and focus on an object about the same distance as where the subject will pass, to anticipate the shot, and then lift your finger. This means you need to hold your Tab completely still for a little bit longer. Anticipating moving subjects to capture dynamic, moving shots can take some practice.

The Tab's slow shutter makes it prone to producing blurry photos if you do not remain perfectly still during capture. Even the smallest movement can have an adverse effect on your photographs; this is especially true in low-light situations. A photo might appear to be fine when you review it on the Tab A display, but when you download it and view it on a larger display, you can see the problem.

Navigating Image Viewer

Image Viewer provides a quick-and-easy way to review the photos you have just taken. It also enables you to quickly share your pictures as soon as you capture them or set them as wallpaper. You can also edit and delete unwanted photos in Image Viewer.

As soon as you take a picture, a thumbnail of that photo appears next to the camera button. You can tap that thumbnail to review the picture you have taken and browse other photos.

1. Tap the Image Viewer to review the image.

2. The image opens full screen, the controls appear, and then they fade away. Tap the middle of the screen to access the controls again.

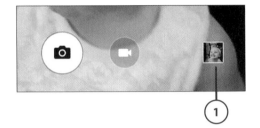

3. Tap the Favorite icon to add the photo as a favorite that you can view in the Gallery app, which is covered later in this chapter in the "Working with Gallery" section.

4. Tap the Share icon to access many options for sharing your photos through services such as OneDrive, Google Drive, OneNote, Wi-Fi Direct, Bluetooth, Samsung Quick Connect, Photos, Google+, Hangouts, Skype, S Note (or Memo), Scrapbook, Gmail, and Email. You can also view the content on another device, mirror your screen on another device, or print the photo.

5. Tap the Edit icon to edit the currently displayed photo in the Photo Editor app.

6. Tap the Delete icon to delete the currently displayed photo.

7. Flick the image from left to right to navigate through all the photos you have captured.

8. If your photo is contained in an album, tap Album to view all photos within the album.

9. Tap More to access more options.

10. Tap to view details about the photo, including the time it was taken, aperture, and exposure settings upon capture.

11. Tap to begin a slideshow of your photos. After the slideshow begins, you can tap anywhere on screen to end the slideshow.

12. Tap to open the Contacts app and set the photo as a contact photo within a new or existing contact.

13. Tap to set the current picture as wallpaper for the Home and/or Lock screen.

14. Tap the Back icon to return to the Viewfinder and take more pictures.

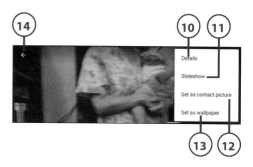

Working with Gallery

Gallery offers a more robust photo and video management system than Image Viewer, but it has similar options for viewing, sharing, and editing photos.

Manage Photos with Gallery

By default, you can access the Gallery icon by flicking the main Home screen from left to right, or you can access it from the Apps menu.

1. Tap the Gallery icon on the Home screen.

2. Content is arranged in categories/ albums. If you have downloaded videos, such as video podcasts or recorded videos, with your Tab and transferred images from your computer, they are in here, too. Tap Camera in the menu bar to access the Camera feature within Gallery.

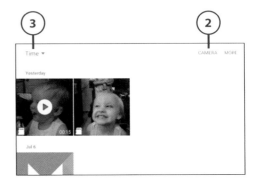

3. Tap Time to group your photos and videos in other ways. The name of this particular menu changes depending on which grouping method you have selected.

4. Tap Time to arrange photos based on the time they were captured. The most recent photos appear in the row at the top of the screen.

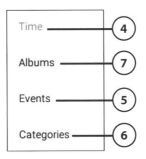

5. Tap Events to arrange photos by event, such as a birthday party. You can create events within the Events screen by tapping More in the menu bar, tapping Create Event, and then selecting the photos to add to your event.

6. Tap Categories to arrange photos based on various preset catego- ries, such as People to show pho- tos of people.

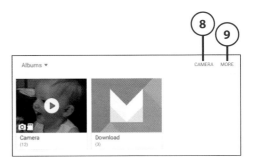

7. Tap the Albums option to arrange photos based on the folder in which they are stored. This exam- ple shows photos in albums.

8. Capture another photo by tap- ping Camera in the menu bar.

9. Tap More in the menu bar.

10. Tap Edit in the menu to select one or more complete albums to delete in the Select Items screen.

11. Tap on one or more album thumbnail images to select one or more complete albums to delete. The selected album has a green check box with a white check mark located in the upper-left corner of the album thumbnail image.

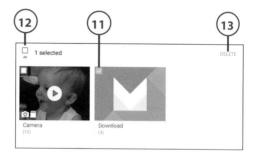

Deleting an Album from the Albums Screen

You can also delete an album from the Albums screen by tapping and holding your finger on an album thumbnail image for a couple of seconds. The selected album has the green check box with the white check mark inside it within the upper-left corner of the thumbnail image. Then tap Delete in the upper-right corner of the screen.

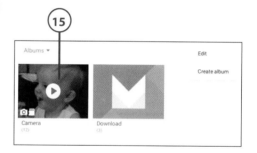

12. Tap the All check box to select all albums.

13. Tap Delete to delete the selected album or albums.

14. If you decide against deleting an album, return to the Albums screen by tapping the Back touch button (not shown).

15. Tap an album to view all photos in it.

16. If you have more photos in the album than can fit on the screen, swipe up and down on the screen to view all thumbnail-sized photos in the album (not shown).

17. Tap and hold your finger on a photo for a couple of seconds to select it. The selected photo has a green check box with a white check mark in the upper-left corner of the photo.

18. View the photo on the entire screen by tapping the double-arrow icon in the lower-right corner of each photo.

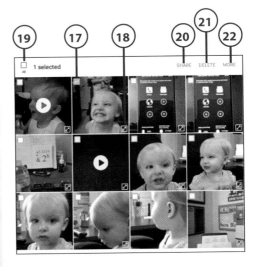

19. Tap the All check box to select all photos in the album.

20. Tap Share to view options for sharing the selected image(s) in an email or Gmail message; on Google Drive, OneDrive, or Scrapbook; in an S Note (or Memo) document; in OneNote; to another device using a Wi-Fi Direct, Bluetooth, or Samsung Quick Connect connection; on Hangouts, Google+, or Skype; or within the Photos app. You can also print the photo, such as to a Bluetooth printer.

21. Delete the selected photo(s) by tapping Delete.

22. Tap More to either copy or move the photo to another album.

23. Turn off the image selection feature by tapping the Back touch button (not shown).

24. View the photo on the entire screen by tapping on the thumbnail-sized photo.

25. Return to the Gallery home screen by tapping the Back icon.

Email Photos from Gallery

Emailing your photos to friends and family can be accomplished in just a few taps on your Galaxy Tab A.

1. Open the album that has the photo you want to email, and then touch and hold your finger on that photo to access more Gallery options (not shown).

2. Tap on more photos that you want to share. A white check mark appears within the green check box that appears in the upper-left corner of each thumbnail-sized photo, letting you know that it is selected. Email providers have varying file size limitations, so make sure you are aware of your provider's limitations before emailing photographs.

3. Tap Share to access the options in the Share Via window.

4. Tap Gmail or Email in the list. This example uses Email.

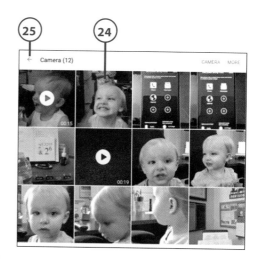
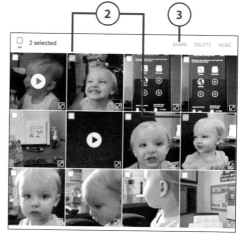
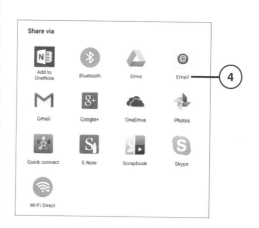

5. The Email app opens and asks if you want to resize all the selected images when you include them in the email message. Tap the size you want. The resize options are Original, Large (70% of the original size), Medium (30%), and Small (10%).

6. A list of the photo files you've attached appears below the Subject field and includes a small thumbnail image of each photo as well as the filename.

7. Remove the attachment from the message by tapping the red minus icon located to the right of the photo name.

8. Type the recipient's email address into the To field. If you see the name of the recipient in the drop-down list as you type, tap the name of the recipient. After you add a recipient to the list, you can add another one by typing the recipient name; you don't need any separator characters, such as a semicolon.

9. Tap in the Subject field and then type a subject for the email.

10. Tap in the Compose Email field to compose a message.

11. Tap Send to send the message.

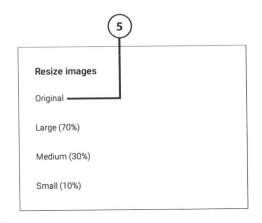

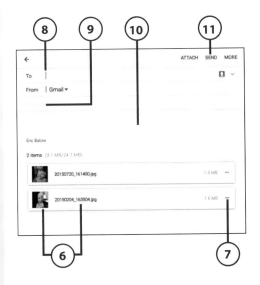

EMAILING FROM CAMERA

You can also email a photo from Camera within the Image Viewer. After you tap the Camera button to capture the image, a thumbnail of the image appears in the Image Viewer. Tap the Image Viewer to review the image, and then tap the Share icon to access your email. Email providers have varying file size limitations, so make sure you are aware of your provider's limitations before emailing photographs.

Creating Screen Captures

Your Galaxy Tab A has a very helpful feature that enables you to take screen captures of its interface. The ability to take screenshots can come in handy for educational purposes, especially if you want to post a few Galaxy Tab tips online.

1. Open the screen that you want to take the screenshot of and position the Tab A into the orientation in which you want to grab the screen capture: vertical or horizontal. This example uses the second Home screen.

2. Press and hold the Power button and Home button at the same time (not shown). You hear the shutter sound effect as it takes the screen capture.

3. The screenshot is saved to the Screenshots album in the Gallery app, and the image is also saved to the Clipboard.

It's Not All Good

Difficulties Taking Screen Captures

It might not be possible to capture some of your Tab's menus using the Screen Capture function. For example, if you're playing a video, and then press and hold the Power button and Home button at the same time, the app you're using to view the video (such as YouTube) is minimized and the screenshot is not captured. You can resume playing the video by tapping the Recent touch button and then tapping the video app tile in the Recent Apps screen.

Play and manage
music from the
Google Play Store

Play and
manage your
videos

Record video

Download and
watch movies
and TV shows

Purchase and
download
music to your
Tab A

In this chapter, you find out how to get the most out of the media and entertainment capabilities of the Galaxy Tab A. This chapter covers the following topics:

→ Downloading movies and TV shows
→ Playing videos
→ Viewing YouTube videos
→ Recording video
→ Purchasing music
→ Playing songs
→ Creating your own playlists

Playing Music and Video

Your Galaxy Tab A is a digital media player packed with entertainment possibilities; it is also camcorder capable, which you can use to record 720p HD video. You can play music, movies, TV shows, podcasts, audiobooks, and videos; read e-books; view photos; and access YouTube. Your Tab A is preloaded with a variety of apps for purchasing and downloading media.

Downloading Movies and TV Shows

The Google Play Store makes it easy for you to browse, purchase, and download the latest music, movies, and popular TV shows to your Galaxy Tab A. If you want to find movies and television shows within the Google Play Store more quickly than shopping in the Play Store itself, try using the preinstalled Play Movies & TV app.

The Play Movies & TV app enables you to shop for movies and television shows, pay for a movie or show if necessary, download the movie or show, and then watch the movie or show within the app.

Download a TV Show

In this example, you find out how to download a free television featurette.

1. Tap the Google icon on the Home screen.

2. Tap Play Movies & TV within the Google window.

3. Tap Next in the lower-right corner of the first introductory screen. If you've opened the Play Movies & TV app before, you won't see this introductory screen and you can skip ahead to step 6.

4. Tap Next in the lower-right corner of the second introductory screen.

5. Tap Done.

6. Tap Shop Movies & TV in the Watch Now screen. The Movies & TV page displays.

7. Tap TV to view TV shows. In this example, I download one of the free TV show featurettes.

8. Swipe up on the TV page until you see the Free Featurettes section. Tap More.

9. Swipe up on the page until you see the tile that contains the featurette you want to download and then tap the tile.

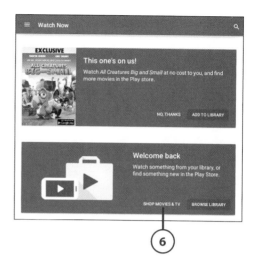

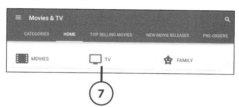

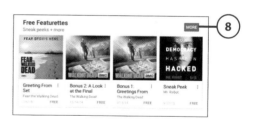

10. Swipe up on the page to read more reviews.

11. Tap Free to the right of the featurette title.

12. The video begins to play in horizontal screen orientation (not shown).

13. When you finish viewing the featurette, tap the Back touch button. View the featurette again by tapping the tile.

14. Return to the My Library screen by tapping the Back icon. You learn more about the My Library screen in the next section.

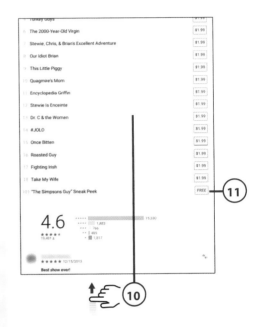

Play the TV Show

The TV show you downloaded appears within the My Library section so you can play it whenever you want.

1. On the Watch Now screen, open the menu by tapping the Menu icon at the left side of the menu bar.

2. Tap My Library.

3. Tap the My TV Shows tab. The shows you downloaded appear in each section; the most recent videos you downloaded appear at the top of the screen.

4. Tap a tile to view more information about each video within the section.

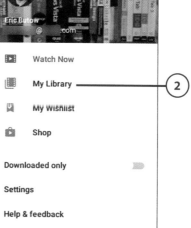

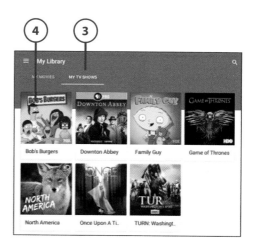

5. Tap a tile to begin playing the video in horizontal screen orientation.

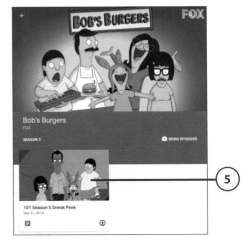

Shop for a Movie

It's easy to shop for movies that you can buy and keep on your Tab A so you can watch them any time you want.

1. From the Watch Now screen, open the menu by tapping the Menu icon at the left side of the menu bar.

2. Tap Shop.

3. Tap Movies.

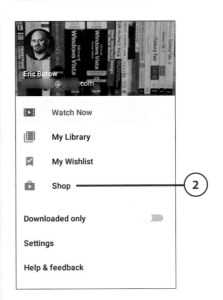

4. Tap the Categories tab.

5. Tap the category you're interested in.

6. Swipe up and down in the page to view all the Top Selling movies in the category you selected. You can view new releases in the category by tapping New Releases.

7. Tap the tile with the movie you want more information about.

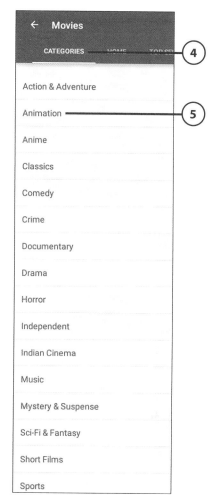

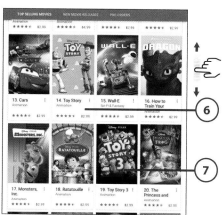

8. The name of the movie, the release year and movie rating, the movie run time, and buttons to either rent or buy the movie at the stated price appear on the screen.

9. Swipe up and down the information area to view the video trailer; rate and review the movie; view user reviews; read the synopsis, cast, and credits; and get rental period information.

10. Tap the Buy From button to purchase the movie and download it to your Galaxy Tab A so that you can watch it whenever you want.

11. Tap one of the Buy options.

12. The Buy window shows you the credit card that you have on file with Google Play, which you need in order to buy a movie or TV show (even free ones) from the Play Store. If you don't have a card on file, Google Play takes you through the steps to register your credit card.

13. Buy the movie by tapping Buy. Google Play charges the card you have on file and downloads the movie to your Tab A so you can view it.

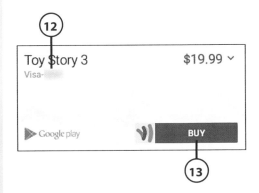

Playing Videos

There are two ways to view movies, TV shows, and other videos on your Galaxy Tab A. One is to watch in the Play Movies & TV app. The other is to use the Video app, which makes it easy for you to browse and play your downloaded and recorded videos.

Play Movies and TV Shows in the Play Movies & TV App

The Play Movies & TV app makes it easy for you to watch movies and TV shows from the Google Play Store directly within the app.

1. Tap the Google icon on the Home screen.

2. Tap Play Movies & TV in the Google window.

3. Swipe up and down in the Watch Now screen to view movies and TV shows you downloaded as well as get recommendations for movies and TV shows from Google Play.

4. Open and watch the video by tapping the movie or TV episode tile.

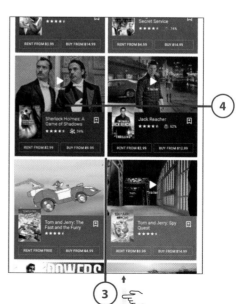

Play Videos in the Video App

If you've downloaded movies to your Tab A or if you've recorded videos using the device's video camera, you can play videos even without access to the Internet within the Video app.

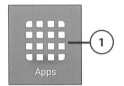

1. Tap the Apps icon on the Home screen.

2. Tap Video.

3. By default, the Video Player screen displays thumbnail-sized images from the video in the list so you can get an idea of what's in the video.

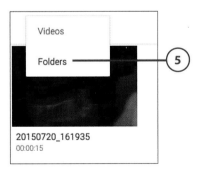

4. Change the screen view by tapping Videos.

5. Tap Folders to view your video files and the folder that contains those files.

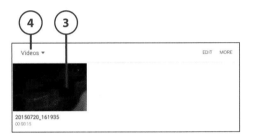

6. Select a folder in the Folders screen to view all videos; in the Camera screen that appears, begin playing the video by tapping the thumbnail-sized video image in the list as you did in step 3.

7. After the video has started, tap in the middle of the screen to bring up the playback controls.

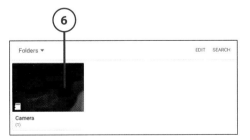

8. Tap the Full icon to view the video on the entire screen instead of viewing the video in its correct aspect ratio, which is the proportional relationship between the video width and height.

9. Tap the Pop-Up icon to view the video in a small video player window that you can move around on the screen. Pause video playback by tapping the window and then tapping the Pause button.

Close the Small Video Player Window or Return to the Video Player Screen

If you decide that you don't want to view the video in the small video player window on the screen, you can close the window by tapping the window and then tapping the Close icon (it looks like an X) in the upper-right corner of the window. You can also view the video in the Video Player screen by tapping the window and then tapping the double-arrow in the upper-left corner of the window.

10. Adjust the volume of the video by tapping your finger on the Volume icon and then sliding your finger on the Volume slider.

11. Tap List to view a list of other videos in a window at the bottom of the screen while the video you're currently viewing continues to play at the top of the screen.

12. Drag your finger across the Movie Timeline to advance through the video or jump to a new location. You can also tap the timeline in a new location to jump to that location.

13. The Play button, located in the Playback controls, turns into a Pause button as the video plays. Tap the Pause button to pause the video.

14. Tap the Rewind or Fast Forward icon to move to the beginning or end of the video, respectively.

15. Tap More.

16. Tap Delete to delete the video from the playlist.

17. Tap Share to share the video using OneNote, OneDrive, Google Drive, Skype, Google+, Bluetooth, Wi-Fi Direct, Samsung Quick Connect, YouTube, Scrapbook, S Note (or Memo), Photos, Gmail, or Email. You can also view the video on another device.

18. Tap Listen via Bluetooth to share the video with other devices via Bluetooth.

19. Tap Turn On Play Audio Only to hide the video on the screen and play only the audio that was recorded with the video.

20. Tap Play Speed to change the play speed of the video so it plays faster or slower than the speed at which you recorded the video.

21. Tap Subtitles (CC) to set the app to view closed-captioned subtitles on the screen as you view the video.

22. Tap Details to view details of the video, such as Name, Size, Resolution, Format, and Last Modified.

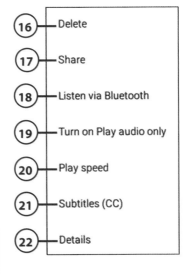

16 — Delete

17 — Share

18 — Listen via Bluetooth

19 — Turn on Play audio only

20 — Play speed

21 — Subtitles (CC)

22 — Details

Viewing YouTube Videos

The high-resolution screen of the Galaxy Tab A, along with its portability and built-in video camera, makes it great for viewing and sharing videos online. The preinstalled YouTube widget gives you the capability to browse and view videos posted by users from around the world. You can also upload videos as soon as you shoot them with your Tab A.

1. Tap the Apps icon on the Home screen.

2. Tap YouTube.

3. Skip the introduction by tapping Got It.

4. Tap the Menu icon at the left side of the menu bar.

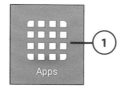

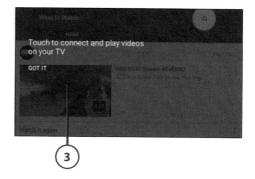

5. A list of your channels appears on the left side of the screen that overlaps a list of videos on the screen. In this example, the list of videos is within the selected What to Watch channel.

6. Swipe down the list and then tap Browse Channels to view channels YouTube recommends for you.

7. View channels by swiping up and down the screen. You can see videos and more information about the artist channel by tapping the channel tile.

8. Tap the Menu icon in the menu bar.

9. Return to the YouTube home screen by swiping down in the list and then tapping What to Watch.

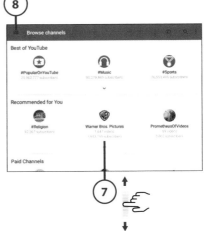

10. Tap the Search icon to search for a YouTube video.

11. Type the search term(s) in the Search YouTube field.

12. When you're finished typing, tap the Search button in the keyboard. The results appear on a separate Search page.

13. Return to the YouTube home screen without completing a search by tapping the Back icon.

14. You can also view the menu by tapping and holding your finger on the left edge of the screen and then swiping to the right (not shown).

15. View videos within a subscription channel by swiping up in the menu and then tapping the channel name in the Subscriptions list.

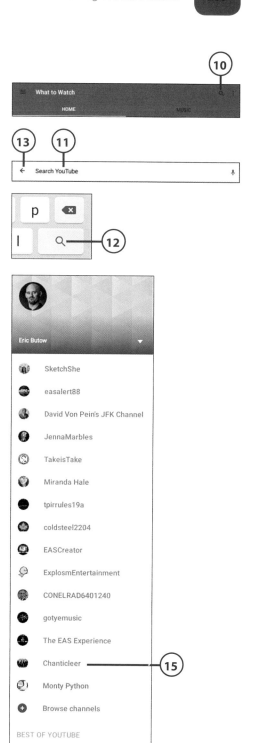

16. Tap the Menu icon below the video thumbnail image and then save the video to the Watch Later list by tapping Add to Watch Later.

17. Add the video to an existing or new playlist by tapping Add to Playlist.

18. Tap Share to share a link to the video via Wi-Fi Direct, Bluetooth, Samsung Quick Connect, Google+, Hangouts, Google Drive, OneNote, OneDrive, Skype, or to the Clipboard, an S Note or Memo document, Scrapbook, Gmail, or Email.

19. Close the menu by tapping the Back touch button (not shown).

20. Tap a video thumbnail image to play the video on the screen.

Other Sharing Options

Other sharing options might appear in this list if you have downloaded apps that allow for additional sharing features, such as BeyondPod.

21. Tap the Menu icon so you can turn closed captioning on and off, change the video quality, and flag the video for inappropriate content so Google can review it.

22. Tap to pause and play the current video.

23. Drag the button in the Timeline slider to move through the current video.

24. The video description appears below the video.

25. Tap to visit the channel of the user who posted this video.

26. Swipe up and down in the page to read more about the artists, view similar videos and artists, read comments about this video from other users, and create a response of your own.

27. Return to the channel screen by tapping the Back touch button (not shown).

28. The video continues to play in the window in the lower-right corner of the screen. View the video screen by tapping and holding in the window and then flicking upward. Close the video screen by tapping and holding in the window and then flicking to the right or left.

29. Return to the main YouTube screen by tapping the Menu icon in the menu bar and then tapping What to Watch, as described earlier in this chapter.

Recording Video

Your Galaxy Tab A is capable of recording 720p HD video with its main 5.0-megapixel camera, located on the rear of the device. The Galaxy Tab A is also equipped with some very helpful features commonly found on dedicated camcorders, including a timer, a video light, and effects.

1. On the Home screen, tap Camera.

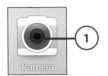

I See a Window When I Start Camera. What Do I Do?

When you start Camera for the first time, you see the Storage Location window that asks you to change the storage location to the SD card. Tap OK in the window. Next, you see the Location Tags window that tells you location tags will be turned on. (You learn more about location tags in step 10.) Tap OK in this window to close it. The next time you start the Camera app, you won't see these windows.

2. Switch to Video mode by tapping the Video button. The Camera app starts recording automatically.

3. Pause recording by tapping the Pause button. After you tap the Pause button, the button changes and shows a red circle in the center. Resume recording by tapping the button with the red circle in the center.

4. Stop recording by tapping the Stop button.

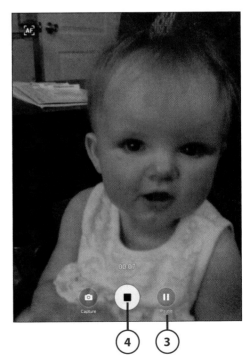

Vertical or Horizontal View?

You can record video in the view that's most comfortable for you: vertical or horizontal. The examples in this section starting with step 2 are in vertical view, so when you use the Camera app, keep in mind that the location of features on the screen in horizontal view will be different from what is described here. For example, in vertical view, the Settings icon is in the upper-left corner of the screen, but in horizontal view, the icon is in the lower-left corner of the screen.

5. Tap the Settings icon.

6. In the Camera Settings window, tap Video Size (Rear) to set a size for the images you capture in the Video Size (Rear) screen.

7. The default video size is HD, or 1280×720 pixels. Change the pixel size to VGA, or 640×480 pixels, by tapping VGA.

8. Return to the Settings screen by tapping the Back icon.

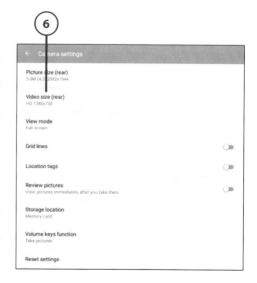

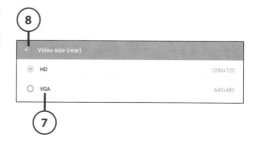

9. Tap the Grid Lines slider to the right (On) or left (Off) to enable or disable, respectively, an onscreen grid that can help you with the composition of the video.

10. Slide the Location Tags slider to the right (On) or left (Off) to enable or disable, respectively, GPS tagging of the photos you capture. Embedded GPS information can come in handy if you use a video-editing and -managing application such as Adobe Premiere, which enables you to use the location information to manage and showcase videos.

11. Tap Storage Location to determine whether the videos you capture are stored on an optional microSD card or on your Tab A.

12. Tap Volume Keys Function and then tap Record Video in the pop-up menu to have the volume key act as the video recording key.

13. Tap Reset Settings to return the camera settings to the default settings.

14. Return to the Viewfinder by tapping the Back icon.

15. Tap to switch between the rear-facing and front-facing cameras.

16. Tap Effect.

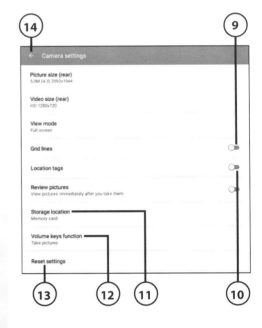

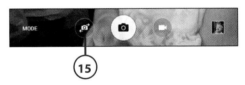

17. Tap to add camera effects to your videos as you capture them. Your choices include Negative, Sepia, and Grayscale. Apply an effect by tapping the effect tile. The selected effect tile has a white box around the tile and a white check mark in the middle of the tile. The Viewfinder applies the effect so you can see how your recorded video will look with the effect. If you don't like the effect, select another or select No Effect.

18. Tap the Back touch button to close the Effects area (not shown).

19. Tap Timer to designate how long the Tab A should wait before the camera starts to record. You can choose from 2 seconds, 5 seconds, and 10 seconds. This is great for allowing time for you to set up the shot and then place yourself in the frame.

20. Close the pop-up menu without making any changes by tapping the Back touch button (not shown).

21. Tap the Video button to begin recording.

Adding Video Effects

Keep in mind that when you record a video and apply any of the video effects, such as Grayscale, Negative, or Sepia, they become a permanent part of your videos. To give yourself more choices in the future as to how you use your images, consider purchasing a video-editing app that enables you to perform such effects but still maintain your original video.

22. When you finish, tap the Stop button.

23. The video you just recorded appears in the Image Viewer in the lower-right corner of the window. Tap the Image Viewer to review the recorded video in the Video Player or Photos app.

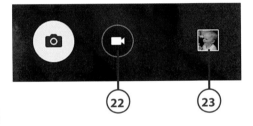

Purchasing Music

The Galaxy Tab A includes the preinstalled Google Play Music app for finding, previewing, purchasing, downloading, and playing music to your Tab A. This app isn't the only one you can use, however—there are plenty of other music apps available for download in the Google Play Store.

1. Tap the Google icon on the Home screen.

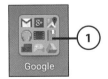

2. Tap Play Music in the Google window.

3. Swipe back and forth to view all the introductory screens. Open the Listen Now screen by tapping Listen Now.

4. Tap the Menu icon in the menu bar.

5. Tap Shop in the list.

6. The Music screen shows the latest free music and exclusive videos. Swipe up and down the screen to view more featured songs and albums in a variety of categories.

How Do I Know If a Song Has Explicit Lyrics?

If you don't want to listen to songs with explicit lyrics (and/or don't want your kids to listen to them), you can easily see which songs and albums have explicit lyrics by looking for the Explicit warning within the song or album tile.

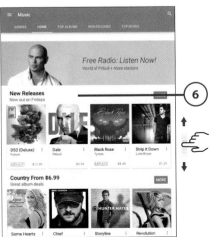

7. Tap More to view more songs and albums in the category.

8. Tap the Top Albums tab to view the best-selling albums in Google Play.

9. Tap the New Releases tab to view the newest albums in Google Play.

10. Tap the Top Songs tab to view the best-selling songs in Google Play.

11. Tap the Genres tab to view categories of music you can choose from.

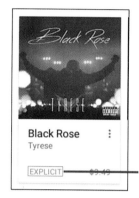

Black Rose
Tyrese

EXPLICIT $9.49

The Explicit warning label in the album tile

12. View all the genres by swiping up and down in the list. When you find a genre you want, tap the genre name in the list.

13. Swipe up and down the screen to view different sections of the genre page.

14. Tap a tab name to view new releases and top songs in the genre.

15. Tap the Genres tab to view a list of subgenres within the main genre.

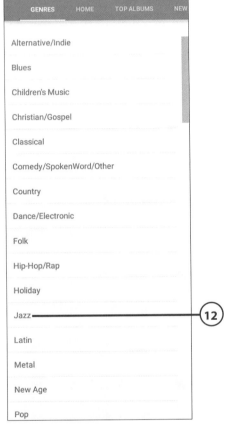

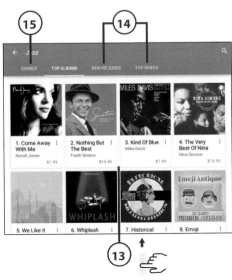

16. Tap a subgenre in the list.

17. Top-selling albums in that subgenre appear on the screen. Scroll up and down the screen to view all the top albums.

18. Tap the Top Songs tab to view the best-selling songs in the subgenre.

19. Tap the New Releases tab to view newly released songs and albums within that subgenre.

20. Tap the Back icon to return to the genre page.

21. Tap an album or song tile on the screen to view more information.

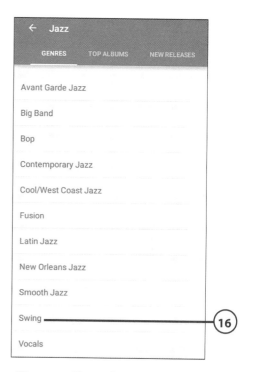

22. The title and album cover appears at the top of the screen. You can purchase the entire album by tapping the orange purchase button that contains the album price.

23. If you want unlimited access to the album and all songs available in Google Play Music for 30 days, tap Free Trial. Then follow the steps in the Get Started screen to sign up. After the first 30 days, Google will charge you $9.99 per month for the same unlimited access to Play Music.

24. Swipe up on the screen to view a description of the album and artist, all songs in the album, reviews from other Google Play users who downloaded the songs or album, more albums by the artist, and similar artists.

25. Tap a song name to play a 90-second snippet of that song.

26. Tap Play All to play all the snippets in the album.

27. Purchase a song on the album by tapping the purchase button that contains the price of that specific song.

28. Swipe down on the screen to view the album cover and title.

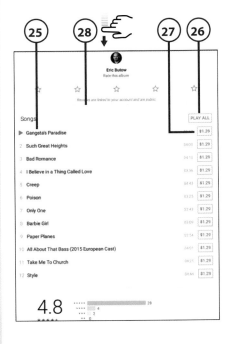

29. Purchase the album by tapping the purchase button located under the album cover.

30. The Google Play window appears with the price of the album and the credit card Google Play will use to process the transaction.

31. Tap Buy to purchase the album.

32. After you purchase a song or album, a Shopping bag with a check mark tells you that you have downloaded the song to your Tab A successfully (not shown).

33. Tap the Listen button to the right of the song you've purchased to listen to the song.

Playing Songs

The Music app on your Galaxy Tab A was designed to make it easy for you to browse and play your music collection downloaded onto your Tab A. A great set of headphones can enhance the enjoyment of your favorite music. The ability to browse your music library and understanding your playback options are big steps toward getting the most out of your many entertainment possibilities on the Tab A.

Play Music in the Music App

In the Music app, you can play songs you added to your play queue within the app. You can also listen to music you downloaded from the Google Play Store within the Music app.

1. Tap the Apps icon on the Home screen.

2. Tap Music.

3. Tap the Playlists tab and then tap Recently Added in the list.

4. The most recent song you listened to appears at the top of the Recently Added list. Swipe up and down in the screen to see other songs in the list.

5. Tap a song in the list to listen to that song in the Music app.

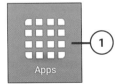

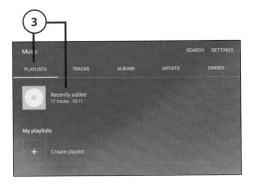

6. The highlighted song plays automatically and the playback controls appear in a window at the bottom of the screen.

7. Tap the Pause button to pause playback. After you tap the Pause button, tap the Play button to resume playback.

8. Tap the Rewind icon to begin playing at the beginning of the song.

9. Tap the Fast Forward icon to move to the end of the song.

10. Tap and hold your finger on the button and then slide the button within the timeline to move to different points in the song.

11. Adjust the volume by tapping your finger on the Volume icon and then sliding your finger on the Volume slider.

12. Tap the Back icon to go back to the Music screen.

Play a Song Even When the Music App Is Closed

After you start playing a song in the Music app, you see the Play icon in the status bar at the top of the screen. Pause the song by opening the Quick Settings and Notifications screen and then tapping the Pause button. When you close the Quick Settings and Notifications screen, you see the Pause icon in the status bar. You can read more about opening the Quick Settings and Notifications screen in Chapter 2, "Setting Up the Galaxy Tab A."

The Play icon in the status bar

13. Tap the Tracks tab to view all the tracks you can play in the Music app.

14. Tap and hold your finger on the selected track in the list to view more options in the song options window.

15. Select another track by tapping the check box to the left of the track image. After you tap the check box, the check box turns green and contains a white check mark.

16. Tap the All check box to select all tracks in the list.

17. Tap Delete to delete the song from the Music app.

18. Tap More to see more options.

19. Tap Add to Playlist to add the track(s) to a playlist, which you learn more about later in this chapter.

20. Tap Add to Favorites to add the song to your Favorites list.

21. Tap the Back touch button to close the menu (not shown).

22. Return to the list of tracks in the Tracks tab by tapping the Back touch button (not shown).

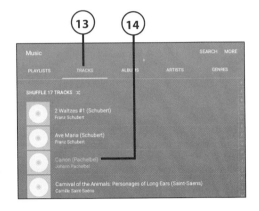

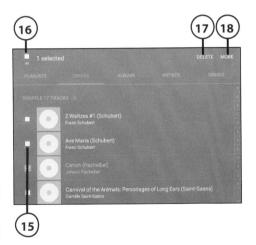

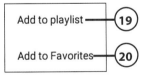

Add to playlist — 19

Add to Favorites — 20

Play Music in the Google Play Music App

The Play Music app makes it easy for you to listen to music within the Google Play Store directly within the app.

1. Tap the Google icon on the Home screen.

2. Tap Play Music in the Google window.

3. From the Listen Now screen, tap the Menu icon at the left side of the menu bar, as discussed earlier in this chapter (not shown).

4. Tap My Library.

5. Tap the Songs tab.

6. Swipe up and down the list of songs in the album (if necessary) and then tap a song title in the list.

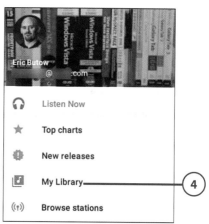

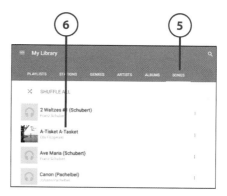

7. Tap the Pause button while you're playing the song to pause playback.

8. Tap the Play button to resume playing the song (not shown).

9. Tap the Rewind icon to begin playing at the beginning of the song.

10. Tap the Fast Forward icon to move to the end of the song.

11. Rate the song so other Google Play users can view it by tapping the thumbs up (good) or thumbs down (bad) icon.

12. View more song options by tapping the Menu icon to the right of the song title in the list.

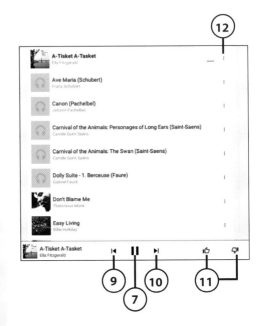

13. Create a new radio station that contains the song by tapping Start Radio. A radio station is a playlist generated by Google Play Music based on songs you have listened to.

14. Have the Play Music app play all songs in the list randomly by tapping Start Instant Mix.

15. Play the next song in the list by tapping Play Next.

16. Download the song to your Galaxy Tab A by tapping Add to Queue.

17. Add the song to a new playlist by tapping Add to Playlist.

18. Within the Add to Playlist window, tap a playlist to add the song to a playlist.

19. Tap New Playlist to add the song to a new playlist.

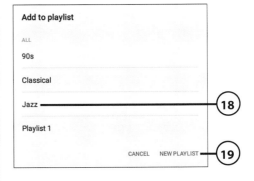

20. Type the playlist name and description in the New Playlist window.

21. By default, any Google Play Music user can view your playlist and listen to songs within it. If you want to make your playlist public so any Google user can see and listen to your music, slide the Public slider button from left (Off) to right (On).

22. Tap Create Playlist. A pop-up box appears at the bottom of the screen that informs you that Play Music added the song to your playlist. Open the song options menu again by tapping the Menu icon to the right of the song title.

23. Tap Go to Artist to view all the artist's albums that you've added to your library.

24. Tap Go to Album to view the album you've added to your library.

25. Tap Delete to delete the song from your Galaxy Tab A and from your playlist within the Play Music app.

26. Tap Share to share a link to the song using Wi-Fi Direct, Bluetooth, Samsung Quick Connect, Google+, Hangouts, Google Drive, OneNote, OneDrive, Skype, or to the Clipboard, an S Note or Memo document, Scrapbook, Gmail, or Email.

27. Tap Shop This Artist to shop for more music from the artist in the Google Play Store.

28. Tap the Back touch button to return to the main Play Music screen (not shown).

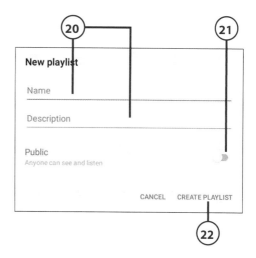

Creating Your Own Playlists

Playlists are a great way to create a compilation of your favorite songs for playback in the Music app. Use playlists as an opportunity to organize the best songs from your favorite artists, acoustic selections, party music, classic rock, orchestral masterpieces, relaxation tracks, and more.

1. Tap the Apps icon on the Home screen.

2. Tap Music.

3. Tap the Playlists tab.

4. Tap Create Playlist.

5. Type the name for your new playlist. The default name is highlighted in the field, but you can replace this name by tapping the Delete key in the keyboard and then typing the new name.

6. Tap Create.

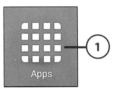

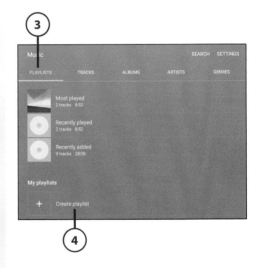

7. Tap the song(s) you want to appear in the playlist. After you tap a song, a white check mark appears in the green check box to the left of the song image. Tap the song title again to clear the check box and delete the song from the playlist.

8. Tap the All check box to select all tracks in the list.

9. Tap Done when you've finished creating the playlist.

10. Your playlist appears on the screen with the tracks you added in the list.

11. Return to the Music app home screen by tapping the Back icon.

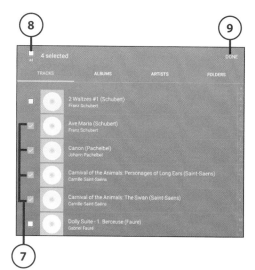

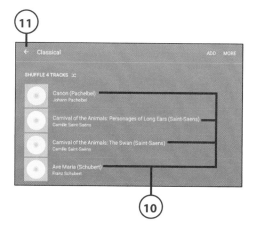

>>>Go Farther

REMOVING AND ADDING SONGS IN A PLAYLIST

You can remove songs from a playlist by selecting the playlist, tapping More in the upper-right corner of the screen, and then tapping Edit in the application menu at the top of the screen. In the removal selection screen, select the track(s) you want to remove by tapping the check box next to each item and then tap Remove in the upper-right corner of the screen. You can add a song to a playlist by opening the playlist to which you want to add the song and then tapping Add in the upper-right corner of the screen. You can then select additional music from the library.

Purchase and read books with Play Books

Purchase and read magazines with Play Newsstand

In this chapter, you find out how to purchase books and magazines using the preinstalled Play Books and Play Newsstand apps and how to read them on your Galaxy Tab A. This chapter covers the following topics:

→ Using Google Play Books
→ Using Google Play Newsstand
→ Shopping for book and magazine readers

Reading and Managing Books and Magazines

Your Galaxy Tab A offers a great outlet for you to enjoy books and magazines. The Play Books app that is installed on your Tab A offers a stylish e-reader that enables you to browse, purchase, download, and read e-books on your device. The Tab A also includes the preinstalled Play Newsstand app so you can read the latest magazines on your device.

Both the Play Books and Play Newsstand apps enable you to enhance your reading experience by offering reading aids such as the ability to increase font size and change background color. If you prefer a different e-reader, you can shop the Google Play Store for other apps and then download and add books from other sources. Consider trying out a few of the available readers to see which one you like the best.

Using Google Play Books

Books are available in the Play Books app for purchase or available for free, and after you download (and purchase, if necessary) a book, you can read it within the app. You can also use built-in reading aids such as changing how the page appears on the screen.

Browse the Catalog

When you open the Play Books app, you can start shopping for books in the Google Play Store right away.

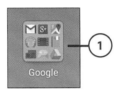

1. Tap the Google icon on the Home screen.

2. Tap Play Books in the Google window.

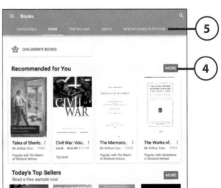

3. Tap More to begin shopping for books.

4. Swipe up and down the screen to view recommendations and books in various categories. View more books in a category by tapping More.

5. Tap New Releases in Fiction to view the newest fiction books.

6. Swipe from right to left within the menu bar to view books in the Top Selling, Deals, New Releases in Nonfiction, and Top Free sections.

7. View a list of book categories by swiping from left to right on the menu bar and then tapping Categories.

8. Swipe up and down in the list to view all categories; tap a category in the list to view featured books within the category.

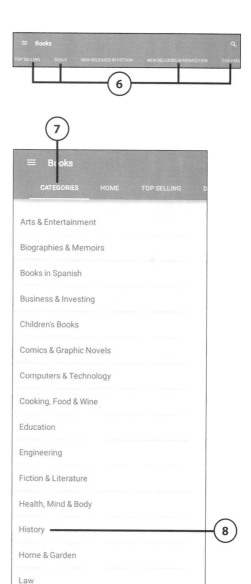

9. View the entire list of featured books by swiping up and down the screen.

10. Tap New Releases to view all the latest books Google has added in the category you're viewing.

11. Open a book in a subcategory by tapping Categories, swiping up and down the category list, and then tapping a subcategory name in the list.

12. Tap a book cover to open the book description page.

Purchase a Book

From the book description page, you can purchase books that are currently available as well as preorder books that will be released soon so you will receive the book on your Galaxy Tab A as soon as possible.

What If the Book Isn't Available Yet?

If the book hasn't been published yet, the estimated publication date appears above the purchase button. When the book is available, a Notification icon displays in the status bar. You can read your delivered book in the Play Books app by opening the Quick Settings and Notifications screen and then tapping the notification on the screen.

1. The title of the book, the book cover, and the Buy button appear at the top of the page. If the book includes a free sample, the Free Sample button appears to the left of the Buy button.

2. Ratings, the book type, and a button link to similar books appear below the Buy button (and the Free Sample button if there is one).

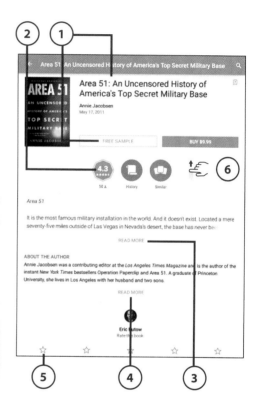

3. Read the entire description by tapping Read More in the Description area.

4. Read more about the author by tapping Read More in the About the Author section.

5. In the Rate This Book section, tap a rating star on a scale from one to five. For example, if you tap the second star from the right, then the first four stars from left to right are highlighted in blue, which signifies that you give the book four stars on a five-star scale. Then you can type your review in the Review window.

6. Swipe upward on the screen to view reviews, more books by the author, related books, and an author biography.

When I Tap the Rating Star, I See an Information Window Instead

The first time you tap a rating star in Play Books, you see a window telling you that reviews in Google Play are linked to your Google+ profile and are public, so anyone on Google+ can read your book review. Close the window by tapping OK, and then repeat step 5 to type your review in the Review window.

7. Read the entire review by tapping the review summary entry in the Reviews section.

8. View all reviews for the book by tapping All Reviews.

9. Tap Wishlist to add the book to your wish list for later purchase.

10. Tap Share to share the link to the book with another device using Bluetooth, Wi-Fi Direct, or Samsung Quick Connect; send the link to someone else in an email using the Email or Gmail app; share the link on your Google+ account; or share the link in a Hangouts or Skype chat. You can also save the link to a Google Drive or OneDrive file; save the link in a OneNote, S Note, or Scrapbook app document; or copy the link to the Clipboard to paste into another app (such as Microsoft Word).

11. Tap +1'd This to let other Play Books users know you like this book.

12. View more information within a section, such as related books, by tapping the More button.

13. Swipe down on the page until you reach the top of the page.

14. Tap the Buy button to begin the purchase process.

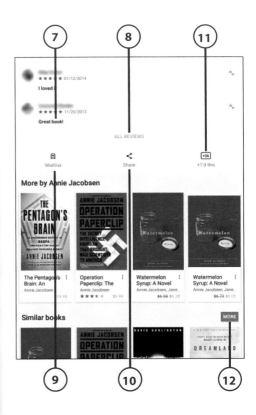

Downloading a Free Book Sample

Some books give you the opportunity to download a free sample
of the book so you can read some
of the book before you decide to
buy it. If a free sample is available,
the Free Sample button appears
next to the Buy button. You can
then read the free sample in Play
Books as you would with any
other book.

15. Tap the price to access more pay-
    ment options.

16. Tap Payment Methods to change
    or add a credit or debit card,
    redeem Google Play credits, buy
    Google Play credits, or add your
    PayPal account information.

17. Tap Redeem to redeem Google
    Play credits to purchase this book
    in whole or in part.

18. Tap Buy to purchase the book.
    After you purchase the book,
    you will see the book in the Play
    Books app so you can read it as
    described in the next section.

Download and Read a Book

There are plenty of free books you can download from the Google Play Store so you can start reading classics and favorites right away.

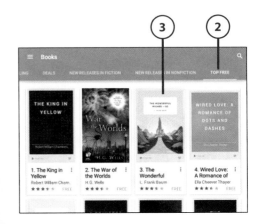

1. Open the Play Books app as you did earlier in this chapter.

2. Swipe from right to left in the menu bar and then tap Top Free.

3. View all books in the list by swiping through the list of books. Tap the tile of the book you want to download.

4. Get information about the book, read reviews, and add your own rating and review as described in the previous section.

5. Tap the Add to Library button to add the book to your Play Books library.

6. The first page of the book appears in the Play Books app. Move to the next page by tapping the right side of the screen.

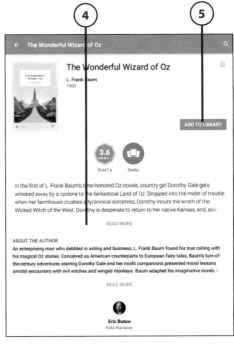

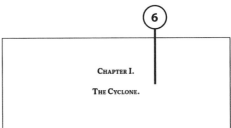

>>>Go Further

CHANGING SETTINGS

If you need to change settings before you start reading the book, such as if you want the screen to rotate when you rotate the Galaxy Tab A, tap in the middle of the screen to view the Reading Aids screen. Tap the Menu icon in the upper-right corner of the screen and then tap Settings in the menu. (You learn more about the Reading Aids screen later in this chapter.)

You can then change the auto-rotation setting for the Play Books app only, determine how you download book files, change how you turn pages, enable uploading of the PDF version of a book to Play Books, tell Play Books to automatically read the book aloud if the correct accessibility setting is on, and download the dictionary to use when the Tab A is not connected to the Internet. Return to the book page by tapping the Back touch button.

Use Reading Aids

The Play Books app contains many options for enhancing your e-book experience, including changing background color and font size, jumping to locations within the book, and organizing your book titles.

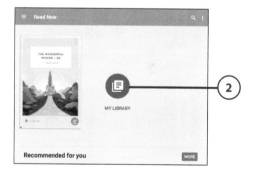

1. Open the Play Books app, as described earlier in this chapter.

2. Tap My Library.

3. Find the book on the My Library page, swiping if necessary, and then open the book by tapping the book cover image.

4. Tap the right side of the book page to progress to the next page. Tap the left side of the page to revisit the previous page. You can also flick left or right to turn pages.

5. Go to a page with text and then tap the middle of the screen to access the Reading Aids screen.

6. Tap the Contents icon to access the table of contents for the book.

7. You can jump to a chapter by tapping its title in the contents.

8. Tap About This Book to read an overview of the book.

9. Close the Chapters list by tapping the Back touch button (not shown).

10. Tap the Search icon to search for text in the book.

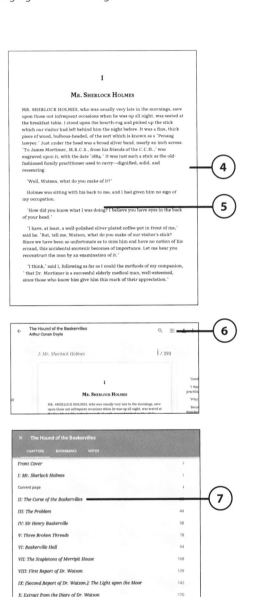

11. Type the search term(s) in the Search in Book field.

12. Tap the Search button in the keyboard.

13. View all the results and the page number on which each result appears by swiping up and down in the list.

14. View the page that contains your desired passage by tapping the entry in the list.

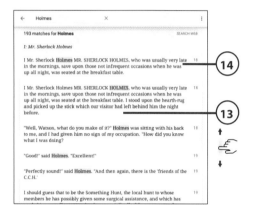

15. The search terms appear high-lighted on the screen.

16. Go to the next page that contains the search term(s) by tapping the right-arrow icon.

17. Return to the search results list by tapping the Back icon in the menu bar. Close the search results list by tapping the Back icon again.

18. View reading aid controls by tapping the Close icon.

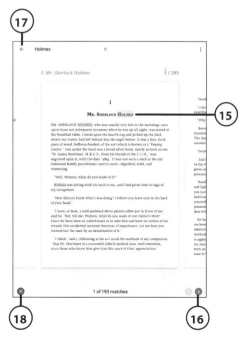

19. Drag the slider to jump to different pages in the book.

20. After you drag the slider to jump to a different location, you can tap the page button to jump back to where you were last reading.

21. Tap the Style icon at the right side of the menu bar to access more options.

22. Tap one of the three theme tiles to change the text and background color theme for the page. Your choices are Day (black text on a white background), Night (white text on a black background), and Sepia (black text on a beige background).

23. Change the screen brightness in the Brightness slider. Set the brightness level to its default level by tapping the Brightness icon (it's shaped like the sun with an A in the middle) to the left of the slider bar.

24. Tap to change the overall font style for the book. Your choices are Original, Sans, Literata, Merriweather, Sorts Mill Goudy, and Vollkorn.

25. Tap to change the overall text alignment for the book. Your choices are Default, Left, and Justify.

26. Tap the small T and large T buttons to decrease and increase, respectively, the size of the book font on the screen. The zoom percentage between these buttons indicates the current setting.

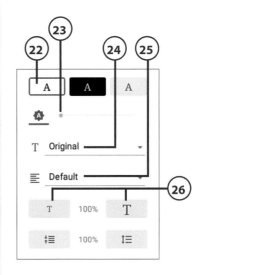

27. Tap the Decrease Line Spacing button to decrease the size of the height between lines in the book.

28. Tap the Increase Line Spacing button to increase the size of the height between lines in the book.

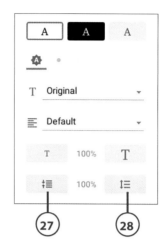

Add Bookmarks, Highlights, and Notes

Play Books provides the convenience of placing a bookmark where you stopped reading so you can begin at the right location later. You also have the capability to highlight text in a book and to leave notes. This section presumes you have already opened the Reading Aids screen, as described earlier in this chapter.

Add a Bookmark and Go To a Bookmarked Page

1. Bookmark the page you're currently reading by tapping the Menu icon.

2. Tap Add Bookmark.

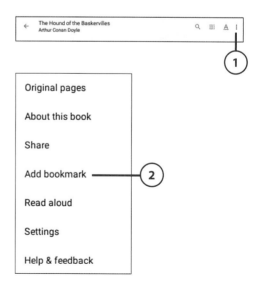

3. A bookmark icon appears in the upper-right corner of the page.

4. Close the book by tapping the left-arrow icon in the menu bar.

5. Open the book in the My Library page by tapping the book cover image as described earlier in this chapter.

6. Tap in the center of the page.

7. Tap the Contents icon.

8. Tap Bookmarks.

9. Tap the bookmark in the list.

Removing a Bookmark from a Page

There are two ways to remove a bookmark from a page. One way is to tap the Bookmark icon in the upper-right corner of the page. After you tap the icon, it moves down the page and then upward until it disappears. The other way is to tap the Menu icon on the Reading Aids screen and then tap Remove Bookmark in the menu.

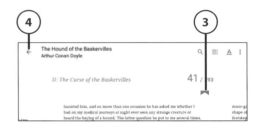

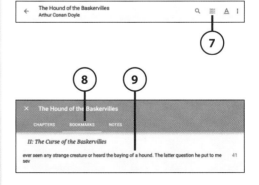

10. The bookmarked page appears on the Reading Aids screen with a bookmark above the slider button. Tap the middle of the page to view the entire page that also contains the bookmark in the upper-right corner of the page.

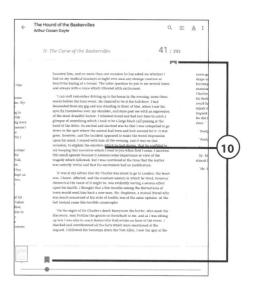

Highlight Text

1. You might want to specify a block of text as a point of interest by highlighting it. Press your finger on the screen and hold. Blue handles appear on either side of the selected word.

2. A dictionary definition appears at the bottom of the screen.

3. Drag the handles of the arrows to specify the text you want to highlight.

4. Tap the Highlight icon in the menu bar in your desired color (from left to right: red, yellow, green, or blue).

5. The highlighted text appears on the page.

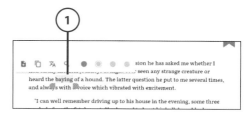

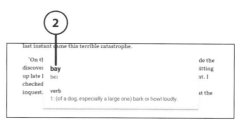

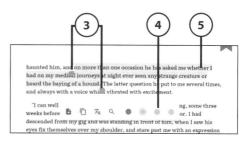

Syncing Highlights and Notes to Google Docs

The first time you highlight a word in a book, you see a pop-up window at the bottom of the screen asking if you want to sync and store your book highlights and notes in Google Docs for safekeeping. If you want to do this, tap Turn On Sync in the window. If you don't, tap No Thanks in the window.

Removing Highlights from Text

You can remove the highlight from text by tapping and holding your finger on a portion of the highlighted text, selecting the text that includes the highlight you want to remove, and then tapping the Delete Highlight icon (a circle with an X inside).

Add a Note

1. You can insert a note for an excerpt of text. Press your finger on the screen and hold. The high-lighted word appears with han-dles on either side of the word.

2. Tap the Add Note icon.

3. Type the note in the Add Note field.

4. Tap the book page when you're finished typing.

5. The passage of text is highlighted and a Note icon appears at the right side of the screen.

Deleting a Note

To modify or delete a note, you can tap the Note icon that appears at the right side of the screen to reveal the associated note. You can then edit your note or select the text in the note that you want to cut, tap the Menu icon in the upper-right corner of the Note field, tap Delete in the menu, and then tap Remove to confirm the deletion.

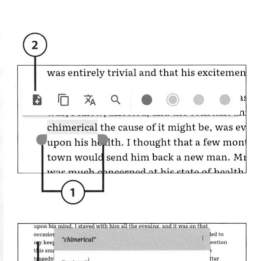

VIEWING ALL NOTES AND MARKS

Your Galaxy Tab A offers a quick and convenient way to view and jump to all notes and highlights you have made in a book. Tap the middle of the screen to reveal the Reading Aids screen. You can then tap the Contents icon. Within the Chapters window, tap the Notes tab to view all of your highlights and notes.

Organize Your Books

After you have accumulated many titles in your Play Books library, you need a method to the madness of organizing your books. By default, your books are ordered by the most recently downloaded on the Play Books home screen. You have a couple other sorting options to choose from.

1. Tap the Menu icon at the left side of the menu bar.

2. Tap My Library to view all the books in your library.

3. Tap the Sort icon to choose from the sorting options. Your choices are Recent, Title, and Author.

4. Tap the Menu icon in the menu bar.

5. Tap Refresh to update your library with all of your latest purchased content.

>>>Go Further

REMOVING AND ARCHIVING BOOKS

You can access the option to remove books from your device by tapping the Menu icon that appears to the right of the book title. A menu opens from which you can choose the Delete from Library option. The book is removed from the library page, but remains archived in your Play Books account.

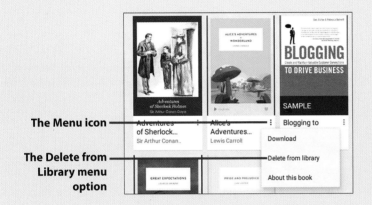

The Menu icon

The Delete from Library menu option

Using Google Play Newsstand

If you want to read magazines without wasting paper, then the preinstalled Play Newsstand app on the Galaxy Tab A is for you. This app enables you to shop for magazines in the Google Play Store, purchase one or more issues of the magazine, and then read the magazine within the app.

Shop for Magazines

When you open the Play Newsstand app, you can start shopping for magazines in the Google Play Store right away.

1. Tap the Google icon on the Home screen.

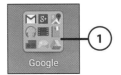

2. Tap Play Newsstand in the Google window.

3. Tap the Menu icon in the upper-left corner of the screen.

4. Tap Explore.

5. Swipe up and down the screen to view magazine topics in various categories. View more magazines in a category by tapping the category tile.

6. Tap Store to shop for magazines in the Google Play Store or tap Featured to view featured magazines in Play Newsstand.

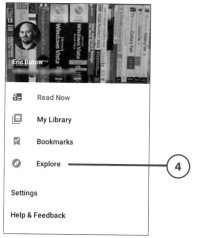

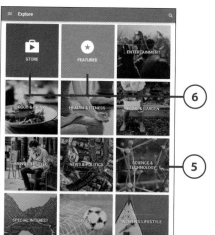

7. Shop for all magazines within the category by tapping More.

8. View the entire list of top magazines by swiping up and down the screen.

9. Tap New Magazines to view all the latest magazines Google has added in that category.

10. Tap a magazine cover to open the magazine description page.

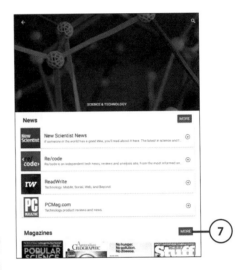

Purchase a Magazine

You can purchase an individual issue of a magazine that you can download to the Play Newsstand app and read at your leisure.

1. The title and issue of the magazine, the cover of the current issue, the Subscribe button, and the Buy button appear at the top of the magazine page.

2. Ratings, the magazine category, and a button link to similar magazines appear at the top of the Description area.

3. View the entire description by tapping Read More in the Description area.

4. Swipe upward on the screen to rate the publication and read magazine reviews from other readers.

5. In the Rate This Publication section, tap a rating star on a scale from one to five. For example, if you tap the second star from the right, then the first four stars from left to right are highlighted in blue, which signifies that you give the publication four stars on a five-star scale. Then you can type your review in the Review window.

6. View all reader reviews by tapping All Reviews.

7. Swipe upward on the screen to perform more tasks, view similar magazines, and view back issues.

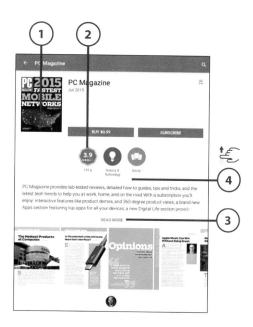

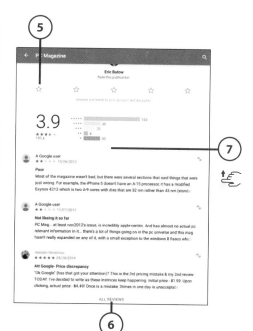

8. Tap Wishlist to add the magazine issue to your wish list for later purchase.

9. Tap Share to share the link to the issue with another device using Bluetooth, Wi-Fi Direct, or Samsung Quick Connect; send the link to someone else in an email using the Email or Gmail app; share the link on your Google+ account; or share the link in a Hangouts or Skype chat. You can also save the link to a Google Drive or OneDrive file; save the link in a OneNote, S Note, or Scrapbook app document; or copy the link to the Clipboard to paste into another app (such as Microsoft Word).

10. Tap +1'd This to let other Play Newsstand users know you like this magazine.

11. Tap More to view more information within a section, such as back issues.

12. Swipe downward on the screen to view the title and issue of the magazine.

13. Tap the Buy button to begin the purchase process.

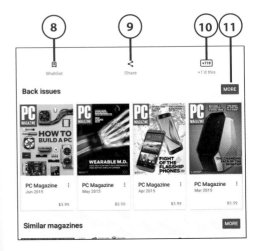

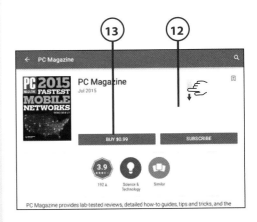

14. Tap the price to access more payment options.

15. Tap Payment Methods to change or add a credit or debit card, redeem Google Play credits, or add your PayPal account information.

16. Tap Redeem to redeem Google Play credits that will pay for the magazine issue in whole or in part.

17. Tap Buy to purchase the issue. After you purchase the issue, a pop-up menu appears in the center of the screen that informs you that you've added the issue to your library. Open the issue by tapping the Open button in the window. If you don't want to open the issue, tap the Back touch button to return to the magazine page.

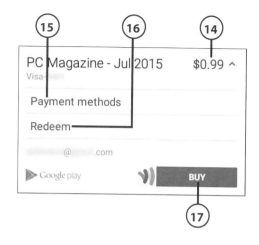

Subscribe to a Magazine

You can also subscribe to the magazine so you can receive new issues on your Galaxy Tab A over a period of time.

1. Open the page to purchase the magazine, as described in the previous section.

2. Tap the Subscribe button to begin the subscription purchase process.

Can I Preview a Magazine Subscription?

If there is a free trial for your subscription, you see the length of the free trial above the Subscribe button. Some magazines make it free for you to purchase if you're already a print subscriber. Some magazine subscriptions also offer a limited-time free trial, although you have to agree to start paying for the magazine after the trial period. You can cancel the subscription before the trial period is over.

3. Tap the price to access more payment options. If the magazine includes a free trial, you see the date the trial expires.

4. Tap the price in the upper-right corner of this window. In this example, the price is Free.

5. Tap Payment Methods to change or add a credit or debit card, redeem Google Play credits, or add your PayPal account information.

6. Tap Redeem to redeem Google Play credits that will pay for the magazine subscription in whole or in part.

7. Tap Subscribe to purchase the magazine subscription. After you purchase the subscription, you see the most recent issue in the Play Newsstand app so you can read it as described in the next task.

Read an Issue

After you download an individual issue of a magazine or the first issue of your subscription, the Play Newsstand app makes it easy for you to browse and read each page in the issue.

1. Open the Play Newsstand app, as described earlier in this chapter.

2. Tap the Menu icon in the upper-left corner of the screen.

3. Tap My Library.

4. Tap Magazines.

5. The first time you open the Magazines tab in the My Library screen, you see an informational window at the top of the screen. Close this screen by tapping Got It. After you tap Got It, you won't see this window any longer when you view the Magazines tab.

6. Swipe up to view the magazine issue you want to read (if necessary) and then tap the cover image.

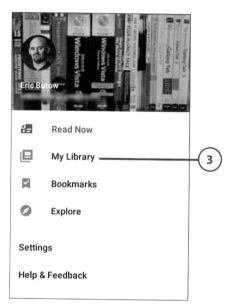

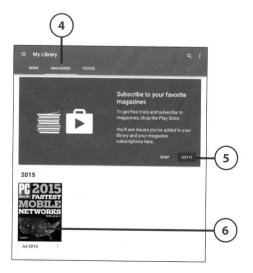

7. The magazine issue cover appears in the Play Newsstand app. Begin reading the issue by tapping the magazine cover.

8. Swipe from right to left to view each page in the magazine on the entire screen.

9. You can return to the issue home screen by tapping the Back touch button (not shown).

I Can't Swipe Left or Right in the Magazine

When you come to the beginning or end of the magazine, you see a blue bar on the left side of the screen for a second or two when you swipe to the right or left, respectively. This blue bar tells you that you've reached the beginning or end of the magazine.

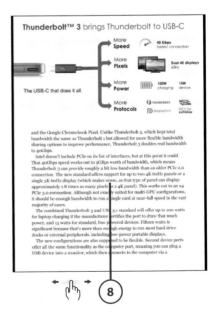

>>>Go Further

ADDING AND REMOVING A DOWNLOAD-ED MAGAZINE

When you purchase the magazine, you have the ability to download it to your Galaxy Tab A so you can read it even when you're not connected to the Internet. Download the magazine by tapping the Play Newsstand icon in the menu bar, tapping My Library, tapping the Menu icon underneath the magazine cover, and then tapping Download in the pop-up menu. After you download a magazine, you see a blue check mark icon (a blue circle with a white check mark) in the lower-right corner of the magazine cover. You can remove the magazine from your magazine library by tapping the Menu icon and then tapping Remove Download in the menu.

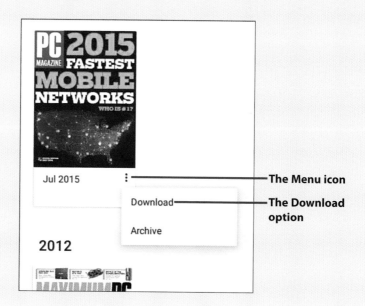

Browse and Read Individual Pages

The Play Newsstand app contains several options that make reading a magazine easier for you.

1. Open the Play Newsstand app, as described earlier in this chapter.

2. Tap the Menu icon in the upper-left corner of the screen.

Why Do I See the My Library Screen?

If you closed the Play Magazines app while viewing the magazines on the My Library screen, when you launch the app again you see the My Library screen with the Magazines tab active. If this happens, you can skip ahead to step 5 in these instructions.

3. Tap My Library.

4. Tap Magazines.

5. Swipe down to view the magazine issue you want to read (if necessary) and then tap the cover image.

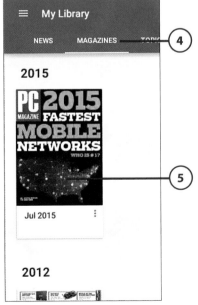

6. Tap the magazine cover as you learned to do in the "Read an Issue" section earlier in this chapter.

7. Tap the right side of the magazine page to progress to the next page. Tap the left side of the page to revisit the previous page. You can also flick left or right to turn pages.

8. Tap the middle of the screen to access the blue menu bar at the top of the screen.

9. Tap the Back icon in the menu bar to return to the magazine home screen.

10. Swipe up and down the page to view thumbnail-sized pages within the magazine. Two pages are shown in each page row with even-numbered pages on the left and odd-numbered pages on the right.

11. Tap the page tile to view the page on the entire screen.

12. View the app menu bar by swiping down on the screen.

13. You can view a list of articles instead of thumbnail images by sliding the View button from right to left.

14. Swipe up and down the screen to view the article title and the first few sentences of each article within each article tile in the list; tap the tile to read the text of the article on the entire screen.

15. You can view the articles as thumbnail images again by swiping up in the article list to view the menu bar and then sliding the View button from left to right.

16. Return to the My Library screen by tapping the Back icon in the menu bar.

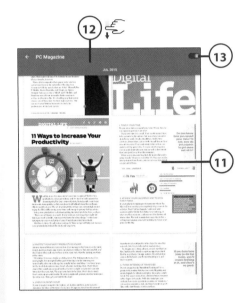

Organize Your Magazines

After you have accumulated many titles in your Play Newsstand library, you need a method of organizing your magazines just as you do with books in the Play Books app. By default, your magazines are ordered by the most recently downloaded on the Play Newsstand home page. You have a couple other sorting options to choose from.

1. Open the My Library screen within the Play Newsstand app, as described earlier in this chapter.

2. View all the magazines in your library by tapping Magazines.

3. Tap the Menu icon in the menu bar.

4. Tap Refresh to update your library with all of your latest content.

5. Tap Manage Subscriptions to manage your magazine subscriptions on the Google Play Store website within either the Internet or Chrome browser.

6. Tap Sort to sort the list of magazines on the Magazines page by publication date (which is the default selection) or by title.

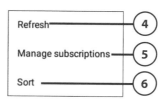

Shopping for Book and Magazine Readers

If you prefer to use another book or magazine reader, you can shop the Google Play Store for other cloud storage apps that are optimized for the Android operating system.

1. Tap Play Store on the Home screen.

2. Tap Apps.

3. Tap the Search icon in the menu bar.

4. Type **book readers** in the Search Google Play field.

5. Tap the Search button in the keyboard.

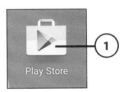

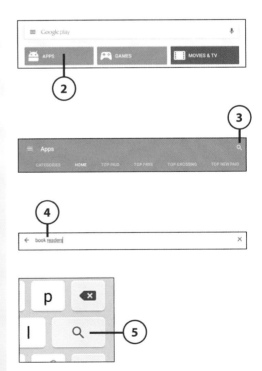

6. Swipe up and down within the list of apps in the search results screen; you also see the Google Play Books app in this list. Tap a tile to view more information about the app. Read more about shopping for apps in the Google Play Store in Chapter 15, "Finding and Managing Apps."

7. Tap the Back icon in the upper-left corner of the screen.

8. Tap the Search icon in the menu bar, as you did in step 3.

9. Type **magazine apps** in the Search Google Play field.

10. Tap the Search button in the keyboard.

11. Swipe up and down within the list of apps in the search results screen. Tap a tile to view more information about the app. Read more about shopping for apps in the Google Play Store in Chapter 15.

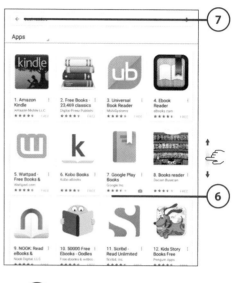

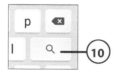

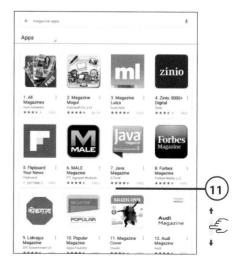

Store and
search all your
contacts

Track your
appointments
and events

Monitor the weather, news, and stocks
from one convenient location

In this chapter, you find out how to organize your daily schedule, news, and information. You also see how to add and search contacts and calendar events. This chapter covers the following topics:

→ Staying up to date
→ Managing contacts
→ Managing your busy schedule

Using Productivity Apps to Simplify Your Life

Your Galaxy Tab A is highly capable of helping you organize your busy life. The preinstalled Contacts and Calendar apps help you improve your daily efficiency by enabling you to manage personal contacts and schedule important appointments. You can also download free productivity apps from the Google Play Store to get the latest weather forecast, learn what's happening on the stock market, and view the latest news stories. This chapter takes a close look at what these productivity apps, as well as the Contacts and Calendar apps, can do for you.

Staying Up to Date

If you want to stay up to date with news, weather, and stock information, there are several well-reviewed free apps available in the Google Play Store:

- The AccuWeather app enables you to get up-to-the-minute weather conditions and forecasts for your area.

- The Stock Alert Tablet Edition app enables you to view all sorts of information about stocks.

- If you're looking for news, search for News360 for Tablets.

This section gives you a brief look at these three apps so you can get the information you're looking for on your Galaxy Tab A. Start by downloading the apps. (You can find out how to download apps in Chapter 15, "Finding and Managing Apps.") You can also explore the Google Play Store to see what other apps might meet your needs.

Choose a Weather Forecast

Follow these steps to display the forecast for a specific city in AccuWeather:

1. On the Home screen, tap Play Store.

2. Tap Apps.

3. Tap the Search icon.

4. Start typing **AccuWeather** in the Address field.

5. Tap AccuWeather in the search list.

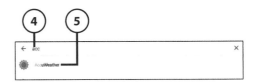

6. Tap Install.

7. Tap Accept.

8. After the Galaxy Tab A downloads and installs the app, tap Open.

9. Tap I Agree on the Terms of Use page.

10. Tap Next in each of the two steps within the introductory slideshow (not shown).

11. Tap No Thanks on the Quick Setup screen (not shown).

Adding Other Forecasts

You can add other forecasts by tapping your current location at the left side of the menu bar, which is located at the top of the screen. In the drop-down menu that appears, tap Add Location. In the Locations column, type a new city and then tap the Search button on the keyboard. You can navigate among the multiple fore-casts by tapping the location at the left side of the menu bar and then selecting the location from the drop-down menu.

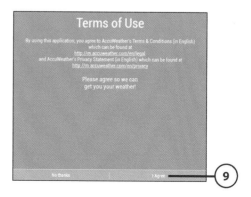

12. Tap My Current Location in the Choose a Location screen.

13. The current conditions appear on the screen.

14. Swipe from right to left to view the 15-day forecast in the Daily column. Within the list of forecast dates and temperatures, you can scroll down the days to see the forecasted conditions for the next 15 days.

Updating Forecasts and Other Settings

By default, you must manually refresh the weather forecast by tapping the Refresh icon at the right side of the menu bar. You can further customize your forecasts by tapping the Settings icon that appears at the far right of the menu bar. For example, you can change the wind speed units (such as km/h) and time format.

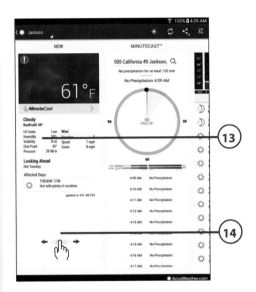

Track Stocks

You can configure the Stock Alert Tablet app so that you can monitor a desired stock for a company.

1. Tap Play Store on the Home screen.

2. Tap Apps.

3. Tap the Search icon.

4. Type **stock alert** in the Search field.

5. Tap stock alert in the list.

6. Swipe up the screen until you see Stock Alert Tablet Edition in the list.

7. Tap the Stock Alert Tablet Edition tile.

8. Tap Install.

9. Tap Accept. The Galaxy Tab A downloads and installs the Stock Alert Tablet Edition app automatically.

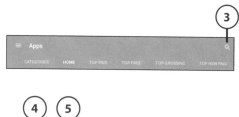

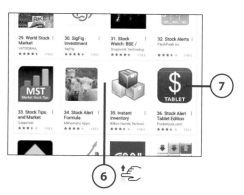

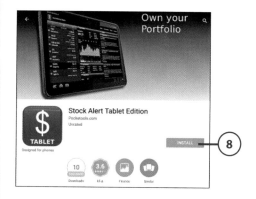

10. After the Galaxy Tab A downloads and installs the app, tap Open.

11. Tap Accept to accept the End User Agreement.

12. Tap the Add Stock icon to add a stock.

13. Type the name of the company with the stock that you want to track. You can also type the stock ticker name.

14. Tap the Search button to view a list of results for the stock.

15. Scroll down the stock list in the window if necessary. Tap the name of the stock that you just added to view the stock summary.

Adding Additional Stocks

You can add another stock by tapping the Add Stock icon, typing in a new stock ticker in the ticker box directly underneath the Search box, and then tapping Add. You can navigate between multiple stocks by scrolling up and down your list of stocks in the left column and then tapping the stock you want to view.

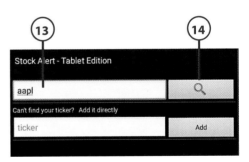

Refreshing Stocks

By default, your stock information must be manually refreshed by tapping the Refresh Rates icon above the list of stocks in the left column on the screen.

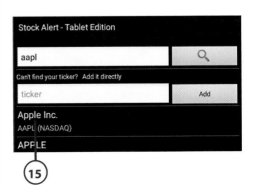

Select Your News Settings

You can browse the latest world, national, and local news stories by customizing your news settings in News360. However, before you can do so, you need to create a News360 account.

1. Tap Play Store on the Home screen.

2. Tap Apps.

3. Tap the Search icon.

4. Type **news360** in the Search field.

5. Tap news360 in the list.

6. Tap the News360: Personalized tile.

7. Tap Install.

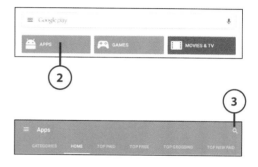

8. Tap Accept. The Galaxy Tab A downloads and installs the News360 for Tablets app automatically.

9. After the Galaxy Tab A downloads and installs the app, tap Open.

10. Swipe up the screen to view news categories and log in to News360 using a social networking or Evernote account.

11. Choose how you want to authenticate with News360 by tapping the appropriate social networking icon. You can use your Facebook, Google, Twitter, or Evernote account information. Within the row of account tiles, swipe from left to right to view the Evernote tile. This example uses a connection through a Facebook account; tap the Facebook tile.

12. In the Facebook window, type your email account and password, and then tap Log In.

13. Tap OK to give News360 access to your public profile and friend list on Facebook.

14. Tap Start Reading at the bottom of the screen.

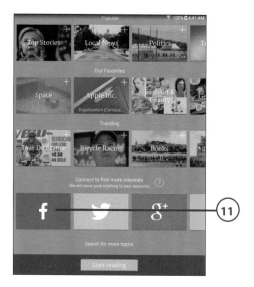

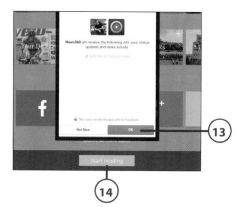

15. Above the default list of stories on the home page, tap the News360 icon in the menu bar.

16. Tap Top Stories.

17. The list of top stories appears. You can swipe from right to left to view more stories and tap a story title to read it.

18. Return to the News360 home screen by tapping the News360 icon in the menu bar.

19. You can search for articles or topics by tapping the Search icon and then typing your search term(s) in the Search field.

20. You can view app settings by tapping the Menu icon and then tapping Settings.

21. Remove one of your existing categories by tapping and holding the category tile and then dragging it over the Remove Topic icon.

22. Add a new topic category by tapping Add Topics.

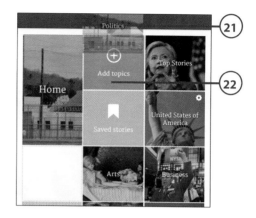

23. Categories appear as rows of tiles within the section name, such as Space, Physics, and Biology within the Science section. Swipe up and down the screen to view all the category sections. Within each category row, swipe left and right to view all category tiles. Add a category to your news feed by tapping the tile.

24. The list of stories within the category appears on the screen. Add the category to the News360 home screen by tapping the Add icon.

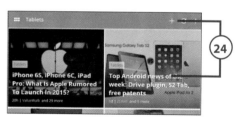

25. The Add icon changes to a check mark icon.

26. Return to the Explore screen by tapping the News360 icon.

27. Your selected category appears with a check mark in the upper-right corner of the category tile.

28. Return to the News360 home screen by tapping the Back icon in the menu bar.

29. The new category tile you added appears on the screen, although you might need to swipe from right to left to see it.

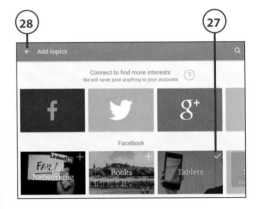

>>>Go Further
HOW DO I REARRANGE MY CATEGORY TILES?

If you want to rearrange categories on the News360 home screen, tap and hold your finger on the category name you want to move. Drag the category name to your desired location on the screen.

As you move the tile, you see where your category tile will appear and other tiles move aside to make room for it. Release your finger to place the tile in that location.

If you want to move your selected tile to another category page, move the icon to the left or right edge to move to the previous or next category page. After the previous or next category page appears on the screen, move the tile to the location on the screen. If the tile page is full, then the tile at the lower right of the screen moves to the top of the next category page.

It's Not All Good

Refreshing News Stories

By default, News360 refreshes news stories when the app finds new stories to post in your headlines list. If you want to refresh your headlines list manually, tap the category tile. In the category screen, tap the Refresh icon at the right side of the blue menu bar that appears at the top of the screen. After a second or two, updated stories appear in tiles on the screen.

Managing Contacts

The Contacts app enables you to manage all the important information you receive from colleagues, friends, and prospective business associates. Think of your Galaxy Tab A as a virtual filing cabinet or Rolodex where you can store contact information such as names, addresses, emails, and notes. If you collect contacts with other social networking services, you can also configure Contacts to sync information between accounts.

Set Up Contacts Accounts

The Galaxy Tab A can synchronize its contacts information with multiple accounts, such as Google, Corporate Exchange, other email providers, and sites such as Facebook and Google+. Information on your Galaxy Tab A is updated when you make changes to information in your accounts. Setting up a contacts account is quite easy.

1. On the Home screen, swipe from right to left to open the second Home screen (not shown).

2. Tap the Settings icon.

3. Swipe down the settings list on the left side of the screen and then tap Accounts.

4. Tap Add Account.

5. Tap an account that you would like to set up.

6. Follow the prompts to set up each account that you would like to add. The account(s) you add appear in the Accounts area within the Settings list.

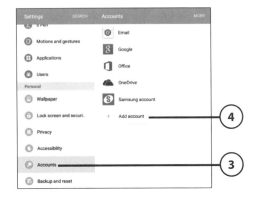

Do I Need to Install an App on the Tab A with an Account?

Some accounts require you to install the associated app on your Tab A. For example, if you add a LinkedIn account, as shown in this example, the LinkedIn app page appears within the Google Play Store so you can install the app on your Tab A. After you install the app, sign in to your LinkedIn account and your account is added to your list of accounts within the Settings screen.

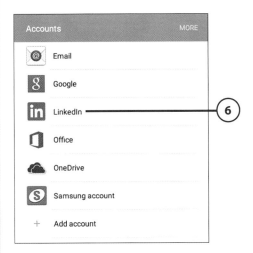

Add Contacts

Using the Contacts app, you can store contact information for family, friends, and colleagues for quick access and to send messages.

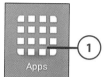

1. Tap Apps on the Home screen.

2. Tap Contacts.

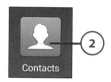

3. A list of all contacts appears. Your own profile information appears by default.

4. Tap the Add button.

5. By default, you save the new contact to Device, which is your Galaxy Tab A. If you want to save the contact to an account, tap Device.

6. Select the account to which you want to save the contact, or tap Device to save the contact to the Tab A instead.

Why Can't I Sync Contacts I Add to the Tab A?

The Galaxy Tab A can't sync contacts you add to the device itself to any other device to which you connect the Tab A. If you want to sync to other devices, you can add the contact to your online contact database stored in your Samsung, Google, or Microsoft Exchange ActiveSync account.

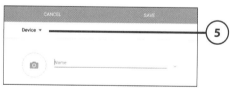

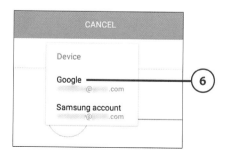

7. Type the first and last name in the Name field.

8. If you want to add the first and last name in different fields, tap the ˅ icon located to the right of the Name field to add a Name Prefix, First Name, Middle Name, Last Name, and Name Suffix to the contact. There is no need to use the Shift key on the keyboard to capitalize the name because the Galaxy Tab A does this automatically.

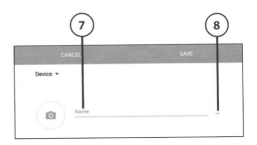

9. Tap the labels within fields to reveal the label field so you can enter information such as the phone number.

10. Tap the label to the right of the field to select the information type. For example, with the phone number the default information type is Mobile, which means the phone number is for the contact's mobile phone.

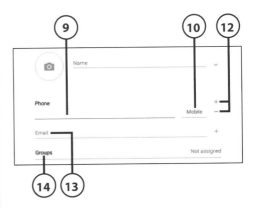

11. Select the type of a pop-up menu with other labels to choose from. For example, tap Mobile to the left of the phone number to open the pop-up menu so you can add other phone numbers such as the person's home phone number.

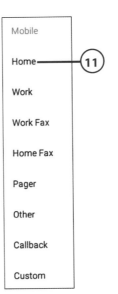

12. Tap the plus icon in the Phone field to add an additional field, or tap the minus icon to remove a field.

13. Add information in the Email section as you did in the Phone section.

14. Assign the contact to a group of contacts, such as your family members, by tapping Groups.

Don't Worry About Formatting

You don't need to type parentheses or dashes for the phone numbers you enter. The Galaxy Tab A formats the number for you.

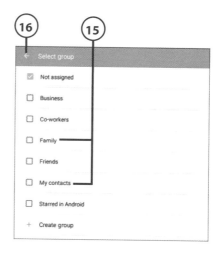

15. In the Select Group window, tap the check box to the left of the group name(s) to which you want to assign the contact. After you tap the check box, the check box turns green and a white check mark appears inside.

16. Return to the Contact screen by tapping the Back icon.

17. The group(s) you added appear in the Groups section.

18. Add another field to the contact by tapping Add Another Field. You can add the user's phonetic name, organization, instant messaging address, physical address, any notes about the user, the user's nickname, website, Internet phone number, events related to the contact, and the contact's relationship to you.

19. Tap the Event check box to add events related to the contact, such as the person's birthday, and then tap Add.

20. Tap the Birthday label to choose the type of event you want to add.

21. Tap Date to add the event date.

22. Add another field to the form by repeating step 18.

23. Tap Save to complete the new contact.

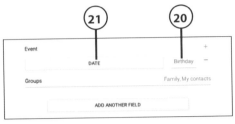

>>>Go Further
UPDATING A CONTACT AND DISPLAYING CONTACTS

You can update a contact by first tapping an existing contact in the Contacts list and then tapping Edit located at the right side of the orange menu bar that appears at the top of the screen. The contact window opens on the right side of the screen so you can edit or add information.

You can control how your contacts are listed by setting sorting and display preferences. After you launch the Contacts app, you can tap Move above the Contacts list, tap Settings, and then tap Sort By. The Sort By menu enables you to list by First Name (which is the default setting) or by Last Name.

Search for Contacts

Your list of contacts is sure to grow the longer you have your Galaxy Tab A. So how do you search your large list of contacts for a specific contact?

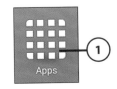

1. Tap Apps on the Home screen.

2. Tap Contacts.

3. Tap the Search field and use the keyboard to type the name of the contact you are looking for. As soon as you begin to type, the screen displays the contact that most closely reflects what you've typed into the field. Continue typing until you have narrowed the search.

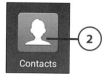

4. View the contact in its entirety by tapping the Back touch button to close the keyboard (not shown).

5. The contact that appears from your search remains visible in the Contacts screen.

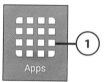

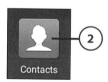

Link Contacts

When you synchronize the contacts on your Galaxy Tab A with multiple accounts, such as Facebook, Twitter, and Google, you can have varying numbers and address information for a single contact. You can see all the contacts' numbers and addresses in a single contact entry by linking contacts. Linking contacts can help you keep your contact information up to date.

1. Tap Apps on the Home screen.

2. Tap Contacts. Your profile information appears on the screen.

3. Swipe up in the contact list until you find the contact to which you want to join another contact. Tap the contact name in the list.

4. Tap the Link icon.

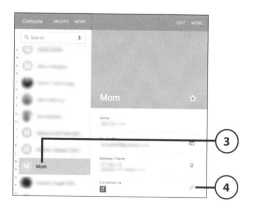

5. In the Linked Contact window, tap Link Another Contact.

6. In the Link Contact window, swipe up in the list until you see the name of the contact you want to link to the primary contact you selected in step 3.

7. Tap the check box to the left of the contact you want to link. The linked contact check box is green with a white check mark inside it.

8. Tap Link.

9. The contacts are now linked and the contact you linked appears underneath the primary contact at the top of the window.

10. Add another contact by tapping Link Another Contact and repeating steps 5 and 6.

11. Close the Linked Contact window and view the merged contact on the Contacts screen by tapping the Back icon.

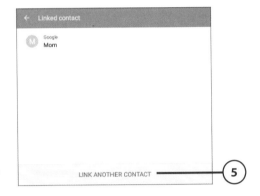

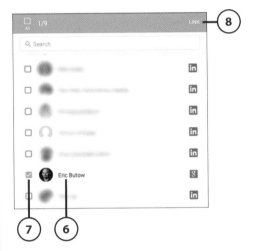

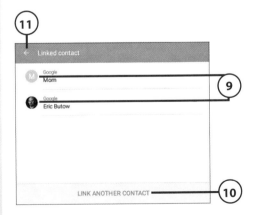

HOW DO I UNLINK CONTACTS?

Unlink contacts by tapping More in the upper-right corner of the Contacts screen. In the menu, tap Unlink Contacts. Within the Linked Contact window that appears, tap the red minus icon to the right of the contact name you want to unlink. The contact name you unlinked no longer appears in the Linked Contact window. Tap the Back icon in the upper-left corner of the Linked Contact window to close the window and view the unlinked contact.

Use Contacts

After you have entered a contact in your Galaxy Tab A, you can utilize a few functions and displays directly from the Contacts page. Start by opening a contact's record.

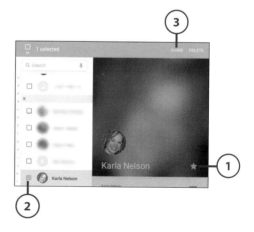

1. Tap the star icon to the right of the contact name to set that contact as a favorite.

2. Press and hold your finger on a contact's name in the contact list. After a second, the name is highlighted in orange and a green check box with an orange check mark appears to the left of the contact name.

3. Tap Share.

4. In the Share Namecard With/Via window, share the namecard via Wi-Fi Direct, Bluetooth, Samsung Quick Connect, Google Drive, OneDrive, Skype, email, or Gmail; you can also add the namecard to OneNote. Think of a namecard as an electronic business card.

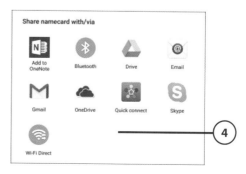

5. Close the Share Namecard With/ Via window by tapping the Back touch button (not shown).

6. Compose a new email to your contact by scrolling down the Contacts screen until you reach the Email section and then tapping the email icon to the right of the contact's email address.

Managing Your Busy Schedule

The Calendar app enables you to manage all your appointments and events from one convenient location. Calendar enables you to view a busy schedule in multiple views such as Day, Week, Month, Year, and Agenda. You can also instruct Calendar to send you a little reminder, in the form of an alert, before an event to help ensure that you never miss a meeting and are always on time.

Create Calendar Events

Your Galaxy Tab A was designed for you to be mobile while still enabling you to manage the important stuff, such as doctor appointments, business meetings, and anniversaries. The Calendar app enables you to add important event dates to calendars to help ensure that you do not overlook them.

1. On the Home screen, tap Calendar.

2. By default, the calendar opens to the Month view. The current date is in green text. Events appear under the date and each event entry has a color that you can assign to an event to categorize your events. For example, you can assign green for marketing meetings. Step 6 explains more about assigning event colors.

3. Tap the date for which you want to add an event. The date becomes highlighted with a green circle around it.

4. Tap the + button at the lower-right corner of the screen.

5. The Title field is selected by default. Type a title for the event in the field.

6. Assign an event color by tapping the palette icon and then tap on one of the 12 color circles within the Select Event Color window. The default color is light blue. After you select a color, the palette icon color reflects your selected event color.

7. If the event will take place all day, slide the All Day slider button from left (Off) to right (On).

8. Tap the date and time in the Start field to enter the start date and time of the event. You can also use the controls in the Set Date and Time window to designate an event for a future date and not just the date you specified in step 3. When you tap the date and time in the Start field, a calendar opens, enabling you to select a future date and time.

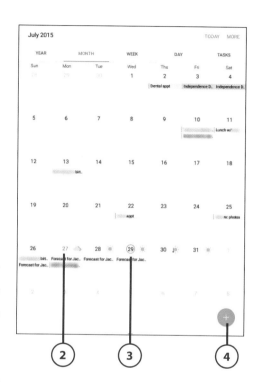

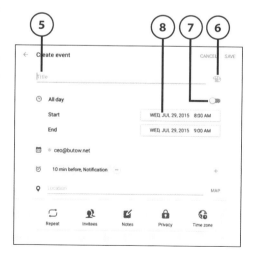

9. The Start button is highlighted in green to indicate that you're changing the event start date and time.

10. The current month appears in the calendar, and the date you set for the event in step 3 is highlighted in the calendar. Change the event date by swiping left and right within the calendar to view months and dates and then tap the date for the event.

11. Tap the controls to enter the start time for the event.

12. Tap Keypad to change the event time using the numeric keypad.

13. Tap Done.

14. Tap the date and time in the End field to bring up the controls and set the date and time for the event as you did when you set the date in the Start field.

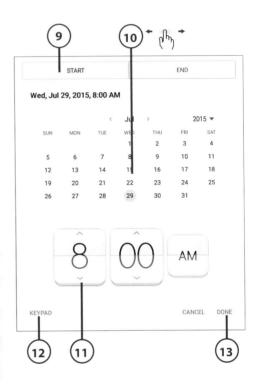

15. Tap your email address to place the event in another account calendar. For example, you can place your event in your Google calendar instead of your Outlook calendar.

16. Tap the Reminder button to choose an alarm time for the event. You can choose the time you want the reminder to appear as a notification in the Notification bar, or you can send the notification to your email account.

17. Tap the minus button to remove the alarm.

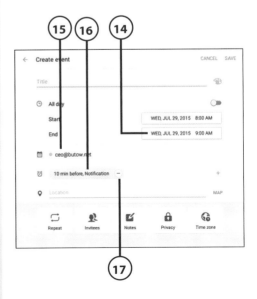

18. Tap the plus icon at the right of the Reminder field to add an alarm if the event doesn't have one, or add another notification that will appear at a different time and/or be delivered in a different manner.

19. Tap the Location field to add a location for the event. If you want to find the location in the Maps app, tap Map to the right of the field. You find out more about using the Maps app in Chapter 9, "Using Maps."

20. Tap the Repeat button if you need to set a repeating cycle for the event.

21. Tap the Invitees button to add names from your contacts so you can invite the contact(s) to your event.

22. Tap the Notes button to type a description for the event.

23. Tap the Privacy button so you can tell others who share your calendar if you're available or busy during the event and to set the event as private. By default, the event is public so anyone who sees your calendar can view the event.

24. Tap the Time Zone button to change the time zone for the event.

25. Tap Save to complete the event and save it to your calendar.

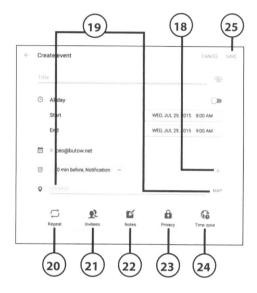

Set Start and End Dates and Times Within the Date and Time Window

There's a faster way to change start and end dates and times for an event without having to close the Date and Time window between setting start and end dates/times. If you need to change the start or end time, tap the appropriate button and make your changes.

How Do I View the Reminder in the Status Bar?

When you receive a reminder, you get an audio reminder and also see a reminder icon at the left side of the status bar. Tap and hold your finger on the top edge of the screen and swipe down to open the Quick Settings and Notifications screen. The reminder displays at the bottom of the Notifications area.

Use Calendar Views

The four views in which you can see the contents of your calendar are Year, Month, Week, and Day. This section examines each view.

Year View

The Year view shows the entire calendar year. Open the Year view by tapping the Year tab in the upper-left corner of the screen.

The current year appears in the upper-left corner of the screen. Swipe right and left within the calendar to view a calendar for the previous or following year, respectively. When you change the year, your selected year appears highlighted in the center. Tap Today in the menu bar to highlight the current date in the calendar.

Current year — 2015

Jump to this year's calendar

Year tab

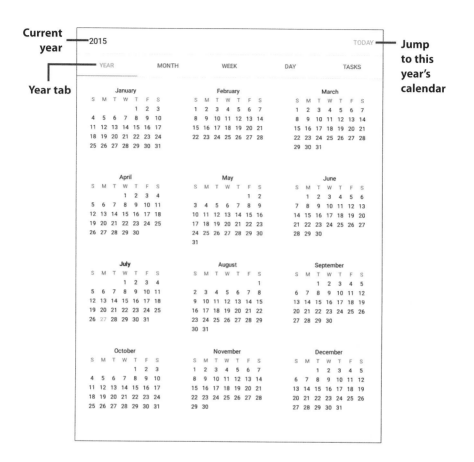

Month View

The Month view provides a broad view of events for a given month. Month view is composed of two sections: the monthly calendar and the day's event schedule. Open the Month view by tapping the Month tab.

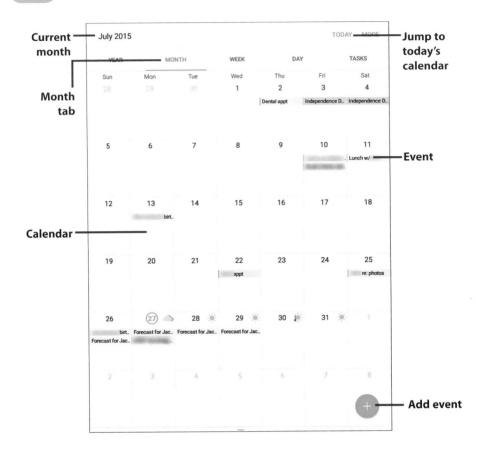

Current month — July 2015

Month tab

Calendar

Jump to today's calendar — TODAY, MORE

YEAR, MONTH, WEEK, DAY, TASKS

Sun	Mon	Tue	Wed	Thu	Fri	Sat
28	29	30	1	2 Dental appt	3 Independence D..	4 Independence D..
5	6	7	8	9	10 Lunch w/	11
12	13 birt..	14	15	16	17	18
19	20	21	22 appt	23	24	25 re: photos
26 birt.. Forecast for Jac..	(27) Forecast for Jac..	28 Forecast for Jac..	29 Forecast for Jac..	30	31	1
2	3	4	5	6	7	8

Event

Add event — +

Each section lists the events scheduled for that particular month. The current day block you are viewing is highlighted within the calendar section with a circle around the date. Any event designated as an All Day Event is highlighted in the day block of the Calendar view.

Tap Today in the menu bar to highlight the current date in the calendar. The current month appears above the calendar. Within the calendar, swipe right and left to view the previous or following month, respectively.

You can tap an event to view notes, edit the entry, delete the event, or share the event as a VCS-format or text file. You can send the file via Bluetooth, Wi-Fi Direct, or Samsung Quick Connect; to an S Note or Memo file; to the Scrapbook app; to a OneNote file; in the Hangouts or Skype messaging service; to the OneDrive or Google Drive online file storage service; to email or Gmail; or to Google+. You can also copy the file to the Clipboard to paste in another app.

Week View

The Week view is arranged into seven-day parts. Open the Week view by tapping the Week tab.

Within the calendar, swipe right and left to view the previous and following week, respectively. Swipe up and down within the calendar to view appointments later or earlier in the day, respectively. Tap Today in the menu bar to highlight the current date.

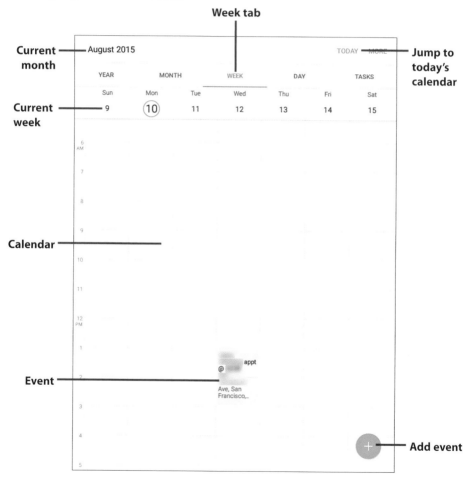

Each event for that week is found in its respective scheduled day block.

You can tap an event to view notes, edit the entry, delete the event, or share the event as a VCS-format or text file. You can send the file via Bluetooth, Wi-Fi Direct, or Samsung Quick Connect; to an S Note or Memo file; to the

Scrapbook app; to a OneNote file; in the Hangouts or Skype messaging service; to the OneDrive or Google Drive online file storage service; to email or
Gmail; or to Google+. You can also copy the file to the Clipboard to paste in
another app.

Day View

The Day view is composed of a list of events over the current and following
day. These events are blocked for each hour. Open the Day view by tapping
the Day tab.

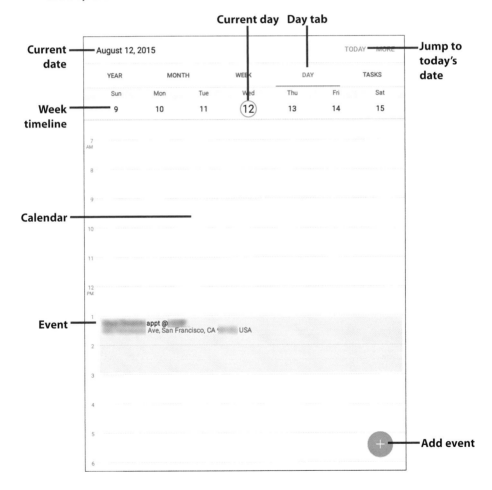

You can press your finger to the calendar and flick up or down to scroll
through the list of events. All events scheduled with a duration of All Day are

located at the very top of the list. The Week timeline located just under the menu enables you to tap specific days during the week.

Within the calendar, swipe right and left to jump to the previous or next day, respectively. Tap Today in the menu bar to return to the current day's schedule no matter where you are in the calendar.

You can tap an event to view notes, edit the entry, delete the event, or share the event as a VCS-format or text file. You can send the file via Bluetooth, Wi-Fi Direct, or Samsung Quick Connect; to an S Note or Memo file; to the Scrapbook app; to a OneNote file; in the Hangouts or Skype messaging service; to the OneDrive or Google Drive online file storage service; to email or Gmail; or to Google+. You can also copy the file to the Clipboard to paste in another app.

Add a Task to Your Calendar

A task is different from an event in that events have specific times attached to them; tasks don't necessarily have time limits but they tell you about important things you need to get done. You can add and view tasks in your calendar within the Tasks tab.

1. Tap the Tasks tab.

2. Tap the Enter New Task field and then type the task title.

3. Tap Today if the task needs to be completed sometime during the current day.

4. Tap Tomorrow if the task needs to be completed sometime during the following day.

5. View more options by tapping the double-arrow icon.

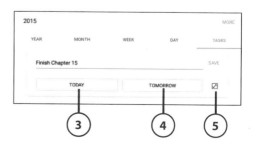

6. If there is a due date for the event, slide the slider button from left (Off) to right (On).

7. Tap the date button to set the due date for the task.

8. Tap the left and right arrow on either side of the month to view the previous and following month, respectively.

9. Change the year by tapping the current year and then selecting a new year in the drop-down list.

10. Tap the due date within the calendar.

11. Tap Done.

12. Tap My Task to place the task in an online account instead of on your Tab A. For example, you can place the task within Samsung Tasks in your Samsung account.

13. Tap the Reminder button to set an alarm to remind you about the task. The alarm date and time can be different from the task due date.

14. Tap the Notes button to type a description for the task.

15. Tap the Priority button to change the priority level to High, Medium, or Low. The default priority is Medium.

16. Tap Save to complete the task and save it to your calendar.

17. The task appears under the due date within the Tasks list.

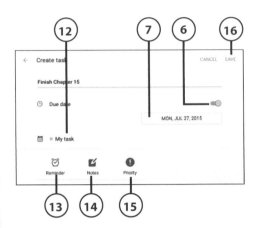

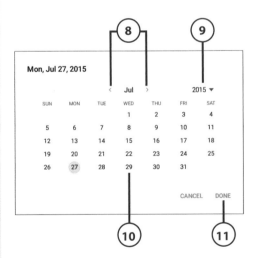

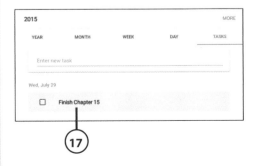

Use built-in apps on your
Galaxy Tab A to enhance
your productivity

In this chapter, you explore a variety of the Galaxy Tab A's preinstalled apps, which you can use to stay productive and get the latest information on the go. This chapter covers the following topics:

→ Staying up to date with Google Now
→ Creating documents with Microsoft Office

Using Apps for Learning, Creating, and Sharing

The Galaxy Tab A gives you plenty of ways to keep abreast of what's going on in your world and the wider world. You can get updates sent to you by the Google Now service and connect with other users through instant messaging and social networking apps. What's more, you can view and create document, spreadsheet, and presentation files with Microsoft Office.

Staying Up to Date with Google Now

Google Now is a feature that monitors your activity on your Galaxy Tab A and shows you features in various tiles, called *cards*, that Google Now thinks you'll be interested in based on your past activity. For example, you might see cards with your local weather, upcoming appointments, and current traffic conditions where you live.

Start Google Now for the First Time

You start Google Now by pressing and holding on the Home button for 2 seconds or by tapping the Google Search box in the lower-left corner of any Home screen.

The Google Search box

After you release your finger, the Google Now setup screen appears so you can set up and get more information about the app.

1. Tap Get Started.

2. Tap "Yes, I'm In" to continue the setup process as described in the rest of this task. The opening Google Now screen displays.

3. Search Google by tapping the Search field, typing your search term(s), and then tapping the Search button in the keyboard.

4. View the current weather information for your city or area by tapping the weather card.

5. Tap the Menu icon (it looks like a group of three horizontal dots) above and to the right of each card to change card settings.

6. Delete a card by tapping and holding on the card and then swiping to the left or right.

7. Swipe up on the screen to see more options.

8. If there are more stories or more information within a card, tap Show More or More Stories.

9. Press the Home button to return to the Home screen (not shown).

Use Google Now

After you finish setting up Google Now, you can access it by tapping the Google Search box in any Home screen. The Google Now screen looks a little different than when you set up the app for the first time.

1. Tap the Google Search box.

2. Type any search term(s) in the Search field. As you type, the first three search results display below the Search field. Three more Chrome search results appear below the first three results.

3. Tap an item in the result list to open a search result. If you search for a name and/or location, any search results in your Contacts database appear in the list of contacts. View more contact information by tapping the name of the contact. You can also search for more contacts by tapping Search Tablet at the bottom of the Contacts list.

4. View more search results by tapping the Search button in the keyboard.

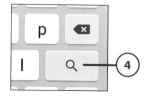

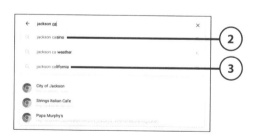

5. The Search results page appears on the screen. Swipe up and down the screen to view the entire list of results on the page.

6. Tap the Back touch button to return to the Home screen (not shown).

7. Tap the Google Search box. Even if you don't search for anything, Google Now remembers your last three searches on the Google search engine and displays them underneath the Search field.

8. Hide the keyboard by tapping the Back touch button (not shown).

9. Swipe up and down the page to view all the other cards on the screen.

10. Tap the Menu icon within each card's section to change the Google Now settings. The type of card for which you want to change settings determines the available options in the Setting screen. This example uses the Weather card.

11. Turn off weather updates in the Weather card by tapping the No button.

12. Keep weather updates on by tapping the Yes button or the right-arrow icon.

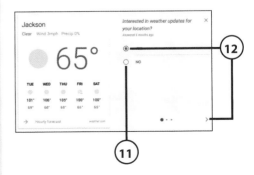

13. Change the temperature unit to Celsius by tapping the Celsius button.

14. To keep the default set to Fahrenheit, tap the Fahrenheit button or the right-arrow icon.

15. By default, the Weather card is visible within the Google Now screen. You can hide the Weather card and tell Google Now you're not interested in weather updates for your location by tapping the No button. After you tap No, the Weather card disappears from the Google Now screen. If you leave the Yes button selected, continue to step 16.

16. Return to the Google Now screen by tapping the Back touch button (not shown).

Can I Add a Widget for Google Now?

A Google Now widget is available on the Widgets screen covered in Chapter 4, "Adding Widgets to Your Home Screen." After you add the widget to your desired Home screen, the widget appears and displays the current weather conditions for your location. Open the Google Now app by tapping the widget.

The Google Now widget on a Home screen

Creating Documents with Microsoft Office

The Galaxy Tab A has several Microsoft Office apps preinstalled on the device, including Microsoft Word, Excel, and PowerPoint. You can use these apps to view and edit Word documents, Excel spreadsheets, and PowerPoint slide-shows right on your Tab A.

This example shows you how to open the Microsoft Word app, open and close a document, access a document from a cloud storage service such as Microsoft OneDrive, and create a new document.

Sign In to Your Microsoft Account

Before you can use Word, you need to open the Word app from the second page of your Home screen. After you open the Word app, you need to sign in using your Microsoft account.

1. On the Home screen, swipe from right to left to open the second Home screen and then tap Word.

2. Swipe from right to left until you reach the third and final introductory screen.

3. Tap Sign In.

What If I Don't Have a Microsoft Account?

This book doesn't discuss creating a new Microsoft account. You can create a new account by tapping Create an Account in the final introductory screen and then following the steps in the Create Account window.

4. Type the email address or phone number associated with your account.

5. Tap Next.

6. Type the account password in the Password field.

7. Tap Sign In.

8. After the Word app downloads any documents you have stored in your OneDrive account, tap Start Using Word.

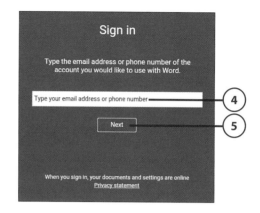

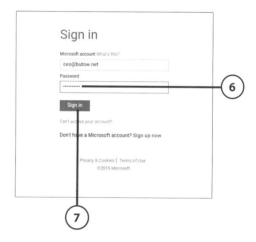

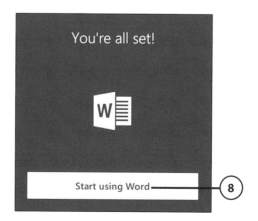

Open and Close a Document

After you start Word, you can begin to browse through a list of documents and open one by tapping the filename in the list. When you finish viewing the document, you can close it and return to the Word home screen to browse for another document.

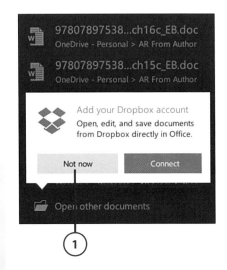

1. In the Word document, you can add your Dropbox account to your list of documents by tapping Connect. For now, tap Not Now.

2. Swipe up and down in the Recent document list to view all the documents available in your OneDrive account. The list shows documents you've opened in OneDrive or the Word app today in the Today section at the top of the list, followed by older documents within the Older section underneath the Today section.

3. Open a document stored on another cloud storage service, on the Galaxy Tab A, or in another location (such as a SharePoint account) by tapping Open Other Documents. You find out how to open other documents later in this chapter.

4. For this example, I'm opening a copy of the novel *Land of Milk and Money* by Anthony Barcellos by tapping the filename in the list.

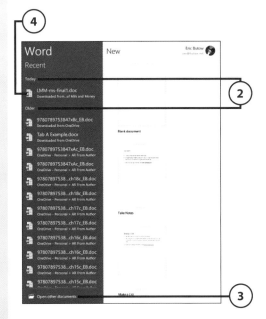

5. After a few minutes, the document screen appears. If you see a yellow Read-Only window above the document asking you to update the file to the newest format, upgrade the file by tapping the Upgrade a Copy button. For now, tap the Dismiss button to view the file in read-only mode.

6. Scroll up and down the document in the screen to read it.

7. Tap on a location within your document to place the cursor at that location. A blue handle appears under the cursor so you can see where the cursor is.

8. Tap the Search icon to find text in the document that matches your search term(s) within the Home toolbar. You can also format your document within the toolbar.

9. Tap the File tab to open a new or existing document, save the document, share the document with others, print the document, change app settings, and close the document.

10. Tap the Insert tab to add features to your document, such as a table or an image, using the tools on the Insert toolbar.

11. Tap the Layout tab to change the document margins, page orientation, page size, column layout, and page breaks using the tools on the Layout toolbar.

12. Tap the Review tab to check spelling, use the thesaurus, view the word count, add and delete comments, and track changes using the tools on the Review toolbar.

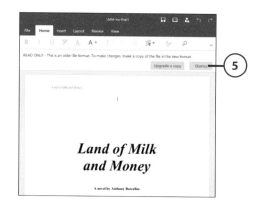

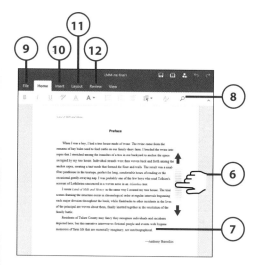

13. Tap the View tab to open the View toolbar and view the document in Read or Edit view, change the view of the file by zooming in and out, view the entire page on the screen, or zoom in so the width of the page appears on the screen.

14. Tap the Save icon to save the file with the same or a different filename on the same OneDrive folder or in a different location, such as in the Documents folder on your Tab A.

15. Tap the Read View icon to hide the tabs, toolbars, and icons and display only the filename in the title bar at the top of the screen. You can return to Edit view by tapping the title bar and then tapping the Edit View icon that's in the same location as the Read View icon in this example.

16. Tap the Share icon to share a link to a file or share the file itself. If you share a link, you must specify whether the recipient can only view the file or has the authority to edit the file.

You can send the link to a One-Drive or Google Drive folder, save the link to a OneNote file, share the link in a Skype chat, include the link in an email message within the Email or Gmail app, or send the file directly to another device using Samsung Quick Connect.

If you email the document as an attachment, you can share the file using all the apps and services as you can when sharing a link, but when you share an attachment, you can also send the file directly to another device using Bluetooth or Wi-Fi Direct.

17. Close the document and return to the Word home page by tapping the Back touch button (not shown).

Why Are Many of the Toolbar Options Disabled?

If you're viewing the document in read-only mode as illustrated in this example, then you don't need to use many of the editing options in the toolbars. Therefore, those options are disabled. You can still perform certain tasks such as searching for a word within the Home toolbar and obtaining the word count within the document in the Review toolbar.

Access Files from a Cloud Service

If you have files on an online file storage service, such as Dropbox, Word makes it easy for you to access and open files from that service.

1. Tap Open Other Documents in the Word home screen.

2. In the Open screen, tap Add a Place to add an online file-sharing service. This example uses Dropbox.

3. Tap Dropbox in the Add a Place window.

4. In the Open With window, tap Internet.

5. Tap Just Once.

6. Type your email address and password associated with your Dropbox account.

7. Tap Log In. If you see a pop-up window asking you if you want to save your password with the associated website, tap Not Now.

8. Tap Allow to give all Office apps on your Tab A access to your Dropbox account.

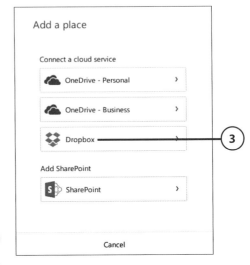

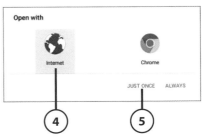

9. The Dropbox folder appears within the list of storage locations.

10. Folders within your Dropbox folder appear at the right side of the Open screen so you can open the file you want within the appropriate folder or subfolder.

11. Navigate to the folder that contains your file and then open the file by tapping the filename.

12. The first page in the document appears in the Word screen in read-only mode so you can read through it by swiping up and down on the screen.

13. Tap Dismiss to close the Read Only window above the document.

14. Tap the Read View icon to maximize the amount of screen space for your document. After you tap the icon, Word hides the tabs, toolbars, and icons and only displays the filename in the title bar at the top of the screen.

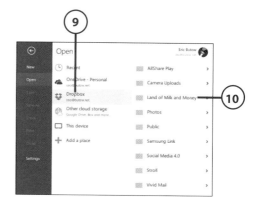

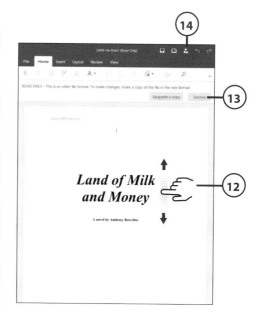

Create a New Document

Word makes it easy for you to create a new document so you can edit, save, and print the document from your Tab A.

1. Open the Word app as described earlier in this chapter.

2. View all available document templates by swiping up and down in the Document Templates list on the right side of the screen.

3. Tap the Blank Document tile.

4. The new document appears on the screen with the keyboard at the bottom of the screen. As you type, your text appears in the default document font.

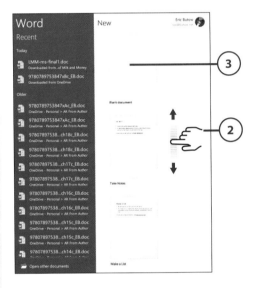

What Appears on the Screen When I Choose Another Template?

When you open a template that isn't blank, the new document opens with the template layout and dummy text. You can replace this dummy text, such as the name of the fax recipient, with the actual recipient's name.

5. The default document title name shows Document1, which is the default name of the document.

6. Tap Undo to reverse the previous action, such as deleting a word.

7. Tap Redo to reapply the previous action you previously undid. For example, if you tapped the Undo icon after deleting a word, tap the Redo icon to delete the affected word again.

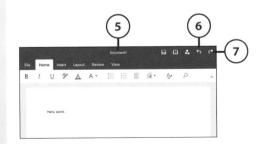

8. Select a word by tapping and holding on the word for a second. The word is highlighted and has two blue handles on either side of the word.

9. Select or deselect characters by tapping and holding on one of the blue handles and then drag your finger until you have selected the text you want.

10. In the Home toolbar, you can change the font size, style, and color; change the appearance and alignment of the selected paragraph; and apply a text style to a selected area of text. For example, you can tap the Styles icon in the toolbar and then apply the Intense Emphasis style by tapping Intense Emphasis in the drop-down list.

11. Open the Open screen by tapping the File tab.

12. Tap Save to save the document.

13. Tap the storage service to which you want to save the document. The default is OneDrive. If you want to store the saved document on the Tab A, tap This Device.

14. Tap the folder into which you want to save the file.

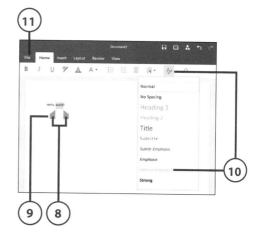

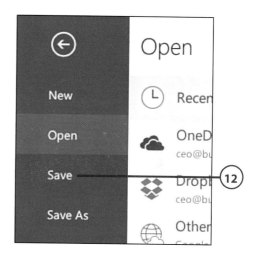

15. A list of documents within the folder appears in the list.

16. If you want to view the list of storage services and devices, swipe from left to right on the screen. View the list of documents in the folder by tapping the folder name as you did in step 14.

17. Tap the Close icon and then type the filename in the box.

18. Tap Save. Word saves the file and the document screen reappears with your new document name in the title bar at the top of the screen.

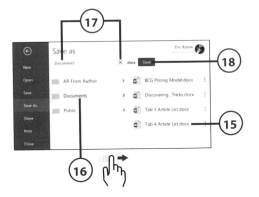

Access Google apps
from the main
Home screen

Search the Google Play Store for
thousands of useful, educational,
and entertaining apps

Shop for Galaxy Tab A apps
in the Galaxy Apps app

Run multiple apps in
Split Screen view

In this chapter, you discover how to expand the capabilities of the Galaxy Tab A by finding and installing new apps from both Samsung and Google. You also learn how to access apps from the Home screen and open multiple apps on the screen. What's more, in this chapter you learn how to browse and make purchases in the Google Play Store and organize application icons on your Galaxy Tab. This chapter covers the following topics:

→ Accessing Google apps from the Home screen

→ Opening multiple apps in Split Screen view

→ Shopping in the Galaxy Apps Store

→ Getting apps in the Google Play Store

→ Managing apps through your Home screens

→ Adding useful apps

Finding and Managing Apps

The Galaxy Tab A is not just about superior hardware craftsmanship. Your Tab's true strength lies in the incredible software that is developed for it. The Galaxy Tab A comes with some truly amazing, preinstalled apps right out of the box, but you can expand its capabilities even further by downloading new apps from the Google Play Store. You can choose from thousands of innovative apps, ranging from games to productivity apps. The number of apps optimized for use on your Tab is growing rapidly.

Android 5.0, also known by its nickname Lollipop, allows you to access all your Google apps from the first page on the Home screen. Lollipop also includes the capability to open multiple apps in one screen so you can switch between open apps easily.

Accessing Google Apps from the Home Screen

The Google icon appears on the main Home screen so you can access any Google app installed on your Tab A within a small pop-up window that appears on the screen. You can also remove any Google app icons within the pop-up window as you would with any other app on a Home screen.

1. Tap the Google app on the main Home screen.

2. Open a Google app by tapping on the app within the pop-up window.

3. Move a Google app icon to a different location within the window by tapping and holding on the icon and then dragging the icon to a new location within the window. The other icons in the window rearrange to accommodate your selected icon's new position.

4. Remove a Google app from the pop-up window by tapping and holding on the icon and then dragging the icon to the Delete icon in the menu bar at the top of the screen.

5. Tap the palette icon to change the window background color.

6. Select a new color by tapping the appropriate tile. The window background color changes and the selected background color tile has a check mark within the tile.

7. Close the pop-up window by tapping the Back touch button (not shown).

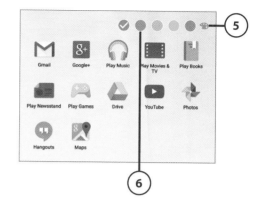

Opening Multiple Apps in Split Screen View

You can view two open apps at one time on the Tab A screen by setting up Split Screen view. If you have no apps open, the Split Screen View screen allows you to open two apps that support Split Screen view. After you open two apps on your screen, you can resize one of the two windows so you can focus on the larger window.

Add Two Apps to the Split Screen View

If you aren't certain about which pre-installed apps can be viewed in Split Screen view, the Tab A shows you the apps you can launch in Split Screen view. By default, one app appears within the top half of the screen and the other app appears within the bottom half of the screen.

1. On the Home screen, tap and hold on the Recent touch button for a second (not shown).

2. The Split Screen View screen is divided in half by a horizontal line. The bottom half of the screen shows the first page of 12 apps you can open in Split Screen view.

3. Swipe from left to right in the bottom half of the screen to view recent apps that you opened that can be opened in Split Screen view.

4. If there are no recently used apps that support Split Screen view, that message appears at the bottom of the screen. The Recent Apps Page icon is highlighted.

5. Swipe from right to left twice in the bottom half of the screen to view the second page of apps denoted by the right page icon at the bottom of the screen.

6. You can select from another 10 apps that support Split Screen view within the second apps page.

7. Swipe from left to right to return to the first apps page.

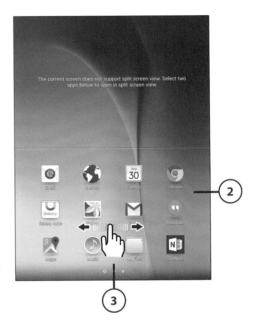

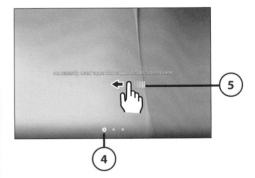

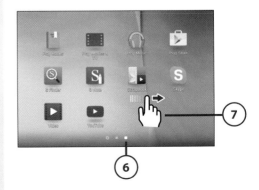

8. This example displays the Gmail and Internet apps in Split Screen view. Tap Gmail in the bottom half of the screen.

9. The Gmail app appears within the top half of the screen.

10. Tap Internet in the bottom half of the screen.

11. The Internet app appears within the bottom half of the screen. It's surrounded by a blue line and has a gray control button at the top center of the window.

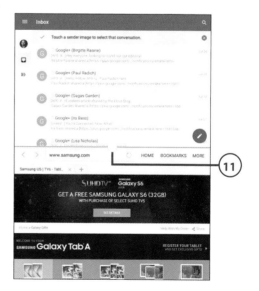

12. Resize the Internet app window by tapping and holding on the gray control button. The button turns blue and you can swipe up or down in the screen to increase or decrease the window size, respectively. When you've moved the blue control button to your desired window height, release your finger. The Tab A resizes the app to the desired size.

13. Open viewing option buttons by tapping the gray control button you saw in step 11. A series of five buttons appears in a bar.

14. Tap to move the Gmail app to the bottom of the screen and the Internet app to the top. After the Internet app window moves to the top of the screen, the gray control button appears at the bottom center of the window.

15. Tap to drag and drop a paragraph of text or a screenshot image from the Gmail app window into the Internet app window. Tap and hold on the image or text paragraph in the Gmail app window and then drag it into the Internet app window. After you drag the text or image, the Internet app window is highlighted; tap the Gmail app window to continue with step 16.

16. Tap to freeze operation of the app in the window and minimize the window on the screen. Open the app in a small window that appears in front of the other window on the screen by tapping the app icon in the upper-left corner of the screen.

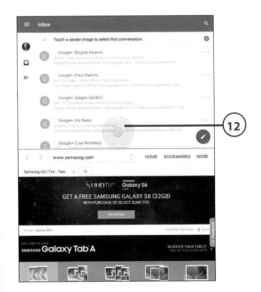

17. Tap to view the Internet app on the entire screen and close Split Screen view. You can only view the Gmail window again by tapping the Recent touch button and then tapping the Gmail screen tile in the Recent Apps window; the Gmail app also appears on the entire screen.

18. Tap to close the Internet window.

19. Tap the Gmail app window to select it; the Gmail app window is highlighted with a blue border, and the white control button appears at the bottom center of the window. Tap the button to perform the tasks discussed in steps 14 through 18.

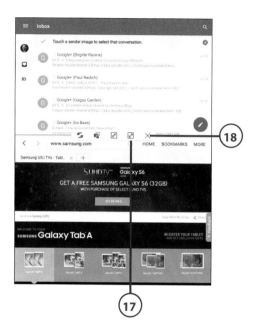

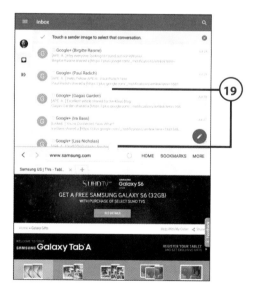

Put Two Open Apps in Split Screen View

If you have apps open but not in Split Screen view, you can open the Recent Apps screen and then display two of those apps in Split Screen view.

1. Tap the Recent touch button to open the Recent Apps screen (not shown). In this example, three apps are open.

2. Tap the app that you want to appear in the top half of the screen by tapping the Split Screen icon within the app tile title bar.

3. The remaining two open apps appear in the bottom half of the screen. Tap the app you want to appear within the bottom of the screen by tapping the app tile.

4. The app appears in the bottom half of the screen.

5. You can change the apps that appear in Split Screen view by tapping the Recent touch button and then selecting two apps within the Recent Apps screen as you did in steps 2 and 3.

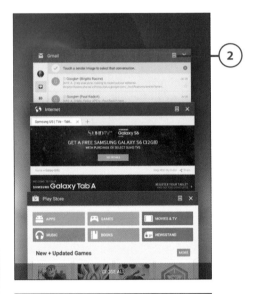

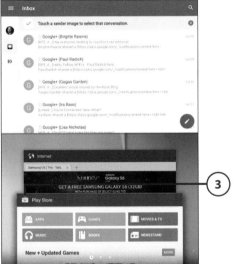

Shopping in the Galaxy Apps Store

A great way to become acquainted with Galaxy Apps is just to start browsing. Many reviews of apps and games are available, so you can make an intelligent choice before downloading.

1. Tap the Apps icon on the Home screen.

2. Tap Galaxy Apps.

3. A page of featured apps displays. Scroll up and down the page to review groups of apps as well as individual apps. You can view more apps in a group by tapping See More.

4. Tap the Category tab in the menu bar and then tap a category to browse the list of results for that category.

5. If you know the name of the app, book, magazine, or movie you want, tap Search to specify a search term.

6. Type a search term into the Search field. Possible matches for your search appear in the list below the field.

7. Tap the app in the list if the product you want is listed as an option.

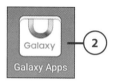

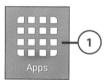

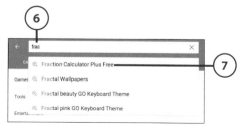

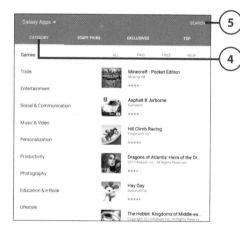

8. Swipe up and down the list of apps in the Results page if necessary and then tap the title of the app you want more information about.

9. Read more about the product. You can purchase—or download, if the app is free—the app on the description page. In this example, install Fraction Calculator Plus Free by tapping Install.

More About Product Descriptions

The description page for an app is chock-full of useful information so you can make an educated decision about whether you want to purchase the app. Sample screenshots of the app are featured on this page along with customer reviews and information about the developer.

Getting Apps in the Google Play Store

The Google Play Store makes it easy for you to browse apps and games that you can download to your Galaxy Tab A. If this is your first time shopping in the Google Play Store, you will find the interface quite intuitive. A great way to become acquainted with the Google Play Store is just to start browsing.

Many reviews of apps and games are available, so you can make an intelligent choice before downloading. A Google, Bing, or Yahoo! search for "Best Android apps for Galaxy Tab A" can help you identify the most popular apps. Tab A users from around the world are writing articles about their experiences with apps that you might find useful. After you download and try out an app, consider giving your feedback so that new Tab A users can learn from you.

Search for Android Applications

To access the Google Play Store for the first time, you must use your Google account to sign in to the Google Play Store. After you launch the Google Play Store app, there are several ways for you to search apps from the Google Play Store home page. The home page search options change position on the page, depending on which orientation you hold your Tab A: vertical or horizontal.

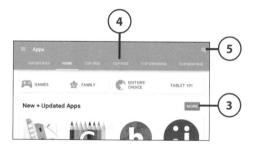

1. Tap Play Store on the Home screen.

2. Tap Apps on the Google Play Store home page. A page of featured apps displays.

3. Scroll up and down the page to review groups of apps as well as individual apps. You can view more apps in a group by tapping More.

4. Tap a category to browse the list of results for that category.

5. If you know the name of the app, book, magazine, or movie you want, tap the Search icon to specify a search term.

6. Type a search term into the Search Google Play field. Possible matches for your search appear in the list below the search field.

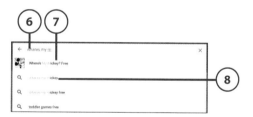

7. Tap the app link in the list if that link is available.

8. For this example, tap the app name in the list to get more search results.

9. Swipe up and down the list of apps in the Results page and then tap the title of the app you want more information about.

10. Read more about the product. You can purchase—or download, if the app is free—the app on the description page. In this example, install "Where's My Mickey? Free" by tapping Install.

Find Great Apps

You can download thousands of apps to your Galaxy Tab A, so use your storage space wisely by finding only the great ones. Finding the best apps might be the biggest challenge of all as you wade through your many options. This task gives you some tips on how to locate the highest-performing apps.

1. Tap Apps in the Google Play Store app.

2. Take a look at the featured apps on the Play Store home page. Keep in mind that large companies, usually with well-established names, tend to dominate the featured list. Lesser-known developers are also producing outstanding apps, so look deeper.

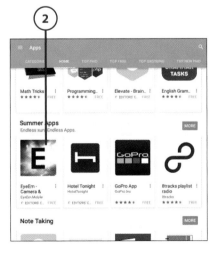

3. Some apps have trial versions you can test-drive before purchasing. Look for Lite or Free versions of applications to test before you buy. This example shows results after you search for the word **lite**.

4. Tap an app in the list that you want to learn more about.

5. Scroll down to check out customer reviews for products, but don't trust everything you read. Some reviews might not be in-depth or unbiased, and therefore they are less helpful. View all reviews on the screen by tapping All Reviews.

6. Swipe up on the screen until you reach the bottom of the page and then view the full version of the app that you can purchase if you like what you see in the Lite version. Tap the tile to learn more and purchase the app.

7. Below the More By section, take a look at the Similar Apps list. You see apps that are similar along with their ratings next to them. You might find a higher-rated app that you want to look into.

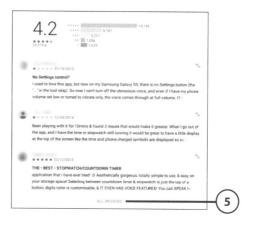

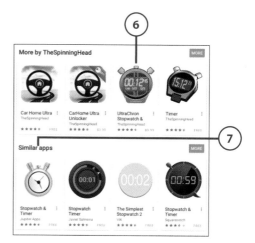

USING OTHER RESOURCES TO FIND APPS

You can use other solid resources outside the Google Play Store for finding great apps.

Perform a Google search. For example, if you are looking for an app suited for taking dictation, type **Galaxy Tab A App Dictation.**

Search for sites that feature and post reviews for apps. Be aware that some of these sites are sponsored by the developers and might not convey completely objective views.

Find a Galaxy Tab forum. There are many of these popping up every day. In a forum, you can post questions to other Galaxy Tab A owners regarding apps. Be aware that experienced Tab users might not moderate all of these forums, and the advice you receive can be questionable.

Purchase Android Applications

Software developers from around the world have developed thousands of apps for you to take advantage of with your Galaxy Tab A. You can choose from many free apps in the Google Play Store, and you can also purchase a variety of more sophisticated apps for a fee. The process for downloading free apps and paid apps is similar, but you need to designate a payment method to make purchases.

1. Tap Play Store on the Home screen.

2. Locate and then tap the app that you want to download. The product description page opens.

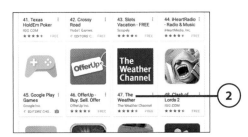

3. Tap the price of the app to see the permissions for this app. If this app is free, as in this example with The Weather Channel app, tap the Install button. A page that lists the permissions the app is requesting opens.

4. Tap Accept to begin installing the app.

Accepting Permissions

If the application you have selected requires control of your Tab or access to data, the Google Play Store displays the information in this area. The list of permissions changes from app to app. When you accept permissions, you are essentially allowing the application you are purchasing to access your Galaxy Tab A, including Internet access.

5. Tap Open to launch the application.

>>>Go Further

UPDATING APPS

The Google Play Store periodically searches for updates for apps that have been downloaded to your Galaxy Tab A. If an update has been found, a notification appears in the status bar. You can open the Quick Settings and Notifications screen and then tap the item in the Notifications list to be taken to the Google Play Store so you can begin the update. You can learn more about opening the Quick Settings and Notifications screen in Chapter 2, "Setting Up the Galaxy Tab A."

>>>Go Further

DISABLING UPDATE NOTIFICATIONS

If you prefer to manually check for updates, you can configure the Google Play Store to stop notifying you about updates. Just launch the Google Play Store app and then tap the Menu icon in the left side of the menu bar at the top of the screen. Select Settings in the menu, and then deselect the App Updates Available option. You can view a list of installed apps in the My Apps screen by tapping the Menu icon in the left side of the menu bar at the top of the screen and then tapping My Apps in the menu. The list of installed apps also lets you know which apps have an update available.

Get Help with Apps

Many new apps are being added to the Google Play Store daily from well-known companies, small companies, and individual developers. Bugs and other problems are likely to arise in such a fast-moving market. There are ways for you to contact developers so that you can ask questions.

1. Tap Play Store on the Home screen.

2. Tap the Menu icon.

3. Tap My Apps.

4. Tap the app for which you need help.

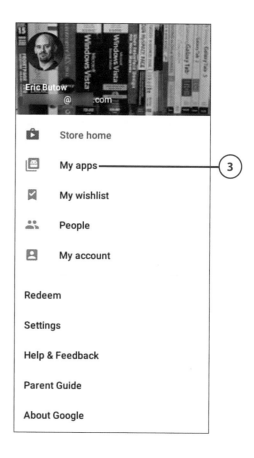

5. Tap Read More to view the entire description.

6. Scroll down and then tap Visit Webpage in the Developer section to visit the developer's site and search for information.

7. Tap Send Email to compose an email message asking your question(s).

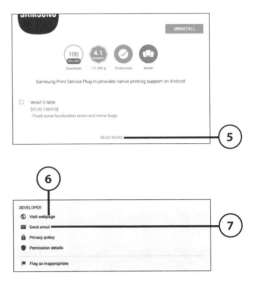

Managing Apps Through Your Home Screens

You begin many of your activities on the Home screen of the Galaxy Tab A. As you purchase new apps, the number of icons in your Apps screen multiplies, which might prompt you to rearrange them according to the ones you use the most. You can manage your apps through your Home screens by creating new Home screens, deleting existing Home screens, and grouping and arranging apps as you see fit on the respective pages.

By default, when you download an application from Google Play Store, a shortcut is placed in the Apps screen that is accessible from any Home screen. You can easily move shortcuts from the Apps screen to a Home screen and then rearrange them.

1. Tap the Apps icon on the Home screen.

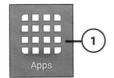

2. Tap and hold the app icon that you want to add to the Home screen.

3. An overlay of the main Home screen appears on the page and icons of all Home screens display below the main Home screen overlay. The main Home screen icon is shaped like a house.

4. Move the shortcut to the desired Home screen overlay. Your selected Home screen appears as an overlay on the screen.

5. Move the shortcut to your desired location on the Home screen.

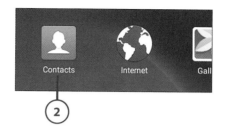

6. Release your finger. The shortcut is placed on the Home screen.

7. Repeat steps 2 through 6 to move more app shortcuts from the Apps screen to the Home screen.

8. By default, your Galaxy Tab A has two Home screens with Home screen 1 the default Home screen you see. Home screen 2 is filled with the Samsung Galaxy Apps and Google Play widgets, so you can move the new shortcut to a new Home screen.

9. Drag the icon with your finger to the right until you see the icon in the new Home screen overlay.

10. Remove your finger from the shortcut when you reach the spot where you would like to leave the shortcut.

Removing Shortcuts and Widgets

When you remove a shortcut or widget icon, this does not delete or uninstall the app from your Galaxy Tab A; it simply removes it from that panel. If you want to create a shortcut for that application again, it is still located in the Apps screen.

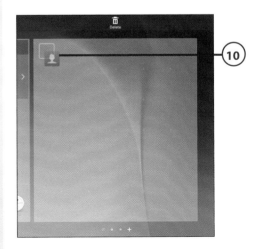

11. The icon appears in the upper-left corner of the Home screen.

12. When you hold your finger on a shortcut and after it pulsates once, the Delete icon (a trashcan) appears in the top of the screen. Drag a shortcut to the Delete icon to remove it from a Home screen.

>>>Go Further

CUSTOMIZING HOME SCREENS

Each Galaxy Tab A can be customized as unique as its individual owner. You can arrange your icons on any Home screen for shortcuts or widgets that you frequently use. For example, you can arrange all your games on one Home screen and all your productivity apps on another.

>>>Go Further

UNINSTALLING APPS FROM YOUR TAB A

After you purchase an app from the Google Play Store, you own it forever. You can uninstall a paid app from your Galaxy Tab A and then choose to reinstall it later (at no additional charge). To uninstall an app, swipe from right to left on the main Home screen and then tap Settings on the second Home screen. Tap Applications in the Settings list and tap Application Manager on the right side of the screen to view a list of your applications. Tap the app that you want to uninstall to open the App Info screen and then tap Uninstall. You can also uninstall apps by using the Uninstall option for the application on the Google Play Store.

Adding Useful Apps

The true power of the tablet revolution lies not only in the simplification of computing, but also in personalization. Apps enable you to optimize your Galaxy Tab for your unique lifestyle. Your Galaxy Tab A can be a virtual dictionary or thesaurus. Add an RSS reader and transform your Tab into a news-gathering device so that you are always up to date on current news and events. Many practical apps on the market enhance the capabilities of your Galaxy Tab A, freeing you from having to purchase and carry a second device such as a digital audio recorder or scanner. There are too many options to list them all here, but let's explore a few practical apps that you might want to consider.

Use the Merriam-Webster Dictionary App

Adding a simple dictionary app to your Galaxy Tab A is a very handy and practical solution for having to lug around an actual paper reference book.

The Merriam-Webster Dictionary app is free on the Google Play Store and delivers content that is trusted. The following steps presume you have already downloaded the Merriam-Webster Dictionary app from the Google Play Store:

1. Tap the Merriam-Webster app on the Home screen.

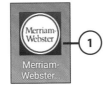

Use Any Dictionary App

Many other free options are available for dictionary and thesaurus reference apps. If you prefer another, don't hesitate to use it. This is just a recommendation for the usefulness of such a reference to exist on your Galaxy Tab A. The Dictionary.com app is also a great application and gets the job done.

2. Tap in the Search field and enter a word to look up. Search suggestions appear in the list beneath the field.

3. Tap the correct word in the list. The definition(s) for the entry appear.

4. You can tap the Speaker icon to hear the pronunciation of the word.

5. Tap the star to add this word to your Favorites.

6. Tap to view all words you have marked as Favorites.

7. Tap to view a list of recently searched words.

8. Tap to open the app menu.

9. You can learn a new word every day. Tap Word of the Day to view the word of the day.

10. Tap Recommended Apps to get a list of apps recommended to you by Merriam-Webster, such as the Britannica Encyclopedia app.

11. Tap Feedback to provide feedback to the developers of this app.

12. Tap Rate This App to rate this app in the Play Store.

13. Tap Share This App to share information about this app in an email message, on social networks, on cloud storage services, in other apps such as Memo, or to other devices.

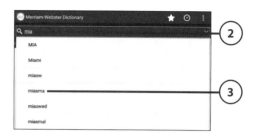

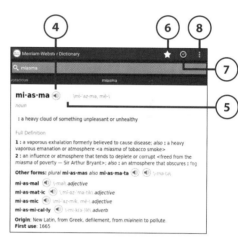

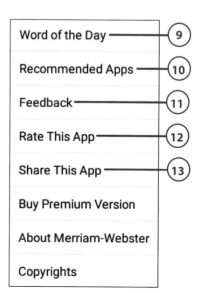

14. Tap Buy Premium Version to learn about and purchase the premium version of the app in the Play Store.

15. Tap About Merriam-Webster to get information about Merriam-Webster.

16. Tap Copyrights to get copyright information for the app.

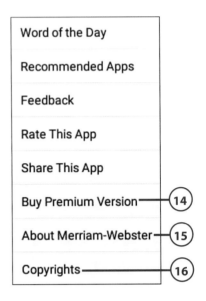

Use Note Everything

A digital voice recorder can be a priceless tool if you ever need to record some notes for yourself. Or have you ever wished you had the capability to scan barcodes on a product so that you could store the information?

Note Everything is a free app that can do all of this and more, including taking handwritten notes and tucking information away neatly in folders. This section presumes you have already downloaded the Note Everything app from the Google Play Store.

1. Tap Note Everything on the Home screen.

Receiving Help

When you first use certain functions, a help screen appears and provides you with tips.

2. Tap Close in the What's New screen.

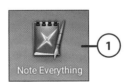

3. Add a new note by tapping the Add icon in the menu bar.

③

4. Tap Textnote to make a note using the keyboard. This is similar to how the preinstalled Memo widget works on your Tab, but you might find it more beneficial to have all your notes in one location.

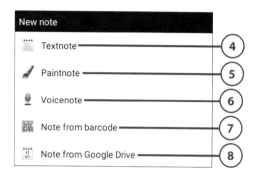

5. Tap Paintnote to make a note using your finger as a pen. You can tap the Menu button on your Galaxy Tab A and change the color of ink, erase marks, change stroke width, clear colors, work full screen, and more. This is a great option for jotting down a quick visual note.

6. Tap Voicenote to record voice memos. Each recording is stored as an individual file that you can play back on your Galaxy Tab.

7. Tap Note from Barcode to use your Tab A camera to read barcodes and note the barcode for later reference. This option requires you to install another free app named Barcode Scanner for it to work. The installation process is streamlined within the Note Everything app and takes only a few moments.

8. Tap Note from Google Drive to import and export text notes from Google Drive. This option requires you to install another free app named Note Everything GDocs. These two apps can work seamlessly together or independently.

9. After you write a note, tap the Back touch button (not shown). The note is placed in the main (root) menu. Tap and hold your finger on any note that you would like to move to a different folder, and a pop-up menu appears.

10. Tap Move to Folder.

11. Tap Close after you read the help screen. Help screens appear when you access a function for the first time.

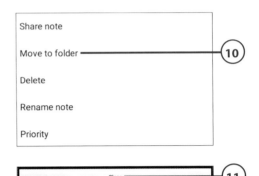

Recording Voice Notes

After each recording, you can choose whether to use or discard the recording. If you choose to keep it, you are taken to a page with a notepad where you can play back the voice memo and take text notes at the same time.

12. Create a folder by tapping the Add icon in the menu bar.

13. Type the name in the Foldername field.

14. Tap OK to move the note to the new folder.

It's Not All Good

Not Always Accurate

Be advised that not all barcode scanners on your Galaxy Tab A are 100% accurate. That goes for any product, not just the one featured here. Sometimes these scanners might not recognize the product, or the price that's provided for the product might be way off the mark. Use all these apps with caution. If you don't like this app, you can choose from many other free options.

Pair Bluetooth devices
with your Galaxy Tab A

Manage a
microSD card

In this chapter, you learn how to get the most from your Galaxy Tab A using hardware accessories such as the optional multimedia desk dock, the keyboard dock, and memory card options. This chapter covers the following topics:

→ Using Bluetooth keyboards
→ Pairing Bluetooth devices
→ Using microSD cards

Adding New Hardware

Your Galaxy Tab A is fully capable of providing an amazing multimedia experience right out of the box, but whether you are viewing movies, capturing photos and video, or composing a long email, you want your Galaxy Tab to be versatile. Accessories such as Bluetooth headsets, desk docks, Bluetooth keyboards, and extra memory cards can offer some much needed practical support for your Tab use.

You can find accessories for the 8.0" and 9.7" Galaxy Tab A models in electronics stores such as Best Buy, or you can try your local electronics store. Online stores, such as Samsung.com and Amazon.com, are also great places to find hardware accessories for the Galaxy Tabs. Always make sure that you pick the right accessory for your Galaxy Tab model. As of this writing, none of the previous Galaxy Tab accessories work with the Tab A.

Limited Accessories to Date

This section covers accessories that were available as the book was written for the Galaxy Tab A 9.7" with S Pen device. It's likely that shortly after this book finds its way onto shelves there will be new accessories for both Tab A models that are not mentioned in this chapter. For example, Samsung does not currently offer a multimedia desk dock for the Galaxy Tab A. I encourage you to keep up to date on what is available for your device by periodically checking the Samsung website, Amazon.com, and tech forums.

Using Bluetooth Keyboards

Your Galaxy Tab A comes with Bluetooth 4.0 technology, which enables you to use devices such as wireless headphones and wireless keyboards.

Bluetooth keyboards provide the convenience of typing with a physical keyboard, which makes it easier to write a lengthy message. This accessory provides a typing experience similar to using a computer keyboard, so inputting information is easier than using the onscreen keyboard. Users who perform extensive writing tasks might find the more ergonomically pleasing Bluetooth keyboard a better alternative to the onscreen keyboard. This accessory is usually in a 2-in-1 package, which means that it serves both as a QWERTY keyboard and also a folding leather case to protect your keyboard. A Bluetooth keyboard case not only protects your Galaxy Tab, but it is also very travel friendly.

Also, limited third-party companies produce accessories such as the Bluetooth keyboard for the 9.7" Tab A device, either with or without the S Pen. One such company is Logitech, and you can find Logitech accessories by performing a product search on Amazon.com.

Pairing Bluetooth Devices

Along with the many other comfort features and conveniences found with the Galaxy Tab A, your Tab gives you the capability to connect some external hardware devices wirelessly. The Tab A is equipped with Bluetooth 4.0 technology, enabling you to connect cable free with Bluetooth-capable keyboards and headphones. By default, Bluetooth is disabled on your Tab. If you have already played with this setting, you can tell if Bluetooth is turned on by verifying that the Bluetooth symbol is visible in the status bar at the top of the screen.

Pair a Bluetooth Device

You can easily connect your Tab A to a Bluetooth device in two phases: discovering and pairing.

1. Turn on the wireless device that you want to pair with your Galaxy Tab and make it discoverable.

Discoverability

Bluetooth devices broadcast their availability only after you instruct them to do so. If necessary, refer to your device's manual to learn how to make it discoverable.

2. On the main Home screen, swipe from right to left and then tap Settings on the second Home screen.

3. Tap Bluetooth to view the Bluetooth options to the right of the screen.

4. Swipe the Bluetooth slider to the right to place the Bluetooth setting in the On position. The switch turns green, and any detectable Bluetooth devices are listed to the right.

5. Tap your Bluetooth device in the list. (If you don't see your device, tap Scan in the menu bar above the list.) Your Tab attempts to pair with the device.

6. The device then appears under a newly created Paired Devices list.

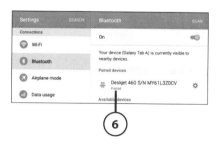

Paired Bluetooth Device Settings

After you have successfully paired your device to your Tab A, a Settings icon appears to the right of the Bluetooth device name within the Paired Devices list. Tap that Settings icon to rename or unpair your device.

Using MicroSD Cards

Your Tab A supports microSD and microSDHC memory cards that come in the following sizes: 4GB, 8GB, 16GB, 32GB, 64GB, and 128GB. Increasing the storage capacity of your Galaxy Tab A is a convenient way to store more music, photos, videos, and other files.

Photo and video files take up a lot of space on your Tab A, and so you might want (or need) to store your photos, videos, or a large quantity of files (like music files) on a microSD card instead. If you're shopping for microSD cards, you should get a card with the most space possible—but not less than 32GB. Be sure to assess your storage needs now and in the future because you might need to purchase more than one microSD card to store all your good stuff.

Format MicroSD Cards

If you buy a new card, you need to format it for your Tab A. Whether you are upgrading a microSD card or adding a new card, follow these steps to format your new memory card:

1. On the main Home screen, swipe from right to left and then tap Settings on the second Home screen.

2. Swipe up in the Settings list on the left side of the screen and then tap Storage.

3. Insert the microSD card into your Tab A. All of the microSD card information appears under the SD Card category on the right side of the screen.

4. Tap the Format SD Card option located at the bottom of the SD Card category.

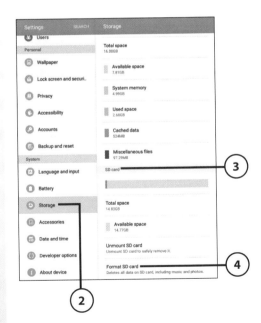

5. Read the warning and then tap Format SD Card.

6. If you type a password to log in to the Tab A, type the password in the Confirm Password screen.

7. When you finish typing the password, tap Continue.

8. Read the warning and then tap Delete All. The SD card is formatted and becomes instantly available for use.

Unmount Before Removing

It is very important that you first unmount the microSD card before removing it from the slot. Failing to do so can result in damage to the microSD card. Simply tap Unmount SD Card in the SD Card category.

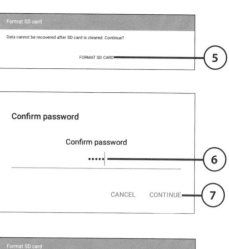

Unmount the microSD card by tapping Unmount SD Card

Troubleshoot Galaxy Tab A software,
hardware, and accessories

In this chapter, you discover ways that you can properly maintain your Galaxy Tab A and troubleshoot basic software or hardware problems. This chapter covers the following topics:

→ Maintaining your Galaxy Tab A
→ Updating Galaxy Tab A software
→ Backing up and restoring your Galaxy Tab A
→ Extending battery life
→ Solving random Galaxy Tab issues
→ Troubleshooting Wi-Fi accessibility problems
→ Getting technical help

Troubleshooting Your Galaxy Tab A

Although problems concerning the Galaxy Tab A software, hardware, and accessories are rare, on occasion you might experience incidents where your Tab does not perform properly. There are a few fixes you can try if you experience the occasional glitch that can occur with any hardware device.

Although your Galaxy Tab A is a sophisticated piece of hardware, it is less complex than an actual computer, making any issue that might arise more manageable.

Maintaining Your Galaxy Tab A

Regular maintenance of your Galaxy Tab A not only helps extend the life of your Tab, but it also helps ensure peak performance. It's important that you make sure your Galaxy Tab A software is up to date and understand basic troubleshooting concepts. Properly cleaning and protecting your Tab's body can be equally important.

The Galaxy Tab was designed to be sturdy, but, like any other electronic device, it can collect dust, and a simple drop on the sidewalk can prove disastrous. The first step in maintaining your Galaxy Tab is prevention. You can start by purchasing a protective case.

A sturdy case designed for the Galaxy Tab A is important for the overall protection of your device. A number of companies have created a variety of cases for the Tab, so search the Internet or go to Amazon.com to see what's out there. The more padded the case, the better it can absorb a shock if you happen to drop your Tab. A case can also help protect your Tab from dust and keep it dry if you happen to get caught in the rain. Make sure you keep the inside of your case clean. Dust and sand can find its way into even the most well-constructed cases. Instead of using your sleeve to wipe off your Galaxy Tab's display, invest in a microfiber cloth; you can find one in any office supply or computer store.

Your first instinct might be to wet a cloth to clean your Galaxy Tab touchscreen. Don't use liquids to clean the touchscreen, especially if they include alcohol or ammonia. These harsh chemicals can cause irreparable damage to the touchscreen, rendering it difficult to view content. Consider purchasing a screen protector at a local store or your favorite online retailer to keep the touchscreen dust and scratch free. Some screen protectors also come with a microfiber cleaning cloth.

Updating Galaxy Tab A Software

Every so often, Google releases software updates for your Galaxy Tab's Android operating system. To get the most from your Galaxy Tab A, it is good practice to update soon after an upgrade has been released. When an update is available, you receive a notification that indicates you can download a system upgrade. At that point, you have the option to initiate the software update. You can also check for system updates manually by tapping Settings on the Home screen, tapping General in the menu bar, tapping About Device, and then tapping Software Update. You are given an option to Update Now. If your system is up to date, your Tab alerts you to this fact. If an update is available, follow the provided directions to upgrade your software.

The Android operating system is not the only software you need to update on your Galaxy Tab. Your Tab also uses software called *firmware* to run its internal functions. When an update is available, use your own discretion as to whether you want to update right away, just in case there are any issues with the update.

Backing Up and Restoring Your Galaxy Tab A

Backing up the contents of your Galaxy Tab A is a good practice for securing your important information and multimedia content. You can ensure that your contacts, photos, videos, and apps are copied to your PC or Mac in case something happens to your Tab.

Ensure Automatic Google Account Backup

Your Google account information— such as your Gmail inbox, Contacts list, and Calendar app appointments—automatically syncs with Google servers, so this information is already backed up for you. To ensure that your Google account information is being automatically backed up, follow these directions.

1. On the main Home screen, swipe from right to left and then tap Settings on the second Home screen.

2. Swipe up in the Settings list on the left side of the screen and then tap Accounts.

3. Tap Google in the list.

4. Tap the Google email account in the list of accounts.

5. Ensure that all the account settings in the list have a green slider and green slider button to the right of the setting name. If they don't, slide the gray slider from left (Off) to right (On).

Multiple Google Accounts

If you have multiple Google accounts, repeat steps 1 through 5 for each account.

6. Tap Backup and Reset.

7. Ensure that the sliders and slider buttons to the right of the Back Up My Data and Automatic Restore entries are green. If not, slide the gray slider button next to one or both entries from left (Off) to right (On).

8. Tap Backup Account.

9. Tap your account in the Set Backup Account window to immediately begin backing up your Google account data.

The Automatic Restore Option

When enabled, the Automatic Restore option ensures that any data or settings placed on third-party apps are restored when you restore those apps to your Galaxy Tab A.

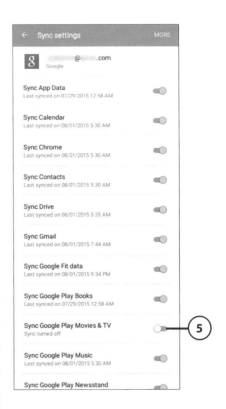

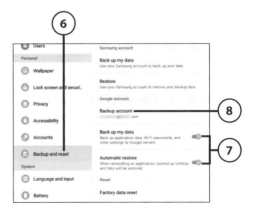

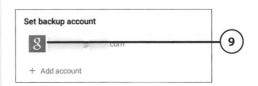

Use Samsung Smart Switch for PCs and Macs

The Samsung Smart Switch application makes it easy for you to manage your music, movies, and photos between your computer and your Galaxy Tab A.

When you connect your Tab A to your PC or Mac, Samsung Smart Switch allows you to back up files on your Tab A to your computer and restore those backed-up files to your Tab A whenever you need them.

Start by downloading Smart Switch for your PC or Mac on the Samsung website at www. samsung.com/us/support/smart-switch-support/.

Can I Use Samsung Kies?

Previous models of Samsung smartphones and tablets used the Kies app to synchro-nize data. With the introduction of the Tab A, Samsung requires that you use Smart Switch. If you try using Kies on your computer with your Tab A, a dialog box appears in Kies that informs you that you can only use Smart Switch with the device. After you close the window, Kies doesn't recognize the Tab A and asks you to connect a device. You need to close Kies before you can run Smart Switch.

1. After you have installed Samsung Smart Switch onto your computer, connect your Tab A to your PC or Mac (not shown).

2. Launch Samsung Smart Switch on your computer (not shown).

3. Click Backup.

4. Smart Switch backs up your data. Cancel the backup by clicking the Cancel button.

5. When Smart Switch finishes backing up files and folders, the screen tells you when the backup was completed, how many files were backed up, and the total amount of file space backed up.

6. Click the Check Backup Items button to view the types of items you backed up and view backed-up files and subfolders within the backup folder.

7. Complete the backup process by clicking the Confirm button.

8. Click the Restore button to restore the data from your last backup to your Tab A.

9. Click the Outlook Sync button to synchronize your Outlook contacts, schedule, and/or to-do list with your Tab A.

10. Click the More button to access more options. You can try to recover the Tab A from a catastrophic failure, view and update the Tab A firmware if necessary, reinstall the Tab A device driver on your PC or Mac, view and change Smart Switch preferences, and get Smart Switch online help and information.

11. Close Smart Switch by clicking the Close icon.

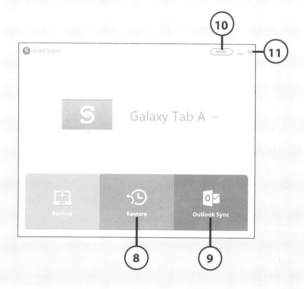

>>>Go Further

SYNCING AND USING MANUAL BACKUP

You can also back up content that is outside of your Google account information on your Galaxy Tab A, such as your apps and multimedia content, onto your computer. Connect your Galaxy Tab A to your PC as a mass storage device and manually drag and drop files. Your Tab A appears as a removable disk in the folder tree within the File Explorer window in Windows or within Finder on the Mac.

When connected to your PC as a mass storage device, you can view all of the data on your Tab's internal storage and optional microSD card. The content is categorized into specific folders that you can copy from your card and internal storage, such as DCIM, Download, Music, Pictures, Movies, Podcasts, and more. You can also copy all folders with the names of apps installed on your Galaxy Tab A.

Extending Battery Life

Your Galaxy Tab A is capable of up to at least 9 hours of battery life, depending on the model you have. Battery life can also vary depending on how you use the Galaxy Tab. Strenuous tasks, such as playing HD video, dramatically lower your battery life more than surfing the Web does. You can monitor your battery power at the top of the screen in the Status area. The white battery status icon located on the right side of the status bar lets you keep an eye on how much battery power you have left. When the battery gets low, a warning appears, informing you of the percentage of battery power you have left and instructing you to connect the charger. When the battery is too low, your Tab automatically shuts down. There are a few things you can do to extend the life of your Tab's battery between charges.

Monitor Power Usage

On the Galaxy Tab A, you can use the Battery Usage screen to see which of the apps you use consumes the most power, and then you can reduce the use of those apps. Your battery power savings are small, but if you're running low on power with no way to recharge, every little bit counts. Follow these directions to access the Battery Usage screen.

1. On the main Home screen, swipe from right to left and then tap Settings on the second Home screen.

2. Swipe up in the Settings list on the left side of the screen and then tap Battery.

3. The Battery settings list on the right side of the screen displays your current battery level and how long you used the battery before you plugged the Tab A into the charger.

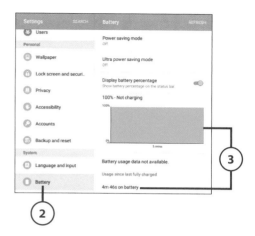

Adjust Screen Brightness

The high-quality touchscreen of the Galaxy Tab A can consume plenty of battery power. The higher the brightness level set on your Galaxy Tab A, the more power the touchscreen uses. If you are viewing the screen in very bright conditions, you probably do not need a very high brightness setting. Consider dimming the screen to extend the battery life.

1. On the main Home screen, swipe from right to left and then tap Settings on the second Home screen.

2. Tap Display.

3. Slide the Brightness slider to the left to lower the brightness level or to the right to increase the brightness level.

4. Change the brightness level to the default level by tapping the Auto check box.

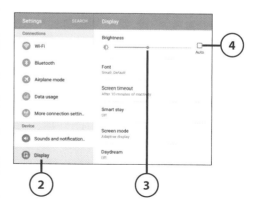

Quick Settings for Brightness

The Galaxy Tab A offers a quicker way for you to access the brightness controls by providing quick settings in the notification panel. Open the Quick Settings and Notifications screen by swiping down from the top of the screen and then use the slider below the S Finder button to adjust screen brightness.

Utilize Sleep Mode

Your Galaxy Tab A goes to sleep after a specified period of inactivity, but you don't have to wait for it to fall asleep—you can put it to sleep manually. When your Tab is awake, it is consuming battery power. Press the sleep button on the side of your Tab when you have finished using the device to conserve battery power.

Conserve Power by Turning Off Wi-Fi

When the Wi-Fi antenna is activated on your Galaxy Tab, your device is incessantly looking for available Wi-Fi networks to join, which uses battery power. To see if Wi-Fi is turned on, check the right side of the status bar of your Galaxy Tab for the Wi-Fi symbol. If you do not need a Wi-Fi connection, turn it off to conserve battery power. If you are not wandering and are using Wi-Fi in a single location, look for a power outlet and plug in your Tab.

1. On the main Home screen, swipe from right to left and then tap Settings on the second Home screen.

2. Turn off Wi-Fi by sliding the Wi-Fi slider to the left.

3. The slider and slider button colors turn gray, and a message on the right side of the screen asks you to turn on Wi-Fi to see available networks.

Quick Settings for Wi-Fi

The Galaxy Tab A offers an even quicker way for you to access the Wi-Fi setting by providing quick settings in the notification panel. Simply swipe down from the top of the Home screen and tap the green Wi-Fi setting to turn it off (or on).

Conserve Power by Turning Off Bluetooth

When Bluetooth is activated on your Galaxy Tab, your device is constantly checking for other Bluetooth devices, which drains battery power. To see if Bluetooth is turned on, check the status bar in the top-left corner of your Galaxy Tab for the Bluetooth symbol. If you are not using a Bluetooth device, turn this function off. There are also security reasons why you should turn off Bluetooth when you are not using it, so get in the habit of turning Bluetooth off as soon as you finish using a wireless device with your Galaxy Tab. You can easily deactivate Bluetooth in the notification panel.

1. On the main Home screen, swipe from right to left and then tap Settings on the second Home screen.

2. View all Bluetooth devices to which the Galaxy Tab A is connected by tapping Bluetooth.

3. Turn off Bluetooth by sliding the Bluetooth slider to the left.

4. The slider button and slider colors turn gray, and a message on the right side of the screen asks you to turn on Bluetooth to see available devices.

Quick Settings for Bluetooth

The Galaxy Tab A offers an even quicker way for you to access the Bluetooth setting in the Quick Settings and Notifications screen. Turn off Bluetooth by simply tapping the green Bluetooth button at the right side of the button bar.

Conserve Even More Power Using Power Saving Modes

If you would rather not tweak individual settings to save battery life, the Galaxy Tab A comes with two power saving modes: Power Saving mode and Ultra Power Saving mode. Each mode restricts the performance of the Tab A and requires few setting changes on your part.

Set Up Power Saving Mode

The standard Power Saving mode gives you the options of slowing down the performance of apps and services on the Tab A and/or putting the display in Grayscale mode so the Tab A doesn't spend battery life creating all the wonderful colors on the screen.

1. On the main Home screen, swipe from right to left and then tap Settings on the second Home screen.

2. Swipe up in the Settings list on the left side of the screen and then tap Battery.

3. Tap Power Saving Mode.

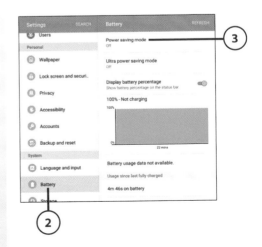

4. In the Power Saving settings list, turn on Power Saving Mode by moving the slider to the right. The slider and slider button colors turn green. By default, the Tab A saves battery power immediately by limiting CPU performance, reducing screen brightness, and reducing the time before the screen is turned off after you receive a notification.

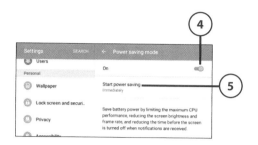

5. Tap Start Power Saving.

6. You can choose when to start saving battery power in the menu. You can start when you have 5%, 15%, 20%, or 50% battery power. Or you can continue to save power now by tapping Immediately.

7. Return to the Power Saving settings list by tapping the Back icon.

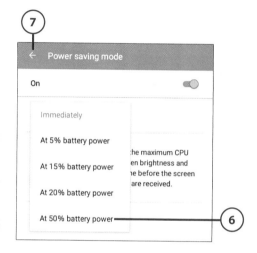

Set Up Ultra Power Saving Mode

Ultra Power Saving mode automatically puts your display in Grayscale mode and goes further by severely limiting the apps and services you can use on the Tab A. You can still access your Wi-Fi network and Bluetooth connection from your Tab A in Ultra Power Saving mode. If you already have Power Saving mode active, the Tab A closes Power Saving mode so you can get the benefits of Ultra Power Saving mode.

1. On the main Home screen, swipe from right to left and then tap Settings on the second Home screen.

2. Swipe up in the Settings list on the left side of the screen and then tap Battery.

3. Tap Ultra Power Saving Mode.

4. In the Ultra Power Saving Mode settings list, turn on Ultra Power Saving mode by moving the slider to the right. The slider and slider button colors turn green.

5. Tap the check box in the Terms and Conditions window. You only see this window the first time you start Ultra Power Saving mode; if you don't see this window, proceed to step 7.

6. Tap Agree.

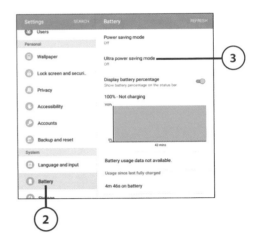

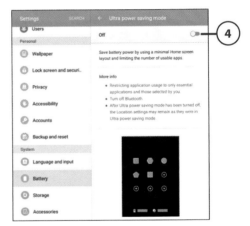

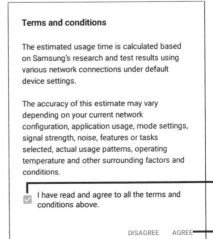

Terms and conditions

The estimated usage time is calculated based on Samsung's research and test results using various network connections under default device settings.

The accuracy of this estimate may vary depending on your current network configuration, application usage, mode settings, signal strength, noise, features or tasks selected, actual usage patterns, operating temperature and other surrounding factors and conditions.

I have read and agree to all the terms and conditions above.

DISAGREE   AGREE

7. The Tab A turns on Ultra Power Saving mode by dimming the screen and turning off the screen after 15 seconds of no activity. The Ultra Power Saving Mode screen appears, and this screen opens every time you wake the Tab A from Sleep mode.

8. By default, you can use the Internet, Calendar, and Clock apps. Run the app by tapping the app icon; when you finish using the app, tap the Back touch button.

9. Add an app to the list of apps you can run by tapping one of the Add (+) buttons. In the Add Application window that appears, tap Calculator or Google+; the app icon appears, replacing the Add icon.

10. Tap More to open the menu so you can remove one or more apps from the list of apps you can run; change various settings, including Wi-Fi, Bluetooth, Airplane mode, Location, Sound, and Brightness; and turn off Ultra Power Saving mode.

11. After you tap Turn Off Ultra Power Saving Mode in the menu you opened in step 10, the Tab A takes a few seconds to display the Home screen in full color. Most apps and services return to normal operation; however, you will need to turn the Location service back on by opening the Quick Settings and Notifications screen and then tapping the Location button (not shown).

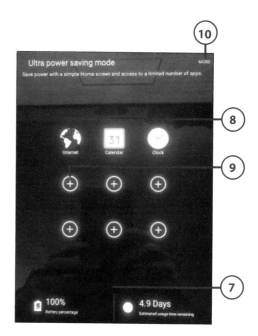

Solving Random Galaxy Tab Issues

The occasional hardware or software glitch happens to even the best of electronic devices. You might encounter an issue, although rare, where an app you are using freezes, a wireless device proves difficult to pair with your Galaxy Tab A, the touchscreen becomes unresponsive, or landscape orientation is not available at all times. Fortunately, it is not very difficult to troubleshoot some of these issues. If you should happen to come across a problem that you can't solve yourself, there are plenty of channels for you to find technical support.

Difficulty Turning Your Tab On or Off

On rare occasions, you might find that your Galaxy Tab A is stubborn when you try to turn it on or off. It might appear that the device has locked or become unresponsive. If this happens to you, hold the Power button for 8 seconds to see if it responds. If this does not work, you might need to let your Tab A sit for a few seconds before you again try holding the Power button for 8 seconds.

Touchscreen Becomes Unresponsive

This tip assumes that your Galaxy Tab A and any app you are using is responsive, but the touchscreen is not responding to your touch. If you attempt to use your Tab A touchscreen while wearing conventional gloves, it does not work. This can prove inconvenient on a very cold day, so you might want to consider a capacitive stylus for your Tab A.

Your Tab uses a capacitive touchscreen that holds an electrical charge. When you touch the screen with your bare finger, capacitive stylus, or special static-carrying gloves, it changes the amount of charge at the specific point of contact. In a nutshell, this is how the touchscreen interprets your taps, drags, and pinches.

The touchscreen might also be unresponsive to your touch if you happen to have a thin coat of film on your fingertips. So no sticky fingers, please.

Force Stop an App

Sometimes an app might get an attitude and become unruly. For example, an app might provide a warning screen saying that it is currently busy and is unresponsive, or it might give some other issue warning to convey that a problem exists. If an app is giving you problems, you can manually stop the app.

1. On the main Home screen, swipe from right to left and then tap Settings on the second Home screen.

2. Tap Applications in the Settings list.

3. Tap Application Manager in the Applications settings list.

4. In the heading area above the list of apps, swipe right to left until you see the Running header. The Running list appears under the Running header and shows only the apps that are currently running.

5. Swipe up in the list of apps if necessary and then tap the problem app.

6. Tap Stop. The app stops running.

7. Tap Report to send a problem report to the app's developer.

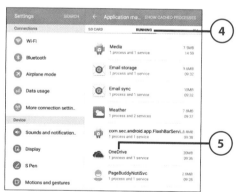

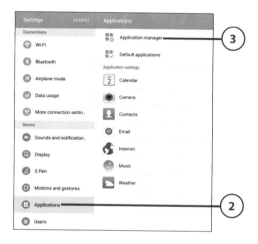

Battery Does Not Charge

If you find that your battery is not charging, first start with the power outlet. Is the outlet supplying power? Is the power strip turned on? Plug something else into the outlet to see if it works, or try another outlet.

Make sure that everything is connected properly. Is the adapter secure on both ends? If the outlet supplies power and the cables are connected properly, but the battery still does not charge, try another cable. If this does not solve the issue, your battery might be defective. Contact Samsung technical support. (See the "Getting Technical Help" section later in this chapter for more information about how to contact Samsung.) There is no way for you to remove the battery yourself.

Overheating

Overheating is rare, but if your Tab A becomes too hot and regularly turns itself off, you might need to replace the battery. You can tell if your Tab A is getting too hot by holding it in your hands. Use caution.

Landscape Orientation Does Not Work

The orientation setting on your Galaxy Tab A could be set so that your Tab A stays in either portrait or landscape mode, regardless of how you hold the device. If your Tab no longer utilizes landscape orientation, first check the setting for screen orientation.

The Galaxy Tab A has a Screen Rotation setting that must be selected for the screen to adjust from portrait to landscape mode, depending on how you hold the device. You can easily confirm that the Screen Rotation setting is selected from the Quick Settings and Notifications screen.

1. Open the Quick Settings and Notifications screen from the Home screen by tapping and holding on the top edge of the screen and then swiping downward.

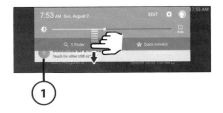

2. Locate the Screen Rotation setting button and confirm that the
button above the Screen Rotation
text is green. If the icon is gray,
activate the setting by tapping
the button. Your Galaxy Tab A
screen should now adjust to the
orientation in which you hold the
device.

Landscape Orientation and Apps

Not every app on the Android Market was developed to take advantage of the
landscape orientation of your Galaxy Tab. If you notice this issue while using an
app, close the app and then see whether your Tab can situate itself in landscape
orientation.

Troubleshooting Wi-Fi Accessibility Problems

Your Galaxy Tab A provides you the convenience and flexibility of wireless
Internet access via Wi-Fi connectivity. Along with this convenience and flexibility comes the potential for connectivity issues regarding wireless networks.
If you are unable to access a Wi-Fi network, or if your connection is sporadic,
there are some troubleshooting tips you can use to pinpoint basic accessibility options.

Make Sure Wi-Fi Is Activated

First and foremost, make sure that the Wi-Fi antenna is on. You can determine
this by looking on the right side of the status bar at the top of your Galaxy
Tab A screen to see whether the Wi-Fi icon is visible. If it is not on, you can
open the Quick Settings and Notifications screen by swiping down from the
top of the screen and then activate Wi-Fi by tapping the Wi-Fi button.

Wi-Fi antenna

Check Your Range

If Wi-Fi is activated on your Galaxy Tab A and you still cannot connect, take note of how far away you are from the Wi-Fi access point. In general, you can be only 150 feet from a Wi-Fi access point indoors or 300 feet from an access point outdoors before the signal becomes weak or drops altogether. Structures such as walls with lots of electronics can also impede a Wi-Fi signal.

However, the type of wireless protocol you're using in your Wi-Fi network also affects your range. For example, if your wireless network uses the 802.11n protocol, which the Tab A supports, you'll have much better range and signal coverage than with the older 802.11a/b/g protocols. If you still have trouble, check your network information for protocol and coverage data. Also, make sure you are close to the access point or turn on the access point's range booster, if it has one, to improve your connection.

Reset Your Router

The issue of Wi-Fi accessibility might not be related to your distance from the Wi-Fi access point, a signal-impeding barrier, or your Galaxy Tab A. As a last resort, you might need to reset the router. After you reset your router, you have to set up your network from the ground up.

Reset the Galaxy Tab A Software

If all else fails and your technical problems still persist, as a last-ditch effort you might need to reset the Galaxy Tab A software. Resetting your Tab A software restores your Tab to the factory defaults, just like when you took it out of the box for the first time. Consider contacting support before you reset your Tab, but if you must, follow these directions to reset the device:

1. On the main Home screen, swipe from right to left and then tap Settings on the second Home screen.

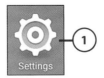

2. Swipe up in the Settings list on the left side of the screen and then tap Backup and Reset.

3. Tap Factory Data Reset.

4. Tap the Reset Device button.

5. If you use a password to log in to your Tab, type the password in the Confirm Password field.

6. Tap Continue.

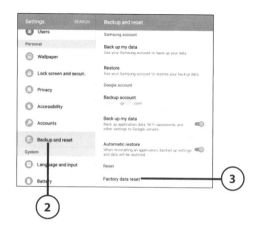

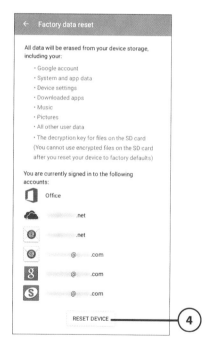

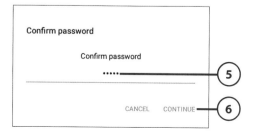

7. Tap the Delete All button to confirm. Your Tab A is returned to its
factory state.

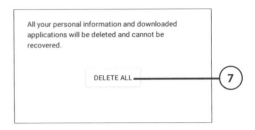

All your personal information and downloaded
applications will be deleted and cannot be
recovered.

DELETE ALL

⑦

Getting Technical Help

Many outlets are available where you can find help if you run across a Galaxy
Tab technical problem that you can't seem to beat. Although limited, the
user's manual is a good place to start. You can download the correct manual
for your Galaxy Tab A model online from the Samsung website (www.
samsung.com), in the form of a PDF, and scan the table of contents or perform searches in the document for words that pertain to your problem. In
most user manual PDFs, topics in the table of contents are often linked to the
section they pertain to within the document, so when you find what you are
looking for, just click the topic to jump to the pertinent page.

Websites and Galaxy Tab forums are also a great way for you to get support
for your device. Type a search phrase, such as "Galaxy Tab Google Calendar
sync problem," into Google. Chances are that plenty of other people are expe-
riencing the same issue. Doing some online research of your own could save
you a few minutes on the telephone with technical support and help you
solve your problem more quickly.

Contact Your Cellular Provider or Samsung

The Samsung website is a great resource for getting help with technical
issues with your Galaxy Tab A. The Samsung website (www.samsung.com/us/
support/) offers support via Twitter, Facebook, Google+, as well as by phone
(1-800-726-7864). Before you call, you need to have your device's model number so that you can give it to the technical support representative.

Locate the Tab Model Number

You can find the model number on the box that your Tab A shipped in, and you can also find it in the Settings menu.

1. On the main Home screen, swipe from right to left and then tap Settings on the second Home screen.

2. Swipe up in the Settings list on the left side of the screen and then tap About Device.

3. Locate your Tab's model number in the Model Number field on the right side of the screen.

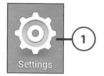

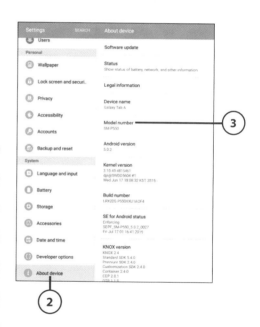

This appendix offers options on how to accessorize your Galaxy Tab A with protective cases, screen protectors, chargers, and adapters. It also covers ways to maximize the longevity of your Galaxy Tab A. Accessories covered in this appendix include the following:

→ Protective cases

→ Screen protectors

→ Chargers and adapters

Finding Galaxy Tab A Accessories

Many accessories are available for the 8.0" and 9.7" models of the Galaxy Tab A, ranging from those that increase its usability to those that protect your Tab A or enhance its style. You can start on the Samsung website to explore which accessories are right for you, but don't stop there. Many other companies create high-quality accessories for the Tab A. Amazon.com is a great place to browse the many offerings for the Tab A and read product reviews from other buyers. Let's take a look at a variety of accessories to see how they can benefit you.

Protective Cases

Perhaps the most fundamental duty you have as a Galaxy Tab A owner is to protect your Tab from becoming damaged. There are many cases on the market to choose from, and all provide some degree of protection for your Tab. Samsung offers cases for both Tab A models and you can also browse many third-party vendors on Amazon.com and other electronics stores that offer an assortment of options for your 8.0" or 9.7" Tab A.

Skins are stylish and provide a thin layer of protection around your Tab A, which can be effective for protecting your Tab against dust, nicks, and scratches. A skin by itself is less effective for absorbing shock, such as from a drop, than a padded case that remains on your Tab A at all times.

Some padded cases, such as the MoKo Slim-Fit Cover Case, also act as stands. Cases are available for both the 8.0" and 9.7" Tab A models and it's easy to fold the cover so you can view your Tab A screen hands-free:

1. Fold the front cover of the case underneath the Tab A.

2. Set the Tab down on a flat surface so the screen is in landscape orientation.

3. Angle the Tab A display so that it is easy to view. This is a great orientation in which to watch videos or movies.

4. Set the Tab A up in portrait orientation by positioning the folded cover behind it.

>>>Go Further

ALTERNATIVES TO CASES

Protective cases aren't the only way to keep your Galaxy Tab A safe from the elements and damage. Protective pouches, sleeves, or slipcases are other alternatives. If you prefer the tactile experience of the Galaxy Tab A body in your hands while you use it, you can use a pouch when you're carrying your Tab and then slip the device from the pouch when you're ready to use it. A leather or cloth pouch can also act as an extra layer of protection for that stylish skin you have been eyeing for your Tab A.

Screen Protectors

Most cases, skins, and pouches do not include a protective screen cover to keep your high-resolution screen from getting scratched, so you might have to purchase one separately. You can choose from a variety of protective screens; the most popular are clear (invisible), mirrored, and antiglare.

A clear protective screen performs the basic duty of preventing your Tab's glass screen from being scratched or collecting dust. A protective film offers three layers of protection after you apply one using its self-adhering surface, and it's barely noticeable. Some screen protectors, such as the ArmorSuit

Military Shield, even protect against moisture and self-heal (minor scratches to the shield's surface repair themselves over time). To remove the protector, just peel off the film.

A mirrored screen does exactly what it says. When your Galaxy Tab A screen is off, the screen reflects as a mirror. When the Tab A screen is on, the mirror goes away. This option not only protects your screen but also adds a stylish aesthetic to your Tab. One thing to keep in mind when choosing this option is the glare factor when using your Tab A in the sun. A substantial glare can impede screen visibility.

Antiglare screen protectors make it easier for you to view your Galaxy Tab A display indoors or outdoors in direct sunlight. While protecting your screen, they also help to reduce annoying surface glare caused by bright indoor lighting.

When you clean your screen, be sure to use a microfiber cloth. You can order one or more microfiber cloths online or pick them up at any office supply store. Then you can use the dry cloth to gently wipe smudges, dust, and lint that accumulate as you use the Tab A. Never use paper towels because they can scratch your screen.

If you have bigger stains on your screen, such as food, you can dampen the cloth lightly and gently wipe the screen. Dry the screen with a dry microfiber cloth. (This is a good reason why you should get at least two cloths.) Never use window cleaners to clean the screens because the chemicals in those cleaners can permanently damage the screen.

Chargers and Adapters

The Galaxy Tab A was designed for a person who is on the go. Just put your Tab A 8.0" or 9.7" under your arm and go. Many accessories are available to the power user, including additional power chargers and adapters. For example, you might want to charge your Tab A at the office as well as at home. Instead of remembering to transport a single cable, wall jack, or dock, why not invest in two? You can also have the convenience of charging your Tab A while in a car. Here are a few accessories you might want to consider:

- **Galaxy Tab 11-pin travel charger**—You can use this data cable to connect your Tab A to a PC, Mac, or Samsung charger. This offers a two-in-one solution for charging power and transferring data simultaneously via a USB data sync cable. You can also use it to connect your Tab A to your computer.

- **Galaxy Tab 30-pin Vehicle Power Adapter with detachable cable**—
  The Vehicle Power Adapter, with data cable, enables you to charge your
  Galaxy Tab A while in your car. You can plug it into your car's 12-volt cigarette lighter socket. If you have to transfer data from your Tab A to your
  laptop, or vice versa, this car charger provides a detachable USB cable
  that enables you to connect to your laptop and make the transfer. You
  can also simultaneously charge your Tab A through the same connection
  to your laptop. Note that you can't purchase the Vehicle Power Adapter
  through the Samsung website (at least as of this writing), but you can
  purchase it through third-party sellers such as Amazon.com.

- **Galaxy Tab travel adapter with detachable USB-to-30-pin data
  cable**—Charge your Tab A while on the go or at home with this adapter
  that plugs in to any standard wall outlet. This adapter includes a USB port
  for universal charging and a 2A charger.

>>>Go Further
OTHER CHARGERS AND ADAPTERS

When it comes to accessories, perhaps the biggest decision to make is choosing from the variety of available manufacturers' products. There are many
options for the power user, such as worldwide travel plug adapters, mini
surge protectors, and dual cigarette lighter sockets. Always make sure that
the accessories you use are compatible with your Galaxy Tab A. Not all manufacturers' accessories are of equal quality.

This appendix provides definitions of terms discussed in this book. Terms are listed in alphabetical order.

B

Glossary of Terms

A number of terms are used throughout this book, and if you want to read a list of definitions before you start reading the book—or just need a quick refresher—this appendix is for you. Though this book contains all the important definitions you should know about, this list isn't exhaustive. Other definitions appear throughout this book and may also appear on the book web page on the Que Publishing website (www.quepublishing.com).

adapter   A device that connects two different pieces of equipment that cannot be connected directly.

Airplane mode   A setting on the Galaxy Tab A that enables you to quickly turn on and off wireless connectivity.

Android   An operating system for smartphones and tablets produced by Google.

apps   Short for *applications*. Apps are programs that are written to perform different tasks on the Galaxy Tab A.

Apps screen   A screen that contains icons for all apps installed on your Galaxy Tab A.

aspect ratio   The proportional relationship between the screen width and height.

back up   The process of copying and archiving computer data, usually to another device or remote file storage service.

Bluetooth   A technology standard to connect computers, smartphones, tablets, and other computing devices (for example, printers) wirelessly over short distances.

book reader   An app that enables you to read e-books on your Galaxy Tab A. The Google Play Books reader app is preinstalled on the Tab A.

bookmark   In a browser app, this is a favorite website saved in the app so you can access it easily. In a book reader app, a bookmark is a page in your book that you can tag so you can go back to that page easily.

brightness sensor   A sensor that measures the ambient light around the Galaxy Tab A so the Tab A can automatically adjust the light level of the screen to help you see the screen clearly.

browser   An app that enables you to view websites and web pages. The Internet and Google Chrome browser apps are preinstalled on the Tab A.

button bar   An area that contains icons for performing specific tasks within an app.

cloud storage   A service that enables you to upload files onto its server computers. Cloud storage services make it easy for you to share large files with others.

contact   A file that stores contact information such as names, addresses, emails, and notes.

contact account   A contact file for a specific person that contains all the information associated with that person.

drag   You can view content on the screen by touching the top of the screen and moving your finger to drag the content the length of the screen. You can also drag from left to right within an app screen if the app allows it.

e-book   An electronic version of a book designed specifically for reading in a book reader app.

email   A method for distributing messages to one or more people on a computer network.

episode   A separate program that is part of a larger video or podcast series.

feed   A data format for providing you with regularly updated content that you subscribe to, such as news headlines.

flick   The method of scrolling up and down the screen in the Galaxy Tab A. After you touch the top (or bottom) of the screen, move your finger quickly down (or up) and then lift your finger at the last moment so the content scrolls after you lift your finger.

Flipboard Briefing   A social media aggregation service that's preinstalled on the Galaxy Tab A so you can get the latest news and updates of interest to you from within one app.

force stop   Manually stopping an app that is no longer working correctly.

Galaxy Tab   The name for Samsung's line of tablets that run the Android operating system.

Google   A multinational computing company founded in 1998 that's head-quartered in Mountain View, California. Google is most popular for its web search engine and for its Android operating system.

Google Chrome   A web browser app that is preinstalled on your Galaxy Tab A.

Google Cloud Print   A web-based service that allows any web-enabled device, including the Galaxy Tab A, to access a printer that is connected to the Cloud Print service. Access the Google Cloud Print website at www. google.com/cloudprint/learn.

Google Drive   A cloud storage app that is preinstalled on your Galaxy Tab A.

Google Hangouts   The instant messaging app for the Galaxy Tab A.

Google Now   An intelligent personal assistant app that's preinstalled on your Galaxy Tab A. Google Now can perform tasks for you based on your location and how you're using your Tab A.

Google Play Store   A preinstalled app on the Galaxy Tab A that enables you to shop for apps, purchase an app, and download the app to your Tab A so you can use it.

Google+   A social networking website designed and operated by Google for sharing updates and multimedia files as well as chatting with other Google+ users.

GPS   An acronym that stands for Global Positioning System, which makes it possible for specific apps (such as Google Maps) to use GPS satellites so those apps can find out where you are and provide location-specific information.

HD   An abbreviation that stands for high-definition video, which is typically 1,280×720 (720p) or 1,920×1,080 (1080p) pixel resolution.

history list   A list of all web pages you've visited during your browsing session stored in the browser app.

Home screen   The screen that appears by default after you swipe on or enter your password, PIN, or pattern in the Lock screen. There are also two other Home screens that you can access by swiping back and forth: One Home screen shows the Flipboard Briefing app, and the other Home screen shows the Galaxy App widget, the Milk Music widget, and more app icons.

hypertext   Text or images in a web page that are linked to text or images on another web page. Tap the linked text or image on the page to open the linked page that contains the other text and/or image.

Ice Cream Sandwich   The nickname for Android version 4.0.x.

icon   An image on the screen that represents a specific application, file, folder, or option.

IMAP   An acronym for Internet Message Access Protocol, which makes the server the place where all messages are stored. Therefore, your Galaxy Tab A and computer display all email messages on the server.

instant messaging   Real-time transmission of text messages between two or more users.

Internet   A global system of interconnected networks that you can use to access websites as well as other services such as email.

iTunes   A media player and media library app that enables you to download, play, and organize audio and video files. iTunes is available for both the Windows and Mac OS platforms.

Jelly Bean   The nickname for Android versions 4.1.x, 4.2.x, and 4.3.x.

KitKat   The nickname for Android version 4.4.x, which is named after the Nestlé candy bar.

Lock screen   The default screen that appears on the Galaxy Tab A when it first boots. This screen shows the current date and time as well as the Wi-Fi connectivity status, battery charge status, and Smart Stay feature status in the upper-right corner of the screen.

Lollipop   The nickname for Android version 5.0.x. The Galaxy Tab A uses Android 5.0.2.

magazine reader   An app that enables you to read online versions of magazines on your Galaxy Tab A. The Google Play Newsstand reader app is preinstalled on your Tab A.

Maps   A preinstalled app on your Galaxy Tab A that gives you the capability to get directions and pinpoint locations.

megapixel   One million pixels, where a pixel is the smallest component of a digital image. A megapixel is the standard measure of the resolution of digital cameras; the higher the megapixels, the higher the resolution.

microSD   An acronym for micro secure digital, a standard memory card format for portable devices such as the Galaxy Tab A.

mount   The process of inserting the microSD card into the microSD slot on your Galaxy Tab A.

multitouch screen   A screen that recognizes gestures using multiple finger touches to perform certain tasks, such as enlarging the size of text within a document.

network   A system of connected computing devices that enables users to share data and resources such as printers.

news reader   An app that enables you to view news stories from a variety of sources within the app.

notifications   Messages that appear in the status bar at the top of the screen. You can also view notifications in the Quick Settings and Notifications screen, which you can open by tapping and holding your finger on the top edge of the screen and swiping your finger down.

OneDrive   A remote file storage service from Microsoft that is preinstalled on the Galaxy Tab A so you can back up your Tab A data to the OneDrive server and share files with other OneDrive users.

parental controls   You can set usage restrictions for one or more users on your Galaxy Tab A. For example, you can restrict the apps a user can shop for in the Google Play Store based on the maturity level setting for that app.

password   A secret string of characters or a word that you must enter on your Galaxy Tab A to gain access to the resources on your Tab A.

pinch   A gesture where you touch the screen with both your thumb and forefinger and bring them together in a pinching motion.

playlist   A list of favorite songs that you can access easily in either the Music Hub or Music Player app. You can also add songs to and delete songs from your playlist.

podcast   An episodic series of multimedia files (such as audio and/or video) that users can download to their computer, tablet, or smartphone.

POP   An acronym that stands for Post Office Protocol. POP retrieves and removes email from a server. Therefore, the server acts as a temporary holding place for email.

protective screen   A protective film that keeps the glass screen on your Galaxy Tab A from being scratched or collecting dust.

Quick Briefing   A series of two Home screens that contain information about upcoming events, links to various apps, and information within certain apps such as email messages.

Quick Settings   Settings you can turn on and off within the Quick Settings and Notifications screen, which you can open by tapping and holding your finger on the top edge of the screen and swiping your finger down.

Remote PC   A remote control service that is preinstalled on the Galaxy Tab A so you can view and control your desktop or laptop PC screen on your Galaxy Tab A.

reset   Restore the Galaxy Tab A to its factory defaults so it's just like it was when you took the Tab A out of the box for the first time.

router   A small physical device that connects computers and devices to the Internet and to each other through a wired and/or wireless connection.

RSS   An abbreviation for Rich Site Summary (or Really Simple Syndication), which is a standard format for publishing frequently updated information such as news stories.

Scene mode   One of several options in the Camera app that enables you to optimize your camera for special shooting situations.

screen capture   A photo you create of the Galaxy Tab A screen interface. Take a screen capture by holding down the Power and Home buttons simultaneously.

screen orientation   The way features on a page appear on the screen for normal viewing. In vertical screen orientation, the screen is higher than it is wide. However, features on the page change when you rotate the unit 90 degrees so the screen is horizontal (wider than it is high).

SD   An abbreviation that stands for standard-definition video, which is either 720×486 or 720×576 pixel resolution.

server   A computer and software designed to manage requests for network services, such as a data repository.

sharing   Making files available on your Galaxy Tab A for others to download and view on their smartphones, tablets, or computers.

shortcut   An icon placed on a Home screen so you can access an app or widget easily.

SideSync   A connection app that is preinstalled on the Galaxy Tab A so you can connect the Tab A with an Android smartphone to share information between the two devices.

signature   Text that you can save to the Email app or Gmail app and use when you want to place this text at the end of your email message.

skin   A thin cover around your Galaxy Tab A that can help protect your Tab A from dust, nicks, and scratches.

Sleep mode   A state in which the screen turns off after a period of inactivity to conserve battery power.

slider   A horizontal line with a button; you can hold your finger and move the button along the line to change the setting level, such as the level of brightness on the screen.

Smart Stay   A feature in the Galaxy Tab A that uses the camera to track your eye movements. If the Tab A recognizes that your eyes are looking at the screen, the Tab A screen will remain on and won't go into Sleep mode.

Smart Switch   An application produced by Samsung for Windows and Mac OS that makes it easy for you to back up to your computer, restore files from your computer to your Galaxy Tab A, and synchronize data between your Tab A and Microsoft Outlook.

social aggregator   An app or website that combines all your social networking feeds onto one screen so you can view all your updates at a glance.

social network   A dedicated website or app that enables users to exchange information with each other.

spam   An inappropriate or irrelevant email message sent to you (and usually a large number of other recipients).

Super AMOLED   Samsung technology that integrates touchscreen functionality into AMOLED (active-matrix organic light-emitting diode) display technology.

swipe   The process of moving elements on the screen by sliding your finger across the screen and then lifting your finger off the screen.

sync You can synchronize a single set of data between two or more devices. For example, you can back up data on your Galaxy Tab A to your desktop or laptop every time you sync both devices. This way, if you lose your data on the Galaxy Tab A (or lose the Tab A itself), you can restore the data from the backed-up copies on your computer.

tab area An area on the screen with buttons that enable you to perform specific functions within an app.

tablet A mobile computer that contains the display, battery, and circuitry in a shape that resembles a stone or paper tablet.

Timer A feature in the Camera app that enables you to determine how long the Tab A should wait before the camera takes a picture.

touchscreen A screen that enables users to control the device by touching areas on the screen with one or more fingers.

unmount The instruction you give the Galaxy Tab A to prepare to remove the microSD card from its slot.

URL An abbreviation that stands for uniform resource locator, which can be a website name or a specific page in a website—for example, http://www.quepublishing.com.

USB An abbreviation that stands for Universal Serial Bus, which is an industry standard for cables and connectors that enable computing devices to communicate with each other.

user account A small file that contains information about you so you can authenticate yourself on the Galaxy Tab A and gain authorization to access various files and services on the Tab A.

VPN An abbreviation that stands for virtual private network. A VPN enables users in a public network (such as the Internet) to transfer private data by making it appear to the users that they're in a private network of their own.

wallpaper An image that appears in the background on your Home, Apps, and/or Lock screens.

Web Short for World Wide Web, which is a system of interlinked hypertext documents you access through the Internet.

web page A document that is suitable for viewing on a browser app (usually written in Hypertext Markup Language, or HTML) that is stored on the Web.

website   A location on the Internet that manages one or more web pages.

widget   A small, portable piece of code that you can interact with like a miniature application. Dozens of widgets come preinstalled on your Galaxy Tab A.

Wi-Fi   The technology standard by which computers and devices can connect to the Internet and/or one another wirelessly.

Wi-Fi Direct   A wireless connectivity standard that allows devices to communicate with each other wirelessly without having to use a wireless access point, such as a wireless router.

Windows Media Player   The default multimedia player app for Microsoft Windows that you can use to sync audio, photo, and video files between your connected Galaxy Tab A and Windows computer.

XGA   An abbreviation that stands for Extended Graphics Array, which is 1,024×768 pixel resolution. Both models of the Galaxy Tab A use an XGA-resolution screen.

YouTube   A website for storing, sharing, and playing videos. You can access YouTube videos using the preinstalled YouTube app on the Galaxy Tab A.

Index

Q–R

X-Y-Z

More Best-Selling **My** Books!

My
Android Tablet

My Samsung
Galaxy Note 4

My
Android Phone

My
Samsung Galaxy S6
for Seniors

My
Office 2016

My
Samsung Galaxy S6

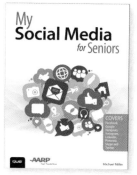

My
Social Media
for Seniors

My
Excel 2016

Learning to use your smartphone, tablet, camera, game, or software has never been easier with the full-color My Series. You'll find simple, step-by-step instructions from our team of experienced authors. The organized, task-based format allows you to quickly and easily find exactly what you want to achieve.

Visit quepublishing.com/mybooks to learn more.